SISTER LUCIA OF JESUS AND OF THE IMMACULATE HEART

'CALLS'

FROM THE MESSAGE OF FATIMA

English translation by Sisters of Mosteiro de Santa Maria
and Convento de N. S. do Bom Sucesso, Lisbon

Authorized by the Congregation for the Doctrine of Faith, Rome

Published by: Secretariado dos Pastorinhos
2496-908 Fatima – Portugal

Title of the original: *Apelos da Mensagem de Fatima*
(Appeals of the Message of Fatima)

8 th Edition: September 2017

Legal Registration nº 431 060/17
ISBN 978-972-8524-23-4

Front Cover: Sister Lucia on 16th May, 2000.

PRELIMINARY NOTE

The author of this work is Sister Lucia (Sister Maria Lúcia of Jesus and of the Immaculate Heart to give her her full religious name), who is so well known that there is no need for a preliminary word of introduction. Nevertheless, in order to avoid any doubts or misunderstandings, I wish to assure readers of this book that it was her idea and was written by her. All that remains for me to do is to explain the purpose and the limitations of this publication, which we now place in the hands of pilgrims and of all those devoted to Our Lady of Fatima.

Finding herself inundated with constantly repeated questions concerning the apparitions and the visionaries, the message they received and the reason for some of the requests contained in that message, and feeling that it was beyond her to reply individually to each questioner, Sister Lucia asked the Holy See for permission to write a text in which she could reply in general to the many questions that had been put to her.

This permission was granted, hence the present work entitled in English: *'Calls' from the Message of Fatima**.

The work is, in effect, a long letter, written entirely by Sister Lucia and addressed by her to all those who have written to her concerning their doubts, questions, and difficulties, and their desire for greater fidelity in living up to what was asked for from Heaven in the Cova da Iria.

The work naturally enjoys those freedoms of expression which are legitimate in the epistolary style, one such being the highlighting of some aspects without thereby diminishing or excluding others. Thus, the author reflects on twenty requests, recommendations and warnings – to all of which she gives the generic title *call (apelo)* – taken verbatim from the Message as already made known. These she presents in catechetical style, interpreting them, mainly, in a moralistic and exhortatory way, in accordance with the wishes of her interlocutors.

The central core of the Message and the point of reference, the backbone, almost, of the whole book is Our Lady's recommendation: "Do not offend the Lord our God any more because He is already so much offended" (Apparition, 13th October, 1917). We offend God when we diso-

---

* Title of Portuguese original *APELOS DA MENSAGEM DE FATIMA*

bey his law, his commandments, the path mapped out for us to attain to eternal life. It was out of love that God gave his law and commandments to us, as a good father gives his children the instructions they need to enable them to follow the paths of righteousness and find happiness. The entire Message of Fatima is a call to abide by this divine Law.

However, in order to avoid disillusionment, it is necessary, in this as in other parts of the Message, to distinguish between Sister Lucia the 'seer' and instrument of God, and Sister Lucia the 'interpreter', with her own intelligence, and her own undoubtedly noble and generous heart. Whatever she may say as 'seer', although, like faith itself, carefully sifted by a rigorous theology, must be accepted with that 'must' characteristic of guaranteed private revelations. But anything she may say as 'interpreter', particularly in the case of decisions which may affect the pastoral care of souls, does not come within her competence, but belongs, rather, to the living Magisterium of the Church.

As a guarantee of the truth, I can state categorically that, in the book, Sister Lucia always displays great sureness and conviction when reproducing the Message of Fatima, transcribing words from Heaven that were given to her either directly in the Apparitions or indirectly through her prayerful reading of Sacred Scripture, in accordance with the well-known maxim of St Ambrose cited by Vatican II: «We speak to him [God] when we pray; we hear Him speak to us when we read the divine oracles» (Dogmatic Constitution, *Dei Verbum,* nº 25).

She takes great care to avoid value judgements or interpretations, leaving the last word, and submitting herself unconditionally, to the decision of the ecclesial Magisterium; and she takes the same care when she needs to speak of historic values, or expound a theological reading of the quotations she adduces, whether from the Message or from the Bible, contenting herself with expressing her own personal opinion only in those cases where she cannot fall back on those of experts or specialists which are, understandably, unknown to her. Our Lady asked her to 'learn to read' (Apparition, 13th June 1917); She did not ask her to go to the University!

Except for a few very beautiful and mystically dense passages that occur from time to time, and in which Sister Lucia expresses her own feelings, she displays great reserve in speaking of herself or of the interior graces with which Heaven has favoured her throughout her life. In this connection, it is well to remember that it was not her intention, nor did she ask the Holy See's permission, to write her autobiography. Nonetheless, allow me to say that, in this book, the author appears not so much as a 'seer' or 'interpreter' but rather as a 'confidante', as is evident not only from the degree of attention, dedication and understanding with which she treats those who approach her, but above all from the fact that she offers her own experience of development in her understanding of the various requests contained in the Message which she received.

In fact, as she herself recognises, 'although supernatural revelations are ordinarily accompanied by a special grace which clarifies their meaning, in fact, at the time, the three children were very far indeed from realising its full meaning as we can understand it today and transmit it to souls, as it is God's will that I should, and it is for this that He continues to keep me here at his disposal.' And she states categorically about herself: «Only many years later was I able to read the Holy Bible, and only then did I discover the most intimate meaning of the Message and its connection with the Word of God.». So she patiently goes back over the path she herself has trodden, copying out biblical passages which she feels give the full meaning of the particular *call* she is discussing, always viewed from its abidingly valid and eternal relevance.

We know that the little shepherds of Fatima were favoured with visions of life beyond the grave, related in particular to the ultimate destiny of this earthly pilgrimage: they experienced ineffable happiness when they felt themselves wrapped in God and God dwelling in them (Apparition, 13th May, 1917), and were terrified when they saw the fate of those condemned to hell (Apparition, 13th July 1917). Such a parting of the ways as one leaves this life and enters into the next remains for everyone shrouded in the veil of mystery, which reason can conceive of and faith to some extent penetrate, helped by the word of witnesses given special insight by Heaven. Now, when Sister Lucia transcribes the voice that came to her from Heaven, she displays such sureness and certainty that she still remembers something of the light seen in the faces she contemplated. For this reason, I feel certain that this book will do much good to all those who feel within themselves some anxiety, disquiet, or maybe even despair concerning their eternal destiny.

There are many people who dream of having a face to face meeting with Sister Lucia. Such a dream is unlikely to be fulfilled. However, I believe that such people will find in this book the reply to the deepest questions they would like to put to her; and even if the concrete question they have in mind is not explicitly formulated, they will certainly see the way she would suggest that they approach it in order to find the best solution to their problem, if in fact it were possible for them to have such an encounter with her. My hope is that *Calls from the Message of Fatima* will awaken deep echoes in the hearts of all men and women of good will, encouraging them to tread the path that will lead them to God, the origin and final end of the great human adventure.

With this wish and expressing the Church's sincerest thanks to Sister Lucia, I conclude with a prayer in this blessed Place to the Virgin Mary for Christ's Church and for all human beings, «especially those who are most in need».

Shrine of Fatima, 13th October 1997.

Serafim de Sousa Ferreira e Silva
✠ *Bishop of Leiria-Fatima*

PREFACE

On 13th May, 1982, a year after the attempt on his life in St Peter's Square, Pope John Paul II came as a pilgrim to Fatima. Referring to the Message that had been entrusted by the Virgin Mary to Jacinta, Francisco and Lucia, the Pope said: "If the Church accepted the message of Fatima, it is above all because it contains a truth and a summons which are in essence the truth and the summons of the Gospel itself."

These words of the pilgrim Pope who has spread the message of the Virgin Mary in Fatima throughout the world with such energy and authority, are the key to reading and interpreting the book which Lucia has given to us. Its title, so suggestive for the Church of today, is *Calls from the Message of Fatima* and in it we find the mature and full synthesis of the message Sister Lucia received from the Mother of the Lord.

The publication of this book completes the series of events which, in this year of Jubilee, focussed the attention of the Church and of the world on the blessed place where Mary appeared, and on the extraordinary occurrences which so profoundly marked the century that is just coming to an end. The events I refer to were: the coming of the Pope to Fatima for the beatification of the two little shepherds, Francisco and Jacinta Marto, and the official publication of the last part of the secret of Fatima by those responsible in the Congregation for the Doctrine of the Faith.

Without adding anything to these events and occurrences, the publication of Lucia's book, the fruit of prolonged meditation, and bearing the date of 25th March, 1997, provides what we might call her authorised explanation of the whole of the Fatima message. The intention is not to satisfy the curiosity of devotees, but to help them to explore in depth, in the light of faith, the spiritual importance of the Virgin Mary's words, always in the light of the one and only definitive proclamation of the message of revelation, the Gospel of Jesus, of which his Mother's words are a living memory, an urgent appeal and an indispensable point of reference. Mary, in Fatima, came to evangelise our century.

In tune with the Gospel

Lucia's book is, in a sense, the seer's spiritual testament, and was written especially for all who have asked her for an authoritative interpretation of the message of Fatima. To read it is to feel one's heart expand. With great simplicity and openness, Lucia has sketched out a kind of message of Fatima according to the Gospel, or a Gospel according to Fatima, to express it in the words of John Paul II quoted above. On every page of the book, the words of the private revelation are, in fact, compared with the truths of Scripture, springing from the pure sparkling source of revelation in the Old and New Testaments.

From the very beginning, the reader is amazed by the constant reference to Scripture. The hermeneutic behind Our Lady's message in Fatima is a biblical hermeneutic, so much so that more than half of the text consists in explicit or implicit references to Sacred Scripture. Lucia is very much at home in the books of the Bible from Genesis to the Apocalypse, and especially so in the Gospels. In each chapter, she compares the essence of the Fatima message, or some part of it, with the truth of Scripture which she cites freely and without forcing its meaning. In this way, not only does she make credible the words of the Lady of Fatima and of the Angel which, being private messages, are subject to the authorised interpretation of the Church, but she also views them wholly in relation to the absolute and authorised truth of Revelation. Thus, the private revelation of Fatima is derived from the public Revelation, the word of God interpreted by the Church, so that Fatima becomes a kind of charismatic and prophetic manifestation, in the service of the Word of God, entrusted to the interpretation of the magisterium of the Church under the guidance of the Holy Spirit (*Cf. Dei Verbum, n. 8*).

Like a catechism of Fatima

Another characteristic of Lucia's book is its *catechetical dimension.* One is moved spontaneously to describe it as a *Catechism of Fatima* in both senses of the word.

On the one hand, Lucia once again spells out the main sweep of the Message, very simply, though at the same time in a systematic and ordered pedagogical way, almost as if it were a catechetical explanation adapted for the wise and the simple, with the authorised mediation of Scripture.

On the other hand, the various parts of the book correspond closely to the general pattern of a little *Catechism of the Christian Life according to Fatima.*

The first part is a necessary introduction to the historical and geographical reality of the events of Fatima, expressing in a simple narrative theology what happened, at a particular moment in our history, to a particular family in the tiny unknown hamlet of Aljustrel where the apparitions began. The title given to this first part, *Under the eyes of God,* characterises extremely well the simple and pious atmosphere in the homes of the Fatima seers, an atmosphere where God was certainly present and was pleased to dwell.

Lucia recalls it, as she has done at length in her other writings, reconstructing and recreating almost poetically that little piece of blessed earth and sacred history where God chose to speak, through Mary, to the men and women of our time. Lucia does not hesitate to tackle a subject which is very dear to her: an apologia of the ideal of the Christian family. She also delights in expounding the providential presence of angels in the history of salvation since, for the little shepherds too, angels were messengers communicating to them the mysteries of God, catechists of the divine mysteries, in preparation for the apparitions of the Mother of God.

The second part is *theological and spiritual* in character. In it, Lucia expounds some of the fundamental mysteries of the Christian faith, taking as a basis the theological virtues of faith, hope and charity, which are so central both to the Christian life as such (with their proper object, the mystery of God and his revelation in Christ and in the Church), and to the supernatural vitality of that life. The result is a catechesis on the theological virtues and on the spirit of prayer and adoration, which the seers of Fatima received from the Angel, as a heavenly forerunner of the Queen of Angels.

Next come reflections on fundamental aspects of the faith and spiritual life of Christians: intimacy with the Trinity, the Eucharist, devotion to the Immaculate Heart of Mary, the importance of apostolic mission, eschatology, perseverance in virtue, the universal call to holiness: in the family, in religious life, in the lives of all Christians.

The third part — like the third part of the *Catechism of the Catholic Church* — is *decidedly moral in character*. With the competence of one of God's catechists, and in communion with the Magisterium of the Church, Lucia recalls the ten commandments of God's Law.

She does so with the burning desire that God's commandments should be observed perfectly by all men and women of our time, because in them we find expressed the will of God for our society today, as the Pope himself recalled in his apostolic journey to Mount Sinai.

She explains the commandments in the light of the New Testament with concrete applications of a spiritual character. She then sums up the whole Law of God in that of divine charity.

The necessary complementarity between the ethical and spiritual dimensions of God's commandments makes the message of Fatima effective, concrete and demanding from the moral point view, and so establishes a coherence between the faith and the life of Christians.

Again as in the *Catechism of the Catholic Church* the fourth part is dedicated to *prayer*: prayer which Lucia centres in the daily recitation of the Rosary, of which she knows how to sing the praises and extol the importance, quoting long passages from the teaching of the Popes starting from Gregory XIII and Sixtus V, who were the first to present this devotion to the Church, right down to that of the more recent pontificates, from that of Leo XIII to John Paul II.

In her apologia of the Rosary, Sister Lucia contributes considerably to the catechesis on the mysteries of Christ and Our Lady, meditates theologically on the joyful, sorrowful and glorious mysteries, with a lengthy section devoted to the central mystery of our faith: the Resurrection of the Lord.

All in all, Lucia's book presents the message of Fatima as, essentially, a call to faith, morality and spirituality, with constant reference to Scripture in the form of short chapters which constitute a short but basic Catechism of the Christian life.

A simple style: theology and spirituality

The book, liberally sprinkled as it is with the inspired word of God, is easy to read on account of the coherence and simplicity of the themes discussed and their applications. Moreover, as custodian of the message of Fatima, our author adds to the abundant collection of biblical texts a good dose of that *sensus fidei* and *sensus fidelium,* that simple appreciation of the faith on the part of the faithful which is the spiritual anointing of the Holy Spirit, Master of the faithful with his gifts in the Church (*Cf. Lumen Gentium, n. 12*).

Lucia is thus seen to be in full harmony with the faith of the Church and with the faith of simple people. What stands out most in her is that good sense of the Portuguese peasant which she always displayed throughout her life, even when she undertook important tasks in her community, such as Sub-Prioress of the Carmel in Coimbra. At times her prose takes on a poetic tone, especially when she praises the beauty of God in creation. One should note the wisdom of the contemplative, but also the practical approach of a woman attentive to the vicissitudes of our world and of our history as they affect our daily lives, born of her desire to infuse the lymph of the Gospel into the spiritual and moral problems of our society.

Hence, the seer of Fatima also contrives to be exactly right in the way she applies her spiritual and moral lessons, without, however, either moralising or indulging in a vague spiritualism. This concrete practicality underlies the urgent demand for moral coherence in the Christian life as designed by God, and that runs parallel to the profound theological demands of the Christian life and also the vital breath of a popular, Christological and Marian piety, which is both simple and universal.

This is the piety that one can actually touch in the Cova da Iria in Fatima, almost as if it were a storehouse of the true Christian sense of life, of the true popular sense of the Christian experience, far removed from all intellectualistic deformations of Christianity, as well as from élitist spiritualities and secularising tendencies.

In this, the author reveals one of the most authentic qualities of true Marian piety: coherence with the Gospel, a profound ecclesial sense, the universality of the Christian message, the ability to dedicate both mind and heart, the realistic approach to the problems of life and death, of day--to-day life and the most authentic experiences which have as their point of reference the last realities of Christian eschatology: Purgatory, Hell, Heaven.

The dividing up of the various themes into short chapters, each of which resembles a letter replying to the many questions asked by the devotees of Fatima, make the book attractive, and turn it into a kind of spiritual treatise, that is not meant to be read at one sitting in a fruitless search for novelty, but rather to be pondered day by day, like a kind of daily manna, in order to nourish a true Marian piety, received as a message from the Mother of the Lord for our day to day lives.

Hence, the reader need not go looking for anything in the way of scientific or intellectual points of view, or hidden novelties in the secrets of Fatima, as they are not there to be found! Lucia is also restrained in the use she makes of some of the documents of the Church's present-day Magisterium. This is not because she is not aware of them, but because it is neither her style nor her intention to make use of them.

What she does do, and at great length, is to quote the words of the Popes in favour of devotion to, and the saying of, the Holy Rosary. For the rest, she refers back with conviction to the Magisterium of the Church in our own day, to which she has always been faithful in her religious life and in her serene and trusting obedience to the Pope and to the Holy See, even in all that she says concerning the phenomenon and message of Fatima.

Some themes of greater importance

Many important and original things are woven into Lucia's book. I will glance briefly at some which I consider to be particularly significant.

First and foremost, the great opening call of the Message of Fatima to *prayer* and *penance*. Beyond all moralism or devotional interpretation of a reductionist kind, Lucia presents a fine biblical synthesis on prayer which has, in Jesus, its model and master: in the Our Father, that rich and simple compendium of Christian prayer, and in the priestly prayer of Jesus, contained in the seventeenth and culminating chapter of St John's Gospel, a key page of the Gospel for which Lucia shows her preference and with which she identifies, as can be seen from numerous quotations from the Johannine texts that are scattered throughout the book. In the same way, Lucia handles carefully the question of penance and Christian conversion, such a forgotten subject nowadays, with all the implications that this has in the light of sin and grace, of redemption and the call to salvation. She illustrates her teaching by concrete examples drawn from the ordinary lives of the people of today.

Intimacy with the Trinity and the celebration and adoration of the Eucharist are outstanding theological themes in the spirituality of Fatima, and as such are in harmony with the Magisterium of the Church and with the Trinitarian and Eucharistic inspiration of the Jubilee Year in accordance with the wishes of John Paul II.

It goes without saying that the tone of the entire book, evoking as it does the message of the Lady of Fatima, is predominantly Marian. However, the Marian spirituality that comes to the fore is entirely subordinate to Christ, from the very first pages where Jesus' words in the Gospel of St John are quoted: *"I am the way, the truth and the life"* (Jn, 14,6). Mary is a living image of her Son. Lucia has thus coined a happy expression in speaking of *"Mary's commandment"*, with reference to the words she spoke in Cana: *"Do whatever He tells you"* (Cf. Jn 2, 1-10). Naturally, the seer of Fatima insists on the special nature of the new and renewed devotion to the *Immaculate Heart of Mary*, the pure heart of a Mother watching over this tragic century, which is also a providential time in the history of the Church, a time both of sorrow and of hope, a century entrusted to the heart of a Mother, in order to negotiate the transition to the new millennium with confidence and hope. A heart which helps us to understand the essential Marian nature of the Church.

Lucia's passionate apologia for the *Holy Rosary*, the pledge given by Mary to the little shepherds, is firm and convincing. Here, too, she stresses the biblical inspiration of this Marian prayer *par excellence.* In the Rosary she finds a simple and profound way to a form of devotion to Mary which enables us to tread in the footsteps of Christ and Mary as we go through the joyful, sorrowful and glorious mysteries of our salvation: the *via lucis* of all beginnings, the *via crucis* of Christ's passage to the Father; the *via gloriae* of the Son and of the Mother. A person who is very close to Lucia told me that the three little shepherds understood the value of the Rosary as a call to prayer and an easy way of responding to Jesus' call to us to pray always. When Our Lady told them to pray the Rosary every day, they were already going to Mass, Lucia had already made her first Confession and was receiving Communion regularly; they said their morning and night prayers. The saying of the Rosary enabled them to pray continuously, that Christian ideal long practised in the Church from the earliest times down to our own day. In its simplicity, the Rosary does indeed make it possible to pray continuously: prayer in heart and mind, calling on the name of Jesus and having recourse to Mary now and at the hour of our death.

The devotion to Our Lady that is practised in Fatima is intimately linked with the life of the Church, the faith of the Church, the morality of the Church, fidelity to the Magisterium, the sacramental life of the Church, especially to the sacraments of Christian initiation and penance. Once again, Mary is coupled with the Church, an idea that we could perhaps express as follows: no Mary without the Church and no Church without Mary. One cannot conceive of a presence of Mary that does not point to Christ and his Church, nor can one conceive of an authentic ecclesiality which does not include the presence of the Mother of Christ and of the Church. Fatima is a synthesis of this indissoluble link between Mary and the Church, so dear to the Magisterium of Vatican II and to the post-Conciliar Popes such as Paul VI and John Paul II. This explains how it is that Lucia does not hesitate to speak of Mary as Mother and Mistress of the Apostles in the early Church.

The entire message of Fatima is a *great call to holiness for the Church of our time*. In this, too, it is at one with the great scheme of Vatican II, of the Extraordinary Synod of 1985 and of the Apostolic Letter *Tertio millenio adveniente*.

Lucia sees this call to holiness in some of the details of the apparitions. The presence of St Joseph in one of the apparitions is a pressing invitation to *the sanctification of the family*, a key theme throughout Lucia's book, and also one of the essential currents and main preoccupations of the magisterium of John Paul II. The apparition of Our Lady of Sorrows standing beneath the Cross at the peak moment in her life, is seen by Lucia as an invitation to the *perfection of Christian life*. And, finally, the apparition of Our Lady of Mount Carmel wearing the Carmelite habit suggests the *call to perfection in the consecrated life*, following Christ *in the way* of the evangelical counsels of chastity, poverty and obedience. But, as Lucia affirms and explains, it is also an urgent *call to holiness for all Christians,* a call which comes from Mary, model of the most perfect holiness to which a creature can attain.

We must thank Lucia for giving us, in this book, this lovely theological and spiritual synthesis of the message of Fatima, which strengthens our faith and our Christians lives. Lucia writes as a daughter of Mary and a daughter of the Church.

These two facets of her personality and of her providential mission are expressed with simplicity and clarity in the opening dedication to Mary and in the concluding words of the book in which she entrusts it to the

Virgin Mary for the glory of the Lord, and for the good of souls and of his Church.

I, who am a brother in religion to Sister Lucia of Jesus and of the Immaculate Heart, discalced Carmelite of the monastery of Coimbra, am happy to present this book. It is at one and the same time both Gospel and Catechism of Fatima, and is sure to confirm the faith of all who have a devotion to the white and lovely Lady of the Cova da Iria. It will also serve to make *Mary's commandment* known in this third Christian millennium: the call to return to the pure source of the Gospel in accordance with the words she spoke at Cana: "Do whatever He tells you". It is a message which reveals the desire of the maternal Immaculate Heart of Mary: an urgent and universal call to holiness for the peace of the world and for the salvation of all in Christ.

P. Jesus Castellano Cervera ocd
Consultor of the Congregation
of the Doctrine of the Faith

16th July 2000
Memory of the Blessed Virgin Mary of Mount Carmel

Front page of *O Século* for 15th October 1917, broadcasting the news
of the "Miracle of the Sun" throughout the country

The three little shepherds at the place of the apparitions

The first Chapel of the Apparitions, erected in 1918

The statue in the Capelinha and the crown containing the bullet

The three children in front of the arch
that had been erected at the site of the apparitions
(October 1917)

Painting illustrating the Apparition of 13th June 1917
(Sr Maria da Conceição, OCD)

The parish church in Fatima in 1917

Statue of Our Lady of the Rosary
in the parish church in Fatima

Father Manuel Marques Ferreira,
parish priest of Fatima
from 1914 to 1919

The home of Lucia's parents

Members of Lucia's family

Cova da Iria, beatification of Francisco and Jacinta (13/05/2000)

Lucia, aged 13

Lucia, aged 17

Convent of the Sisters of St Dorothy (Pontevedra – Spain)

Pontevedra. Room of the Apparition on 10/12/1925...

... which was later turned into a chapel

Convent where Our Lady asked for Russia to be consecrated to her
(13/06/1929)

Vision of the Blessed Trinity which occurred
in the course of the June 1929 Apparition (Tuy, Spain)

Pius XII consecrates the world to the Immaculate Heart of Mary
(31st October, 1942)

In St Peter's Square in Rome, before the statue of Our Lady of Fatima
from the shrine chapel, Pope John Paul II,
together with all the bishops of the church, consecrates the world and
Russia to the Immaculate Heart of Mary (25th March, 1984)

D. José Alves Correia da Silva with the envelope containing the 'secret'

Cardinal Sodano reveals the third part of the secret (13th May, 2000)

Drawing illustrating the third part of the secret (J. Gil)

Sister Lucia with Pope Paul VI (13th May, 1967)

Pope John Paul II with Sister Lucia (13th May, 2000)

The Carmel in Coimbra

Statue of the Immaculate Heart
of Mary in the Carmel in Coimbra

Sister Lucia coming out of her old home (16th May, 2000)

I beg you, Mother, to guide my pen
so that it may faithfully transmit the Message which God,
through You, chose to entrust to me.

Ave Maria!

INTRODUCTION

I address this to all those who have faith and also to all who have not the happiness of possessing this gift of God, because we are all pilgrims on our way to eternity, whether we know it or not.

I have received countless letters containing a great many questions and requests. I should have liked to be able to reply to each one separately, but as this was not possible, I am replying now to all in general with «*Calls from the Message of Fatima*» which God chose to entrust to me on behalf of all. I do so in the conviction that this is God's will, recognised as such by legitimate authority, and I offer for all the sacrifice that this work will require of me.

It is not an interpretation of the Message; this pertains to God's Church. Neither is it an historical account of the Apparitions, as this is already known to you. Many authors have told the story better than I could ever have done, and it is contained in many books that have been spread throughout the world. All I wish to do is to reply to the questions, and clarify the doubts, that have been put to me.

Please do not look upon this communication as something that comes from myself. Look upon it, rather as the echo of the voice of God, and let us all willingly endeavour to follow faithfully the path that He has mapped out for us. Yes, because it was out of love that God sent us this pressing call from his mercy, in order to help us along the way of our eternal salvation.

«*I am the way, and the truth, and the life*» (Jn 14,6): said the Lord to his Apostles, and also to us. Those who follow the Way of Truth, who is the Word of God, follow Jesus Christ, and have within them the Source of life. Again, it is Our Lord who has told us «*It is the spirit that gives life, the flesh is of no avail*» (Jn 6, 63). So it is with my eyes fixed on the Way of Truth that I shall endeavour to explain the Message to you exactly as God entrusted it to me, and gave me to understand what it means and to which souls it is addressed.

I would ask you, therefore, not to pay any attention to the poverty and ignorance of the instrument which God chooses to use, because He is in the habit of choosing poor and useless instruments to accomplish the works of his power, knowledge and wisdom. This will be yet another proof He is giving you that the work is his and not mine.

Part One

IN THE PRESENCE OF GOD

1

The three little shepherd children
and their families

I will begin by replying to the questions you have asked me about the atmosphere in the homes of the humble children who were chosen by God so that He might accomplish his mighty purposes through them.

They were two Christian families which were closely related by blood. Aunt Olimpia was my father's sister and her first husband had been a brother of my mother's. They had two children, António and Manuel. After her first husband died, Aunt Olimpia married Uncle Marto, who was also related to my mother, a cousin, in fact, though I'm not sure to what degree. Six children were born of this marriage: José, Florinda, Teresa, João, Francisco and Jacinta.

My own parents, António dos Santos and Maria Rosa, had seven children: Maria dos Anjos, Teresa de Jesus, Manuel dos Santos, Glória de Jesus, Carolina de Jesus, Maria Rosa – whom God took to Heaven while she was still very small so that I never knew her – and Lúcia de Jesus Rosa dos Santos, who is talking to you now.

There was such a close bond between these two families that the children felt as much at home in the house of their aunt and uncle as in their own; and in both would eat for their afternoon snack some of the fresh bread still warm from the oven, made into a sandwich with fresh sardines from Nazaré, or with slices of salted cod or sausage taken from the reserve that had been put aside for consumption in the course of the year. At other times, the filling consisted of pieces of game which provided a family feast at certain times in the year: rabbits caught in clever traps, partridges caught in the hay and in the corn fields, thrushes caught in the snares set beneath the olive trees and baited with ripe olives.

But the whole village was so united that it appeared to be one single family! Everyone knew which was the hole in the wall in which the mistress of the house put the key when she went out. If a neighbour needed anything, she knew that she could go in and look for whatever it was she wanted, faithfully returning it later on. What tended to happen most frequently was for the bread to run out sooner than expected; in which case, one would have recourse to one's neighbour; then, later on, when the new batch had been baked, one would pay her back with some fresh warm bread straight from the oven.

The little village of Aljustrel, which at that time comprised no more than about thirty-five families, was situated in the *Serra de Aire* in the parish of Fatima, council district of Vila Nova de Ourem and the diocese of Leiria; at that time this diocese was extinct so it had been annexed to the Patriarchate of Lisbon. I don't know if there was anyone living there then, even amongst the very oldest inhabitants, who remembered having seen the red clothes worn by a Prelate, or who had received the Sacrament of Confirmation.

Like everyone else in the parish, the two families were poor, hardworking Christians, extracting all that they needed to live on from the cultivation of their own plots of land.

Their homes had been blessed by the Sacrament of Matrimony; and their conjugal fidelity was absolute. They welcomed all the children that God chose to send them, not as a burden but as another gift with which God was enriching their homes, another life to prolong their own into the future, another flower to bloom in their garden, filling it with the perfume and joy of the many scents and shades of fresh smiling youth, another soul entrusted by God to their care so that, by guiding it in the ways of Heaven, it could become yet another member of the Mystical Body of Christ, yet another hymn of praise to eternal glory.

Hence, they made sure to bring them to the baptismal font in order to wipe away the stain of original sin from their souls and make them Christians, children of God and heirs to the Kingdom of Heaven. The baptism, which had to take place no more than eight days after the birth, was a cause of great rejoicing for all the family. All came together to congratulate the parents who had been honoured by another gift from God.

It was on their father's knees and their mother's lap that the children learned to pronounce the Holy Name of God, to raise their innocent little hands in prayer to their Heavenly Father and heard about that other Mother who, with the Child Jesus in her arms, welcomed them, too, with the same tenderness, because she is their Mother also, though much more powerful, holy and beautiful than the earthly mother who rocked their cradle. Thus, the light of faith grew so strong in these delicate, pure and innocent souls that it later illuminated their whole lives in all its meanderings.

The parents were careful to send their children to the catechism classes in the parish church, in order to prepare them as well as possible for the great day of their First Communion. At home, they themselves were the children's teachers, teaching them during the afternoon siesta and after the evening meal. It was usually the father who performed this task, while the mother was busy with the housework, tidying up the kitchen after the frugal supper. The parents were happy to see their little ones jumping up and down round the hearth listening to the stories which their smiling father delighted in telling them, while the chestnuts and sweet acorns from the holm oaks burst open among the embers where they had been carefully placed by an older brother or sister in order to make things even jollier, causing the children to back away and end up laughing.

The parents felt very proud when, either during the catechism lesson or when the adults were being questioned prior to the fulfilment of their Easter duties, the parish priest called upon one or other of their youngest children to answer the questions to which the grown-ups either did not know the answer, or had forgotten it.

The day on which each of their children made his or her First Communion was one of solemn and intimate rejoicing for all the family, for on that day God was once again visiting their home and uniting Himself with one of its members. It marked the return to God of the innocent soul that He had entrusted to them and with them they sang the hymn of thanksgiving:

O Angels sing with me
O Angels praise without end!
To give thanks I am not able,
O Angels, give thanks for me!

In their homes there was no abundance of the earthly goods that the world sets such store by. However, with the little that was needed for each day, there was peace and unity, joy and love, the fruit of mutual understanding, mutual asking and granting of forgiveness for the inevitable shortcomings of human frailty. Thus everyone was happy; everyone was content, because everyone endeavoured to serve and give pleasure to their parents, brothers and sisters. In this way, the little went a long way because it was shared: everything belonged to everyone.

Let me pause here to tell you a little incident which confirms the truth of what I have just said, and of which I preserve a happy memory, as I heard my mother tell it several times with great emotion. She knew that her youngest daughter was very fond of fruit. One day she noticed how the little one was carefully watching the first of the early figs ripening; as soon as she found one that was ripe, she picked it stealthily and ran back to the house to give it to her mother for her to eat. My mother, moved, took the gift into her hands, kissed her daughter and told her to keep the fig until the evening so that it could be shared with her father and the rest of the family! One fig among so many is nothing, but the love that accompanied the little piece that everyone got from the first fig that had ripened on their own fig trees that year was a great deal, and it was this that made everyone happy, instilling in them a feeling of joy and satisfaction.

Herein lies the secret of happiness, on earth and in Heaven: in *Love!* God loved us and delivered Himself for love of us, writes the Apostle Saint Paul. God loves us and for love of us He is in our tabernacles, waiting for our humble return of love. And God is within us, since we are temples of the adorable Trinity: «*Do you not know that you are God's temple and that God's Spirit dwells in you?*» (1 Cor 3,16).

With this spirit of faith, and in spite of their lack of worldly knowledge, these admirable parents took the greatest care in safeguarding the innocence of their children lest anything should soil the whiteness of their infant souls. As Our Lord Himself warns us: «*See that you never despise any of these little ones, for I tell you that their angels in heaven are continually in the presence of my Father in heaven.*» (Mt 18,10).

Yes, my dear pilgrims, the Angels in heaven always behold the face of Eternal Light, and in it – as in an immense mirror before which everything passes – everything is present, everything remains as if carved in indelible characters: the past, the present and the future. Everything that exists and was created by God: heaven and hell, the earth, the stars, the sun, the moon, worlds known and unknown, all animate and inanimate beings, absolutely everything, receives its being and life from the wish, the power, the knowledge and the wisdom of that Infinite Light which is God, the one and only Source from which is derived all life that exists, and of which every other light and life is no more than a tiny particle, a pale reflection, one of his sparks. Thus the Angels in Heaven, gazing into this mirror of light which is God, in Him, see all things, know all things, understand all things through their complete union with God and their participation in His gifts.

Forgive me for this digression. I let the pen put on paper what my heart was dictating. But it will be for your benefit, to strengthen you in your faith, so that you do not allow yourselves to be deceived by those who deny the existence of God. They are wrong. Do not let them trick or deceive you, leading you astray on false trails which could well lead you to eternal damnation. But I will leave this subject for now and come back to it later, when I shall have another opportunity to clarify things of this kind for you. Let us now go back to what I was saying in reply to your requests for information about the three shepherd children's family backgrounds.

Everybody fulfilled the precept of keeping holy the Sundays and the other Holydays of Obligation. In the morning, everyone went to Mass. In the afternoon people relaxed. The young people would meet together and have a good time in our yard, in the shade of the huge fig trees and under the watchful eyes of their parents who, in groups apart, talked about the work in the fields, played cards, and so on.

When the sun went down and the church bells rang, everybody stood up, the men taking off their characteristic cap and holding it in their hands while the Angelus was said, followed by the traditional goodbyes 'Adeus'. It was time to go back home for a family supper after a happy day well spent, and with a good conscience after having kept the Law of God and restored one's physical strength so that, at dawn on the following day, each one could again take up their daily tasks with renewed vigour.

After supper, the father would start the grace after meals followed by a string of Our Father's, Hail Mary's and Glory be to the Father's for all the intentions that came to mind. Then the mother would lead the Rosary, or the Crown of seven Mysteries in honour of Our Lady of Dolours. There would then be a few moments of conversation, discussion of the plans for the next day's work, and then to bed as the night is short.

Early next morning the grown-ups and the older children would get up with the approach of dawn in the light of the rising sun; then off they went, cheerfully singing to the sound of a harmonica, guitar or fife, crunching underfoot the over-ripe olives, thistles, gorse and thorns in order to gather the manna of life, as if for them as for the Israelites in days gone by, it would rain down on them from heaven, together with the fresh morning dew.

43

As soon as the children reached the age of seven, they began to take their share in the running of the house by being taught how to look after the flocks. Like the Patriarchs and Kings of old, nearly every family has its little flock of gentle sheep which the children led out to graze in the green fields belonging to their parents. The flock helped considerably towards the maintenance of the family: milk and cheese, lambs to replace sheep that have grown old, or for sale on the market; wool which the women of the house used to spin, dye and then weave, in order to use it, later, to make warm coloured shawls for the winter, or to make mats for the humble bedrooms, or round blue serge skirts with wide red stripes to adorn the Sunday clothes worn by the girls. Gold earrings reaching down to their shoulders, glistening medals hung round their necks, a scarf over their shoulders and a cool hat covering their heads decorated with gold beads and coloured feathers completed their adornment.

Would that the clothes people wear in our own day had even a touch of the modesty, the respect for human dignity, displayed by those worn by the village women of those days! It will be good for us to recall here what Sacred Scripture has to say on this subject: «*Yahweh God made clothes out of skins for the man and his wife, and they put them on.*» (Gen. 3, 21).

Why did God clothe the first two human beings if, before that, they were naked? Scripture itself tells us the answer:
«*Then Yahweh God gave the man this admonition, 'You may eat indeed of all trees in the garden. Nevertheless of the tree of the knowledge of good and evil you are not to eat, for on the day you eat of it you shall most surely die' (...) The woman saw that the tree was good to eat and pleasing to the eye... she took some of its fruit and ate it. She gave some also to her husband who was with her, and he ate it. Then the eyes of both of them were opened and they realised that they were naked. So they sewed fig-leaves together to make themselves loin cloths. (...) But Yahweh God called to the man. 'Where are you?' he asked. 'I heard the sound of you in the garden;' he replied 'I was afraid because I was naked, so I hid.' 'Who told you that you were naked?' he asked 'Have you been eating of the tree I forbade you to eat?' The man replied, 'It was the woman you put with me; she gave me the fruit, and I ate it'. Then Yahweh God (...) to the man he said, 'Because you listened to the voice of your wife and ate from the tree of which I had forbidden you to eat (...) accursed be the soil because of you. (...) It shall yield you brambles and thistles (...) With sweat on your brow shall you eat your bread, until you return to the soil, as you were taken from it. For dust you*

are and to dust you shall return.' Yahweh God made clothes out of skins for the man and his wife, and they put them on.» (Gen 2,16-17; 3,6-21).

This sacred text shows us that God covered the bodies that had stripped themselves, through sin, of the garment of grace. For this reason, we must all clothe ourselves decently, modestly and with dignity. Those who appear indecently dressed are an incentive to sin, and so are responsible not only for their own sins but also for those that others may commit because of them. Reflect that fashion, if it is indecent – and we see that the world unfortunately follows it as if it were a law – is a trick of the devil, a clever trap in which the devil catches souls, in the same way as hunters catch game in the woods and fields.

God did not give us clothing as an adornment in order to feed our human vanity and frivolity. No! He gave it to us as a protection against sin, as a sign of penance for sin committed, and a punishment for it, as well as to remind us of the laws of God which we are all obliged to obey.

Let us begin by examining how it is a sign of punishment and penance for sin committed, and a protection against temptation. The sacred text tells us that, after they had sinned, Adam and Eve tried to cover themselves with fig leaves; but God did not think this was enough because, Sacred Scripture tells us, He *«made clothes out of skins for the man and his wife, and the put them on.»* (Gen. 3, 21).

Then follows a description of the punishment and the penance imposed on account of the sin: *«Yahweh God expelled him from the garden of Eden, to till the soil from which he had been taken»* (Gen. 3, 23). And this *«until you return to the soil, as you were taken from it. For dust you are and to dust you shall return.»* (Gen. 3, 19). Thus, after clothing them, God expels them from the garden, but only after having imposed on them the penance of work, telling them to cultivate the earth until they return to the ground from which they were taken, in other words until they die.

Human beings brought the sentence of death on themselves by sinning in disobeying the commandment of God, who had told them: *«But of the tree of the knowledge of good and evil you shall not eat, for in the day that you eat of it you shall most surely die».* (Gen 2,17) Yes, your body will die because you sinned and transgressed the law of your God. But, worse still, your soul will be lost for ever unless you repent and do penance. You will die, if you do not change your life, if you do not return to obeying the law of your God.

Notice, however, that it is not only for these two reasons – punishment and penance for our sins – that God clothes us; it served other purposes too. Besides being a protection against sin, the modest clothing with which we must cover ourselves is a distinguishing mark setting us apart in the stream of immorality and enabling us to be, for the world, true witnesses of Christ.

Clothing also serves to remind us of the laws of God, and of our serious obligation to obey them. God, in fact, asked his people to wear, over their clothes, concrete signs which would remind them of his holy commandments: «*Speak to the people of Israel and bid them to make tassels on the corners of their garments throughout their generations, and to put upon the tassel of each corner a cord of blue; and it shall be to you a tassel to look upon and remember all the commandments of the Lord, to do them, not to follow after your own heart and your own eyes, which you are inclined to go after wantonly*» (Num. 15, 38-39)

Let us look at what God is saying here: *The tassels of your clothes will serve to remind you of the commandments of the Lord, to do them, not to follow after your own heart and your own eyes, which you are inclined to go after wantonly.* Our clothes, then, are to be a protection for the eyes and the heart, so that we will not allow ourselves to be caught in the temptations of the flesh, the devil and the world. The tassels mentioned in the text undoubtedly envisage some kind of decoration on our clothing; but such decoration must be in accordance with modesty, with the dignity of the human person, with decency, in short, with morality, prompting us to observe the commandments of the Law of God.

Finally, let us reflect on the expression that God uses: «*throughout your generations*». This makes us think that God was not speaking for the sake of the Israelites of that time alone. What He said to them concerns us too, today, as it will concern those who come after us – not in the external form of the sign chosen which, naturally, changes, but in the meaning and specific purpose we must not lose sight of, if we are to respect the order of things as God created them. Because the Law comes to us from God and does not change; it is immutable as He himself is immutable.

It is the Lord himself who tells us this in the Gospel: «*Think not that I have come to abolish the law and the prophets; I have come not to abolish them but to fulfil them. For truly, I say to you, till heaven and earth pass away, not an iota, not a dot, will pass from the law until all is accomplished*» (Mt 5, 17-

18). Whoever keeps it will be saved; whoever does not keep it will be condemned!

Returning to the passage from the book of Genesis concerning the punishment for the sins of our first parents, let us not go any further without pausing for a few moments to reflect on another penance that God imposed on us in punishment for our sin: *«In the sweat of your face you shall eat bread till you return to the ground for out of it you were taken; you are dust, and to dust you shall return»* and *«the Lord God sent him forth from the garden of Eden, to till the ground from which he was taken»* (Gn 3, 19;23)

It is the punishment of work. We all have to work, to eat our bread by the sweat of our brow. It is a duty that no-one can escape from, for the law of work applies to everyone, rich and poor, wise and foolish, superiors and subjects.

But do we, in fact, work in this spirit of penance? In other words, in reparation for our sins? In a spirit of reparation and charity for the salvation of our neighbour? If so, we are giving its full force to the first and greatest of the commandments: *«You shall love the Lord your God with all your heart, and with all your soul and with all your mind and you shall love your neighbour as yourself»* (Mt 22, 37.39).

The Angel Raphael said to Tobit: *«When you prayed, I brought a reminder of your prayer before the Holy One; and when you buried the dead I was likewise present with you.»* (Tob 12, 12). Will our work, too, be thus clothed with charity, and so worthy to be offered to the Lord as prayer?

Dear pilgrims, if by the work we do, and the lives we lead, we can offer salutary penance to God; if we can by this means earn Heaven and win salvation, why would we want to be lost?

However, now let us return to the family setting I was telling you about. Initiated, as I have said, at an early age into the life of a shepherd, the children grew and developed in the pure air of the fields, breathing in the scent of the simple flowers of the *serra*, of the heather, rosemary and gorse that grow in the thickets, of the lavender and pine trees, of the eucalyptus that crown the hilltops, of the holm oaks, oak and olive trees lining the slopes, of the enormous chestnut trees and fruit trees that grow in the fields and orchards.

In this oasis, the silence is broken only by the cheerful chirping of the birds which flit about among the treetops. They include the gentle voices of the turtle dove and the hoopoe guarding their nests, the clucking of the partridges pecking about among the rocks in the middle of the cornfields, then there is the swoop of the swallows, and the cuckoos which emigrate during the summer months; not to mention the swift flight of foxes and hares when someone disturbs the undergrowth, and the venturesome rabbits hidden in the hay.

Touched by the fresh early morning breezes, the children live happily with the creaking of the heavy carts used to carry home the crops, the music of the labourers' harmonicas, barrel organs and guitars, with the singing of the young men and women returning in groups from gathering olives or grapes, with the singing of the cocks in the chicken runs in the nearby villages and the church bell ringing out the Angelus.

Surrounded by the enchantments of nature, their innocent souls live with a longing for the supernatural which their intuition, prompted by grace, tells them is even richer and more enchanting. Then, when the sun goes down behind the pine trees, they bring their bleating flocks back to their pens, after which they run and play close to their parents whom they are never tired of kissing in order to show their affection. In this way their pure souls shine like the light of the sun, and their smiling eyes are as clear as the crystal-clear water from a spring. Only Heaven holds out a greater hope for them: it is their faith which prompts them to look upwards, giving them a more genuine smile as they look forward to a more valuable treasure. Their souls pray; in their parents' arms they rest peacefully at night, sleeping the undisturbed sleep of those who have no cares.

I think, dear pilgrims, I have now answered all your questions about the family background of the three humble shepherd children whom God chose in order to transmit his Message to you through them. Do not, however, conclude from what I have told you that in these homes there were none of the shortcomings due to human frailty. There were, of course, but there was also understanding, forgiveness, peace and love.

Now, in exchange for having replied to your questions, let me ask you some: if your own homes were not better, were they at least as good as the two I have described? Has your home been blessed and established under the sacrament of Matrimony?

Have you accepted and are you still willing to accept all the lives which God may wish to entrust to you? Remember that getting rid of them is against the law of God who has told us in the fifth commandment: «*You shall not kill: and whoever kills shall be liable to judgement*» (Mt 5, 21).

Do you keep your marriage vows, as you promised to one another before God? This, too, is required of you by the Law of God when it says: «*Be chaste*». This comes in both the sixth and ninth commandments which Jesus explained as follows: «*You shall not commit adultery. (...) everyone who looks at a woman lustfully has already committed adultery with her in his heart*» (Mt 5, 27-28) And God also says: «*You shall not swear falsely, but shall perform to the Lord what you have sworn*» (Mt 5, 33)

Are you careful to bring your children to be baptised in order to make them Christians, remove from their souls the stain of original sin and make them heirs to the Kingdom of Heaven? This too has been ordained for us by God: «*Go into all the world and preach the gospel to the whole creation. He who believes and is baptized will be saved; but he who does not believe will be condemned.*» (Mk 16, 15-16). In truth, this command of Our Lord's imposes a great responsibility on parents. Those who put off having their children baptised are exposing them to the risk of finding the way to happiness barred to them, something far worse than if they were to lose possession of the whole world. Yes, indeed, for nothing can be compared to the supreme good of Eternal Life. And who can guarantee that your children will live while you put off such an important event?

Whoever believes and is baptised will be saved. Obviously, a new-born baby cannot of itself make acts of faith, but the virtue or gift of faith is infused into its soul as one of the fruits of the sacrament of Baptism, which purifies it and releases it from the stain of original sin, making it worthy of eternal happiness. I urge you strongly not to make yourselves responsible, through carelessness or lack of faith, for one of your children being deprived of the immense happiness of Heaven. The fact is that if you were to lose them (and I hope and earnestly beseech God not to allow such a thing to happen), this would be yet another eternal punishment for you.

Now to change the subject. Do you keep the third commandment of the Law of God which requires us to observe Sundays and the Holydays of Obligation? Do you do so by abstaining from servile work and going to Mass ? Remember that God says in Holy Scripture: «*Six days shall work be done, but the seventh day is a sabbath of solemn rest, holy to the Lord*» (Ex 31,15). Note the expression God uses here: a day «*consecrated to the Lord*». Hence, the Lord's Day is not to be passed in idleness, still less in unlawful pleasures, in vice or any kind of sin. Sundays and Holydays are to be used to bring us close to God by taking part in the Eucharistic Liturgy and other devotions, reading good books which will give us a better knowledge of God and of his Laws so that we can fulfil them better, and engaging in wholesome entertainment which will enable us to recuperate our physical and moral energies. Only thus can we have an easy conscience and be certain of fulfilling the Law of the Lord.

Are you careful to bring up your children in the knowledge of God and of his laws ? Bear in mind that this, too, is a sacred duty and forms part of the mission God has entrusted to parents, as we are told in Sacred Scripture: « *When your son asks you in time to come, 'What is the meaning of the testimonies and the statutes and the ordinances which the Lord our God has commanded you?' then you shall say to your son (...) 'the Lord commanded us to do all these statutes, to fear the Lord our God, for our good always, that he might preserve us alive, as at this day'* » (Dt 6, 20 and 24)

Jesus, the divine Master, did not avoid answering the questions that were put to Him about the Law of God, even when they were asked «*in order to trap him, "Teacher, which is the great commandment in the law?" Jesus said to him, "You shall love the Lord your God with all your heart, and with all your soul, and with all your mind. This is the great and first commandment. And a second is like it: You shall love your neighbour as yourself. On these two commandments depend all the law and the prophets*» (Mt 22, 36-40).

And the book of Deuteronomy leaves us in no doubt: «*These words which I command to you this day shall be upon your heart; and you shall teach them diligently to your children, and shall talk of them when you sit in your house, and when you walk by the way, and when you lie down, and when you rise. And you shall bind them as a sign upon your hand, and they shall be as frontlets between your eyes. And you shall write them on the doorposts of your house and on your gates*» (Dt 6, 6-9). In them fathers and children will find their eternal happiness: «*Oh that they had such a mind as this always, to fear me and to keep all my commandments, that it might go well with them and with their children for ever!*» (Dt 5, 29).

These words spell out clearly the mission which God has entrusted to parents in the education of their children. Parents are their children's first teachers. It is in their father's arms and on their mother's lap that little children, while still innocent, must learn to pronounce the Holy Name of God, to raise their pure little hands to Heaven in prayer, to smile their lovely childish smile at the images of their Heavenly Father and Heavenly Mother.

It is the parents who must guide their children's feet in the righteous paths of the Law of God and entrust them, in accordance with their means and circumstances, to competent teachers who will not turn them away from the paths on which they have been set. After all, what benefit would great knowledge be to them if they were to lose their immortal souls? By losing their soul, they will have lost everything, because our life here on earth is over in a flash, whereas eternity abides unchangingly for ever.

Undoubtedly, the human sciences, with all the knowledge they contain, are good, especially when a wise person manages, by means of them, to discover the immensity of the power, the wisdom and the goodness of God who, out of love for us and for our good, created so many marvels. This knowledge will instil in us a profound humility when we realise that after so much effort and study the greatest wise men have still not managed to understand fully even one of the countless marvels that issue from the almighty creative hands of God.

Thus, every home must be the children's first school where they will learn to know God and to draw near to Him by means of the sacraments and prayer; where they will learn to prepare themselves for their First Communion, not only by being taught the precepts that embody the Law of God but also by having instilled into them that lively faith, firm hope and ardent charity which, when engraved in their souls at an early age, will abide there as a light to guide their steps throughout life. In this way, your children will be happy, and the Bread of Angels will be the food that strengthens them: «*This is the bread which came down from heaven; (...) he who eats this bread will live for ever.*» (Jn 6, 58)

When you read these lines, dear pilgrims, some of you may ask yourselves what they have got to do with the Message of Fatima or with the atmosphere in the two homes about which you have asked me questions. Let me tell you that they have a great deal to do with it because, since the Message as a whole is a call to keep the Law of God, I think that it will have been the fact that these families kept these divine laws, in spite of the inevitable weaknesses of human nature, that drew down upon them the gaze of the infinite mercy of God.

Praised be Our Lord Jesus Christ!

Ave Maria!

2

The Guardian Angel

The description of the two homes makes it clear that they were solidly Christian. They were, however, very far from being able to put any mystical ideas into the minds of the children, or any exalted spirituality such as is evident in the Fatima Apparitions. Hence, what happened could only have come entirely from God.

Having replied to the first question, I shall now endeavour to reply to the second, which is the one that has been put to me most frequently: «Tell us, Sister, what exactly happened during the first apparitions about which little or nothing has been said?»

It must have been in 1914 or 1915, shortly after I began to care for my parent's flock of sheep, because I had already begun the life of a humble shepherd together with other children of the area, when we were surprised by an apparition that completely puzzled us. One day when we were on the slopes of the hill known as the *Cabeço*, we saw something like a white cloud in the shape of a human being, which had come down from the sky and was passing slowly in front of us, above the trees that stretched down to the valley at our feet, as if wishing to attract our attention and keep our eyes fixed on it.

Some of the girls who were there told their parents what they had seen, but I said nothing beyond confirming, when asked, what the others had said. I have been asked many questions about this apparition, which happened several times in different places. My reply today is the same as it was then: *I do not know what it was nor what it meant.* But I was left with an interior conviction which I do not wish to conceal, and which tells me that it was the Guardian Angel. Perhaps in that form and without speaking, he wished to make his presence felt and so prepare souls for the accomplishment of God's designs.

Until now, I have not wished to say any more about those apparitions than I needed to say in order to reply to the questions that were put to me. Today, however, I am doing so, not in order to confirm whether or not they were the Guardian Angel, but in order to tell you that Guardian Angels truly exist, and that they were created by God to serve, adore, praise and love Him. It is equally certain that God, in his abundant goodness and mercy has given each of us an Angel to accompany us, help and guard us.

I tell you this categorically, not simply because it was given to me to see; if such were the case, my words would not be very convincing. I am telling you what God has revealed to us in the sacred pages of the Old and New Testaments. You are free not to believe in what I myself say, but you cannot doubt the Word of God contained in Sacred Scripture. So let's have a look at some of the passages in which God reveals to us this truth about Guardian Angels.

When Moses was crossing the desert, leading the People of God to the Promised Land, the Lord said to him: «*Behold, I send an angel before you, to guard you on the way and to bring you to the place which I have prepared. Give heed to him and hearken to his voice, do not rebel against him, for he will not pardon your transgression; for my name is in him.*» (Ex 23, 20-21).

And the sacred text also tells us what happened to Jacob when, in obedience to his parents' wishes and in order to escape the foreseeably violent reaction of his brother Esau, he set off for Paddan-aram: «*He came to a certain place, and stayed there that night, because the sun had set. Taking one of the stones of the place, he put it under his head and lay down in that place to sleep. And he dreamed that there was a ladder set up on the earth, and the top of it reached to heaven; and behold, the angels of God were ascending and descending on it! And behold, the Lord stood above it and said, "I am the Lord, the God of Abraham your father and the God of Isaac; the land on which you lie I will give to you and to your descendants; and your descendants shall be like the dust of the earth, and you shall spread abroad to the west and to the east and to the north and to the south; and by you and your descendants shall all families of the earth bless themselves".*» (Gen 28, 11-14).

I have heard various commentators on Sacred Scripture say that God communicated with the Patriarchs of old by means of dreams, as He spoke to the Prophets by means of visions. It must have been so, because if the dreams were mere dreams, there would have been no reason to attach such importance to them, neither would people have come to realise how, in fact, they were fulfilled in the life of Jacob.

We find the same thing in the life of St Joseph and the Three Wise Men, as the Gospel tells us. When the Wise Men had departed «*An angel of the Lord appeared to Joseph in a dream and said, "Rise, take the child and his mother, and flee to Egypt, and remain there till I tell you; for Herod is about to* search for the child, to destroy him." And he rose and took the child and his mother by night, and departed to Egypt».(Mt 2, 13-14).

As regards the Wise Men, the same Evangelist describes what happened: «*Now when Jesus was born in Bethlehem of Judea in the days of Herod the king, behold wise men from the East came to Jerusalem, saying, "Where is he who has been born king of the Jews?" (...) Then Herod summoned the wise men secretly and ascertained from them what time the star appeared; and he sent them to Bethlehem, saying, "Go and search diligently for the child, and when you have found him bring me word, (...) When they heard the king they went their way (...) and going into the house they saw the child with Mary his mother, and they fell down and worshipped him. (...) And being warned in a dream not to return to Herod, they departed to their own country by another way. (...) Then Herod sent and killed all the male children in Bethlehem and in all that region who were two years old or under*» (Mt 2, 1-12; 16).

Wise and studious men such as the Wise Men would not be inclined to believe in mere dreams or allow themselves to be guided by them. Hence, I believe that what they received were not so much dreams as true revelations of the supernatural. All the more so because dreams, as compared with revelations, are of less value than the night as compared with the day. In fact, whereas dreams leave in us a confused and vague memory of whatever it was we dreamt about, revelations are engraved indelibly in our spirit and leave a clearer memory even than of an ordinary conversation one has had with another person.

A certainty of this kind must have been engraved in the minds of Wise Men and of St Joseph. Otherwise, they would not have attached so much importance to the dream, forcing Our Lady to get up in the middle of the night and set off for a foreign country with a tiny child in her arms, and without giving her time to make any preparations or secure some means of transport.

In addition to the events just described, Sacred Scripture describes many others which prove to us the existence of Angels and how God sends them, sometimes as messengers, at other times as helpers or as guardians and defenders. Here are some passage from the sacred pages:«*Jacob went on his way and the angels of God met him; and when Jacob saw them he said, "This is God's army!" (...) And Jacob was left alone; and a man wrestled with him until the breaking of the day.(...) Jacob asked him, "Tell me, I pray, your name". But he said, "Why is it that you ask my name?" And there he blessed* him. *So Jacob called the name of the place Peniel, saying, "For I have seen God face to face, and yet my life was preserved."* (Gen. 32,2; 24.29-30).

One day when Our Lord was talking to his disciples, he said to them: «*See that you do not despise one of these little ones; for I tell you that in heaven their angels always behold the face of my Father who is in heaven*» (Mt 18, 10).

And St Luke, describing the events surrounding the annunciation and the birth of the divine Word and his precursor John the Baptist, refers to several interventions by Angels: «*While Zechariah was serving as a priest before God when his division was on duty, (...) there appeared to him an angel of the Lord standing on the right side of the altar of incense. And Zechariah was troubled when he saw him, and fear fell upon him. But the angel said to him, "Do not be afraid, Zechariah, for your prayer is heard, and your wife Elizabeth will bear you a son, and you shall call him John*» (Lk 1, 8; 11-13).

«*In the six month the angel Gabriel was sent from God to a city of Galilee named Nazareth, to a virgin; (...) and the name of the virgin was Mary. And he came to her and said, "Hail, full of grace, the Lord is with you!" (...) "Do not be afraid, Mary, for you have found favour with God. (...) "The Holy Spirit will come upon you, and the power of the Most High will overshadow you; therefore the child to be born will be called holy, the Son of God.*» (Lk 1, 26-28; 30.35)

When the time had run its course, Mary's Son was born in the city of David called Bethlehem: Now, in that region «*There were shepherds out in the field, keeping watch over their flock by night. And an angel of the Lord appeared to them, and the glory of the Lord shone around them, and they were filled with fear. And the angel said to them, "Be not afraid; for behold, I bring you good news of a great joy which will come to all the people; for to you is born this day in the city of David a Saviour, who is Christ the Lord. (...) And suddenly there was with the angel a multitude of heavenly host praising God and saying, "Glory to God in the highest, and on earth peace among men with whom he is pleased!"*» (Lk 2, 8-11.13-14).

But already in the very first pages of Sacred Scripture the existence of Angels is affirmed when, after Adam's sin, we are given a description of his expulsion from the garden of Eden: «*He (God) drove out the man; and at the east of the garden of Eden he placed the cherubim, and a flaming sword which turned every way, to guard the way to the tree of life.*» (Gen 3, 24).

All the passages of Sacred Scripture which I have mentioned, and many others, prove to us that Angels really exist and also the purpose for which

God created them, which is exactly the same as the purpose for which He created us: «*To serve Him, praise Him, adore Him and love Him*».

With this conviction, then, let us sing with the psalmist: «*Because you have made the Lord your refuge, the Most High your habitation, no evil shall befall you, no scourge come near your tent. For he will give his angels charge of you to guard you in all your ways. On their hands they will bear you up, lest you dash your foot against a stone.*» (Ps 91/90, 9-12).

Bearing these truths in mind, it will not seem so strange to us that God should have once again chosen to make use of one of his Angels in order to address to us yet another call to obey his law and remember the end for which we were created.

Ave Maria!

Part Two

CALLS FROM THE MESSAGE OF FATIMA

3

The Call to Faith

I want now to go back over the Message which the good God, through his most holy Mother, entrusted to the humble little shepherds of the Cova da Iria, in order to convey once again his perennial calls to the people of today, and in particular to those who come on pilgrimage to Fatima.

To say 'pilgrims of Fatima' is the same as saying 'pilgrims of peace; I am told that there is a language in which the word 'Fatima' means 'peace'. At all events, we are all pilgrims of peace. We all desire and long for peaceful days, to be able to live in peace. But this peace will not be achieved until we use the Law of God as the norm and guide of our steps. Now the entire Message of Fatima is a call to pay attention to this divine Law. For this reason, we will go through it step by step and it will point out for us the way we are to go.

When the Apparitions took place, I did not really know this Law; I only had a limited and very vague idea about it, no different from that of any other simple ignorant child, such as I was then, unable to read and write, and living in a place such as my home village, so far removed from education and culture. Moreover, in spite of having later lived in more educated circles, I confess that I only acquired this knowledge very slowly, through the light that God gave me.

In fact, only long after those events took place, and after I had written about them, was I allowed to read Sacred Scripture. Only then did I understand the true meaning of the Message, although it had been given to me to understand it earlier, but in a less concrete way.

The first Call of the Message:

My God, I believe.

It was the Spring of 1916 ... At least, I think it was, because at that time, being a child, I did not bother my head with dates, and might even not have known what date of the month it was! One day, then, about that time, when the three little Fatima shepherds were on the slope of the hill known as the *Cabeço*, beneath a rock called the *Loca*, they saw, some way off, a young man approaching them who seemed to be made of light. When he reached them, he said: «*Do not be afraid. I am the Angel of Peace. Pray with me*». Then, kneeling down on the ground, he bowed low until his forehead touched the earth and said the following words three times: «*My God, I believe, I adore, I hope and I love You. I ask Your pardon for those who do not believe, do not adore, do not hope and do not love You*». He then straightened himself and said: «*Pray thus; the Hearts of Jesus and Mary are attentive to the voice of your supplications*».

The first call which God addresses to us through his Messenger is thus a call to faith: *My God, I believe.*

Faith is the basis of the entire spiritual life. It is by faith that we believe in the existence of God, in his power, his wisdom, his mercy, his work of redemption, his pardon and his fatherly love.

It is by faith that we believe in God's Church, founded by Jesus Christ, and in the doctrine the Church transmits to us and by which we shall be saved.

It is the light of faith that guides our steps, leading us by the narrow way that leads to Heaven.

It is by faith that we see Christ in others, loving, serving and helping them when they are in need of our assistance.

And it is also our faith that assures us that God is present within us, that his eyes are always upon us. They are eyes of Light, almighty and immense, which extends everywhere, sees everything, and penetrates all things with the unique clarity proper to the Divine Sun alone, as compared with which the sun which we see and which warms us is no more than a pale reflection, a fragile spark emanating from the Light of the immense Being which is God.

What I have just said to you is nothing new: St John had already said it at the beginning of his Gospel: «*In the beginning was the Word, and the Word was with God, and the Word was God. He was in the beginning with God; all things were made through him, and without him was not anything made that was made. In him was life, and the life was the light of men. The light shines in the darkness, and the darkness has not overcome it.*» (Jn 1, 1-5). In this passage, St John speaks to us of the eternal Being of the Word of God; he tells us that everything was created by Him; that everything received from Him the being that it possesses. In his power, goodness and infinite wisdom, God bestows on everything that exists all the gifts it needs for its subsistence. Hence, everything depends on Him and without Him nothing can continue to exist.

St John also speaks to us of the light of God, telling us that this light is our life: «in Him was Life and the Life was the light of men». Hence, our life is a spark from the Light of God shining within us. It came from God and must return to God, unless sin drives it away.

These truths open up paths of light before us. It is up to us to choose whether or not to follow them. Everything that exists is a manifestation of God, of his provident and redeeming creative work.

In our day, when science has made such progress, when daring men have walked on the moon, and the world rejoices in so many advances, let none of the wise men of today forget the name and greatness of the Artificer who created all these worlds which they so much long to explore.

Let me tell you about something that happened to me a few years ago. We had heard the news about two astronauts on their way to the moon who had not managed to reach their destination. I went out into our garden with the intention of going as far as the image of the Immaculate Heart of Mary which we venerate there. As I went out through the door, I paused for a few moments to watch the bees from a hive in front of it. They were furiously busy! Then I noticed an ant crawling up one of the filaments of a spider's web, in an attempt to get from there to the hive. But a bee returning to the hive loaded with pollen knocked against the filament and broke it, and the ant fell to the ground, its aim frustrated.

Then I thought about the two astronauts who were lost in space and was sorry for them; and I thought: this ant falls to the ground and the bee enters triumphantly into the hive with the fruit of its labours! The two are an image of human power and knowledge set alongside the power and knowledge of God.

How much study, how many calculations, how much energy and sacrifices have men put into the effort of setting foot on a star which God created with a single act of his will, his wisdom and his power. Being almighty, He placed it there and keeps it there, always in the same position, always following the same path which God has marked out for it for as long as God wills. And not only the moon. The same is true of all the other stars, too, known and unknown, which travel round in space where men can never dream of going. Here we have, side by side, the greatness of God and the powerlessness of men.

With these thoughts in mind, I took out my Rosary and went down to the image of Our Lady to pray, asking her, since God had not granted to these men the grace of treading on the moon, at least to grant them the grace of returning safe and sound to their country and the bosom of their families.

But faith does not consist solely in believing in the existence of God, in his power and in his wisdom. It has many other facets turned in other directions, and our full adherence must extend to their utmost extremities.

The word of God contained in Sacred Scripture is a revelation which we cannot deny because – as Jesus Christ himself tells us in his Gospel – «*The words that I say to you I do not speak on my own authority; but the Father who dwells in me does his works. Believe me that I am in the Father and the Father in me; or else believe me for the sake of the works themselves.*» (Jn 14, 10-11).

We see that Jesus Christ draws our attention to his works, because what a person does bears true witness to what a person is, and confirms what a person says. Hence, when St John the Baptist sent his disciples to Jesus to ask if He were the Messiah or if they were to wait for another, «*Jesus answered them, "Go and tell John what you hear and see: the blind receive their sight and the lame walk, lepers are cleansed and deaf hear, and the dead are raised up, and the poor have good news preached to them.*» (Mt 11, 4-5).

As no-one other than God can perform miracles, Jesus uses them to confirm his word and his power of life: «*He who hears my word and believes him who sent me, has eternal life; he does not come into judgment, but has passed from death to life.*» (Jn 5, 24).

So we see that the word of Jesus Christ is the word of God, because Jesus Christ is God, equal to the Father in all things and able to say: «*I and the Father are one*» (Jn 10,30). Jesus Christ is truly the Son of God who became man in the womb of the Virgin Mary through the Holy Spirit: «*The Holy Spirit will come upon you, and the power of the Most High will overshadow you; therefore the child to be born will be called holy, the Son of God.*» (Lk 1, 35).

When, at the Annunciation, the Angel addressed these words to Mary, he proclaimed the divinity of the Son who was to take human flesh in her womb and be born in order to make Himself equal to us, visible to our eyes and so able to accomplish the work of our Redemption.

Jesus Christ, then, is true God and true Man. His word is eternal life for those who listen to it and carry it out. To reject it is to carve out one's own sentence of condemnation, as the Lord tells us: «*If any one hears my sayings and does not keep them, I do not judge him; for I did not come to judge the world but to save the world. He who rejects me and does not receive my sayings has a judge; the word that I have spoken will be his judge on the last day. For I have not spoken on my own authority; the Father who sent me has himself given me commandment what to say and what to speak. And I know that his commandment is eternal life. What I say, therefore, I say as the Father has bidden me.*» (Jn 12, 47-50).

He had said earlier on: «*The words that I have spoken to you are spirit and life.*» (Jn 6, 63). The word of Christ is the word of the Father: «*The Father who sent me has himself given me com-mandment what to say and what to speak.*» (Jn 12, 49b). Thus Christ came into the world, not in order to destroy the Law of God but to fulfil it, perfect it and explain to us its true meaning and how we are to understand it and practise it. His words were: «*Think not that I have come to abolish the law and the prophets; I have not come to abolish them but to fulfil them.*» (Mt. 5, 17).

Jesus Christ came into the world as a Teacher in order to teach us, to guide our feet in the way of truth, justice, charity and life. Any way other than the one He has mapped out for us is a way that leads to eternal death.

One day «*Then Pharisees and scribes came to Jesus from Jerusalem and said, "Why do your disciples transgress the tradition of the elders? For they do not wash their hands when they eat." He answered them, "And why do you transgress the commandments for the sake of your tradition? For God commanded, 'Honour your father and your mother,' and, 'He who speaks evil of father or mother, let him surely die.' But you say, 'If any one tells his father or his mother, What you would have gained from me is given to God, he need not honour his father. So, for the sake of your tradition, you have made void the word of God. You hypocrites! Well did Isaiah prophesy of you, when he said: 'This people honours me with their lips, but their heart is far from me; in vain do they worship me, teaching as doctrines the precepts of men.'*» (Mt 15, 1-9).

This text shows clearly the extent to which the law of justice and charity had become distorted, whereas in fact it requires us first and foremost to help our neighbour, all the more so in the case of a father or a mother. And it is equally just, charitable and necessary for us to help one another. That is what Jesus Christ taught us when He said: «*If you had known what this means, 'I desire mercy, and not sacrifice,' you would not have condemned the guiltless.*» (Mt 12, 7).

From this we can deduce how necessary it was for the Law of God to be clarified, because men had misinterpreted it. We have this clarification in Christ, who was sent to us by the Father and so can say to us: «*He who hears my word and believes him who sent me, has eternal life; he does not come into judgment, but has passed from death to life.*» (Jn 5, 24).

His teaching is precise and exact. But in order to carry out the word of Jesus Christ, we need to know it and to believe in Him. How can we fulfil a Law if we do not know it, or if we do not believe in the One who promulgated it? Hence, it is necessary to acknowledge the person of Christ.

In the world, there are unfortunately many people who believe themselves wise, but who know little or nothing about the laws of God. Sadly, moreover, people often argue against these laws, not because they know them well, but because they see in them an obstacle to their own disordered passions, to their lack of justice and charity. And yet, it is the laws of God that we should all be most anxious to know, as it is through them that we shall be either saved or condemned.

There are others who do, in fact, know the laws of God but who interpret them to mean quite the opposite of what Christ said, believing, in this way, that they are justifying the disorderliness of their own disorderly conduct; they thereby cause great harm to themselves and to their neighbour, whom they deceive by their bad example, their outlook and their misleading words. They are like those about whom Jesus Christ said: «*Let them alone; they are blind guides. And if a blind man leads a blind man, both will fall into a pitt.*» (Mt 15, 14).

Hence, we must be on our guard where they are concerned. By applying the rule that Jesus Christ gave us, we can know them by their fruits: «*For no good tree bears bad fruit, nor again does a bad tree bear good fruit; for each tree is known by its own fruit. For figs are not gathered from thorns, nor are grapes picked from a bramble bush. The good man out of the good treasure of his heart produces good, and the evil man out of his evil treasure produces evil; for out of the abundance of the heart his mouth speaks.*» (Lk 6, 43-45). This is the guiding principle given to us by Jesus Christ: to examine the fruits of those who present themselves as our guides in the ways of life and see whether or not they are in accordance with the teaching of the one true Church of God founded by Jesus Christ, which possesses the gift of infallibility in recognising and declaring the Truth of Christ with the help of the Holy Spirit: «*And I will pray the Father, and he will give you another Counsellor, to be with you for ever, even the Spirit of truth, whom the world cannot receive, because it neither sees him nor knows him; you know him, for he dwells with you, and will be in you.*» (Jn 14, 16-17).

This promise made by Jesus Christ to his Church gives us absolute certainty in the ways of faith which we must tread, and which have been marked out for us by the Church of Christ, since the Church in turn is guided by the Holy Spirit; it is the Holy Spirit who speaks to us through the mouth of the Church.

I have been asked the following question a number of times: «*How are we to know the true Church of Christ?*»

The theologians who study these things will be better able to answer this question than I, who am poor and ignorant. I would not even attempt to do so unless the sacred text were there to elucidate the matter for us.

St Matthew describes how Jesus Christ, having come with his apostles into the region of Caesarea Philippi – as they crossed the lake to get there the Master had warned them against the false teaching of the Pharisees who did not believe in Him – asked them the following question: «*"But who do you say that I am?" Simon Peter replied, "You are the Christ, the Son of the living God." And Jesus answered him, "Blessed are you, Simon Bar-Jona! For flesh and blood has not revealed this to you, but my Father who is in heaven. And I tell you, you are Peter, and on this rock I will build my church, and the powers of death shall not prevail against it. I will give you the keys of the kingdom of heaven, and whatever you bind on earth shall be bound in heaven, and whatever you loose on earth shall be loosed in heaven."*» (Mt 16, 15-19).

That was how Jesus Christ appointed St Peter as Head and Leader of his Church on earth, with all the powers to govern, direct and instruct, under the guidance and with the abiding help of the Holy Spirit; and it was for this reason that the divine Master gave him the gift of «infallibility». If this were not the case, Jesus Christ could surely not have promised that whatever his representatives did in his name on earth would be endorsed in Heaven. We all know very well how men and women, mere creatures that they are, are subject to shortcomings and liable to make mistakes; hence, it is the assistance of the Holy Spirit promised to his Church by Jesus Christ that guarantees for us its infallibility: «*"The word which you heard is not mine but the Father's who sent me. These things I have spoken to you while I am still with you. But the Counsellor, the Holy Spirit whom the Father will send in my name, he will teach you all things and bring to your remembrance all that I have said to you"*» (Jn 14, 24-26). And later on, reverting to the same subject, the Lord also said: «*When the Counsellor comes, whom I shall send to you from the Father, even the Spirit of truth, who proceeds from the Father, he will bear witness to me; he (...) will guide you into all the truth*» (Jn 15, 26; 16, 13).

Thus the infallibility of the Church is guaranteed for us by the words of Christ who is the Truth: «*I am the way, and the truth, and the life; no one comes to the Father, but by me*» (Jn 14, 6). Our way is the word of Christ, entrusted to his Church, with the assistance of the Holy Spirit.

But your questions went further than that: *«Among the various Churches that call themselves Christian, which is the earliest and the true one?»*

As we have seen, Jesus Christ chose St Peter as Head and Leader of his Church on earth. He entrusted to him the deposit of his teaching, for him to keep and teach, together with all those who would remain united to him in the same faith, the same hope and the same charity.

St John tells us that one day after his resurrection, Jesus Christ waited on the beach for his apostles who had gone fishing; and that He gave them a meal of grilled fish and bread when they got out of the boat. «*When they had finished breakfast, Jesus said to Simon Peter, "Simon, son of John, do you love me more than these?" He said to him, "Yes, Lord; you know that I love you." He said to him, "Feed my lambs." A second time he said to him, "Simon, son of John do you love me?" He said to him, "Yes, Lord; you know that I love you." He said to him, "Feed my sheep." He said to him the third time, "Simon, son of John, do you love me?" Peter (...) said to him, "Lord, you know everything; you know that I love you." Jesus said to him, "Feed my sheep."*» (Jn 21, 15-17).

Jesus Christ thus entrusted to the care of St Peter the flock which is his Church: the lambs and the sheep, the sheep and the shepherds. Hence, the true Church of Christ is made up of all those who remain united to Peter by the same faith, the same hope and the same love, which is the love of Christ. God is *Love*, and for that reason He elicits from his Representative a triple declaration of *Love*.

In truth, the Church of God is the Church of charity, of *Love*. It was precisely this that Jesus Christ asked of his Father shortly before he gave himself up to death for us: «*Holy Father, keep them in thy name, which thou hast given me, that they may be one, even as we are one. (...) "I do not pray for these only, but also for those who believe in me through their word, that they may all be one; even as thou, Father, art in me, and I in thee, that they also may be in us, so that the world may believe that thou hast sent me. The glory which thou hast given me I have given to them, that they may be one even as we are one, I in them and thou in me, that they may become perfectly one, so that the world may know that thou has sent me and hast loved them even as thou hast loved me."*» (Jn 17, 11; 20-23).

We see that Jesus prays to the Father not only for the Apostles, but also for all of us who would believe in Him and in his word, which would be transmitted to us by the Apostles and their successors. And what is it that He prays for from his Father? That the members of his Church might remain so united as to be one. «*"I do not pray for these only, but also for those who believe in me through their word, that they may all be one"*»; so that «*"the world may know that thou has sent me and hast loved them even as thou hast loved me"*», and «*that they may become perfectly one*».

With these words, Jesus reveals to us the nature of the unity of his one unique Church. One single unity that does not allow of division: «*The glory which thou hast given me I have given to them, that they may be one even as we are one*». United in the same faith, hope and charity.

Before this prayer to his Father, Jesus had spoken at length to his disciples. At one point He had said to them: «*Abide in me, and I in you. As the branch cannot bear fruit by itself, unless it abides in the vine, neither can you, unless you abide in me. I am the vine, you are the branches. He who abides in me, and I in him, he it is that bears much fruit, for apart from me you can do nothing. If a man does not abide in me, he is cast forth as a branch and withers; and the branches are gathered, thrown into the fire and burned.*» (Jn 15, 4-6). In this allegory of the vine and the branches, we see that the life of the members of the Mystical Body, which is the Church, depends on their union with Christ. He is the Head of the Church in the person of his Representative, and we are its members; He is the vine and we are the branches. Just as the branch, if separated from the vine, dries up and yields no fruit; in the same way if we, through sin, separate ourselves from the true vine which is Christ, and cease to be fed by the sap of his grace, we wither and dry up and bear no fruit, becoming good for nothing except to be thrown on the eternal fire.

We have here a very clear statement of the fate awaiting those who are led astray by false ideas, by the temptations of the world, the devil or the flesh and so allow themselves to be turned aside and separate themselves from the true Mystical Body of Christ which is the Church. Without following them, we must pray and make sacrifices for them so that they may return to the right path, because God does not wish sinners to perish but rather that they be converted and live.

This is the reason why Our Lady urged us so insistently to pray and make sacrifices for the conversion of sinners: *«Pray, pray very much, and make sacrifices for sinners. Many souls go to hell because there is none to make sacrifices and to pray for them»* (Fatima, 19th August 1917). Hence, by our union with Christ and with his Church, we must offer ourselves as victims of expiation and petition for the conversion of our brothers and sisters. Herein lies the essence of our charity: to love those who perhaps do harm to us, contradict or persecute us. Our forgiveness, offered to them in the light of faith, hope and charity, will draw them back into the arms of God.

This is how the Church is *one*: one and only, united by the bonds of forgiveness, love and faith. It is one and *catholic* or *universal*, as Jesus taught us and commanded us: *«Go into all the world and preach the gospel to the whole creation. He who believes and is baptized will be saved; but he who does not believe will be condemned.»* (Mk 16, 15-16).

The Church of God is *apostolic*: it was entrusted by Jesus Christ to the Apostles and to their successors who received from them the faithful witness of the Redemption, with the mission of making it present and living in the farthest corners of the earth and of history: *«"All authority in heaven and on earth has been given to me. Go therefore and make disciples of all nations, baptizing them in the name of the Father and of the Son and of the Holy Spirit, teaching them to observe all that I have commanded to you; and Io, I am with you always, to the close of the age."»* (Mt 28, 18-20).

In these words, Jesus Christ assures us not only that He is entrusting his Church to the Apostles but also that He will be with them, in the person of their successors, until the end of the world. This presence of the Lord in his Church strengthens our faith, our hope and our charity, because the Church of God is Christ among us, it is Christ in each one of us inasmuch as we are members of his Mystical Body, of his Church.

We also say that the Church is *Roman,* because St Peter was the first Bishop of Rome. Being the visible Head and Leader of the Church of Christ, he there established the Chair of the Supreme Pontiff, that is, of the visible Head and Leader of the one true Church of God, founded by Jesus Christ. Thus all those who are legitimately elected as Bishops of Rome are the rightful and true successors of St Peter as the Representative of Christ on earth, visible Head and Leader of his Church, the Holy Father.

For all these reasons, we unite our prayer with the prayer of Christ, asking the Father for the unity of his Church, so that the world may believe that Christ was sent by the Father and, united in the same faith, in the same hope and in the same charity, we may together form the one Mystical Body of Christ and, through Christ, we may all be saved.

Thus, convinced that the true Church of God is the Catholic, apostolic Roman Church founded by Jesus Christ and kept in being by the Apostles and their successors, we must all remain united to it in the same faith, the same hope and the same charity, being receptive to its guidance and treading the paths it maps out for us, because the Church is the custodian of the true Law of God and the doctrine taught by Jesus Christ.

We must believe in the Church, trust in it, respect it, love it, pay heed to its teaching, follow in its footsteps, and remain united with its Head, who is Christ in the person of the Supreme Pontiff of Rome, the one true Vicar of Christ on earth, Head of the Mystical Body of Christ of which we are all members by our faith in Christ, as the Apostle St Paul tells us: «*For by one Spirit we were all baptized into one body – Jews or Greeks, slaves or free – and all were made to drink of one Spirit. For the body does not consist of one member but of many.*» (1 Cor 12, 13-14).

And the Letter to the Ephesians explains to us even more clearly this concept of our unity in Christ: «*In him you also, who have heard the word of truth, the gospel of your salvation, and have believed in him, were sealed with the promised Holy Spirit, who is the guarantee of our inheritance until we acquire possession of it, to the praise of his glory.*» (Eph 1, 13-14).

Hence, we were created and chosen by God to be the praise of his eternal glory. To be the praise of his Glory: this is the highest purpose for which God could have destined us! It means that, by participation, we have within us the glory of God with which we can praise Him; that we possess the honour of God with which we can extol Him; and that we are clothed with the dignity of Christ with which we can enhance his dignity, and work for an increase of this dignity in the members of his Mystical Body, so that each one can become ever more worthy. To achieve this we must all give ourselves fully to the Lord in a life of faith, hope and love.

Ave Maria!

4

The Call to Adoration

The second Call of the Message:

I adore.

Here the Message draws our attention to the first commandment of God's Law: « *"I am the Lord your God (...). You shall have no other gods before me. You shall not make for yourself a graven image, or any likeness of anything that is in heaven above, or that is in the earth beneath, or that is in the water under the earth; you shall not bow down to them or serve them, for I the Lord your God am a jealous God."* » (Ex 20, 2-5). And in another place, we read: « *You shall serve the Lord your God, and I will bless your bread and your water; and I will take sickness away from the midst of you.* » (Ex 23, 25)

By this Law, God commands us to adore Him alone, because He alone is worthy to be adored by his creatures. He forbids us to make idols out of the things that were created by Him and which are even more powerless than we are: they can do nothing and are worth nothing, which is why He forbids us to pay homage to them, or to adore them.

But we must distinguish between the idols to which God refers in this commandment and the images of Christ, of Our Lady and the Saints. We do not, nor should we, adore any of these images. We venerate them on account of what they represent and recall to our minds, in the same way as we venerate pictures of our parents, our brothers and sisters or our friends, placing them in the most honoured places in our homes so that we can see them better, and also so that the people who visit us can see them and be reminded of them too. We venerate the images of Jesus Christ, of Our Lady and of the Saints because they remind us of the people that they represent, of their virtues and of their teaching, and so encourage us to follow their example.

Jesus Christ, who is our model in all things, refused to pay homage to anyone other than God. St Luke tells that after He had been in the desert for forty days and forty nights, praying and fasting, He was tempted by the devil who said to Him: « *"To you I will give all this authority and their glory; for it has been delivered to me, and I give it to whom I will. If you, then, will worship me, it shall be all yours." And Jesus answered him, "It is written, 'You shall worship the Lord your God, and him only shall you serve.'"»* (Lk 4, 6-8).

Thus, to adore God is a duty and a commandment imposed on us by God out of love, so that He can shower his blessings on us. This is clear from the following episode: when Moses was leading the Israelites to the Promised Land, they all halted on the slopes of Mount Sinai. God then told Moses to go up to the top of the mountain in order to receive the Tables of the Law from the hands of God Himself. While Moses was there in the presence of God, the people fashioned a golden calf and worshipped it. God was very angry on account of this sin of the people and told Moses that He would destroy that idolatrous people. What did Moses do? He interceded on behalf of the people: «*And Moses made haste to bow his head toward the earth, and worshipped. And he said "If now I have found favour in thy sight, O Lord, let the Lord, I pray thee, go in the midst of us, although it is a stiff-necked people; and pardon our iniquity and our sin, and take us for thy inheritance."*» (Ex 34, 8-9). Thus, by prostrating himself in adoration before God, Moses secured pardon for the people and a renewed alliance with God.

How we are to adore God is described for us by St John in the conversation between Jesus and the Samaritan. At a certain point, the Samaritan says: «*Sir, I perceive that you are a prophet. Our fathers worshipped on this mountain; and you say that in Jerusalem is the place where men ought to worship"... Jesus said to her, "Woman, believe me, (...) the hour is coming, and now is, when the true worshippers will worship the Father in spirit and truth, for such the Father seeks to worship him. God is spirit, and those who worship him must worship in spirit and truth.*» (Jn 4, 19-24).

So we see that what matters is not where a person is; the important thing is for our spirit and our intelligence to recognise God in his infinite greatness, his immense power and in thus paying homage to Him, to adore Him.

Adoration is combined with love, acknowledgement and gratitude, because we owe no one as much as we owe to God. Sometimes, people express their great love for a person by saying: *I love So-and-so so much I adore him/her!* It is no more than an expression of affection, esteem, respect, for a person like ourselves. And ought we not to have it for God? Who deserves it more than, or as much as, God ?

It is true that in Leviticus, the Lord said: «*You shall make for yourselves no idols (...), and you shall not set up a figured stone in your land, to bow down to them; for I am the Lord your God.*» (Lev 26,1), but we also read in Sacred Scripture that in the desert, when the people of Israel were being attacked by a plague of poisonous serpents, whose bite was fatal, God instructed Moses to make a bronze serpent and put it on a pole so that, by looking at it, anyone who had been bitten would not die (Num 21, 4-9). Obviously, it was not the bronze serpent that worked the miracle to save the lives of those people, but their faith in the efficacy of God's word who had promised that it would be so; it was the faith with which they looked at that serpent, who represented Jesus Christ raised up on the wood of the Cross.

It is in this way that we are to look at the images of the Saints, reminding ourselves what it is they represent, believing in what they represent, loving and respecting what they represent. *If you have faith, you will move mountains.*

In the Apocalypse, St John tells us that he heard the Angel that had been charged with announcing the Good News to the inhabitants of the earth saying: «*"Worship him who made heaven and earth, the sea and the fountains of water"*» (Rev 14, 7). After contemplating the marvels of Heaven which God has prepared for the elect, St John wanted to prostrate himself in order to adore the Angel which had shown and explained these things to him, but the Angel said to him: «*You must not do that! I am a fellow servant with you and your brethren the prophets, and with those who keep the words of this book. Worship God*» (Rev 22, 9).

Again it is St John who describes for us the following vision: «*And I saw what appeared to be a sea of glass mingled with fire, and those who had conquered the beast and its image and the number of its name, standing beside the sea of glass with harps of God in their hands. And they sing the song of Moses, the servant of God, and the song of the Lamb, saying, "Great and wonderful are thy deeds. O Lord God the Almighty! Just and true are thy ways, O King of the ages! Who shall not fear and glorify thy name, O Lord? For thou alone art holy. All nations shall come and worship thee, for thy judgments have been revealed."*» (Rev 15, 2-4).

This is the canticle of our adoration before God. We adore Him with faith, because we believe in Him. We bless Him with hope in the conviction that all good things come to us from Him. We give Him thanks because we know that it was out of love that He created us, that it is for the sake of love that He keeps us in being, and that it was for love that He destined us to share in his divine life. Hence, our adoration must be a hymn of perfect praise, because, even before we came into being, God was already loving us, and was moved by this love to give us our being.

Ave Maria!

5

The Call to Hope

The third Call of the Message

I hope

All our hope must be placed in the Lord, because He is the one true God who created us with eternal love and redeemed us by sending his own Son, Jesus Christ, true God and true Man, who suffered and died for our salvation.

It is this that the Gospel of St John tells us in recording for us the following words of Jesus to Nicodemus: «*Are you a teacher of Israel, and yet you do not understand this? Truly, truly, I say to you, we speak of what we know, and bear witness to what we have seen; but you do not receive our testimony. If I have told you earthly things and you do not believe, how can you believe if I tell you heavenly things? No one has ascended into heaven but he who descended from heaven, the Son of man. And as Moses lifted up the serpent in the wilderness, so must the Son of man be lifted up, that whoever believes in him may have eternal life. For God so loved the world that he gave his only Son, that whoever believes in him should not perish but have eternal life. For God sent the Son into the world, not to condemn the world, but that the world might be saved through him. He who believes in him is not condemned; he who does not believe is condemned already, because he has not believed in the name of the only Son of God. And this is the judgement, that the light has come into the world, and men loved darkness rather than light, because their deeds were evil.*» (Jn 3, 10-19).

This sacred text spells out for us the basis of our hope:«*so must the Son of man be lifted up, that whoever believes in him may have eternal life.*» If the Israelites who had been mortally wounded were healed by looking at the serpent which Moses had nailed to a post, how much more we, if we can contrive, with faith and confidence, to lift our eyes and gaze on Christ, raised up on the wood of the cross; if we can unite our own daily cross with his, our work, our toil, the things that go wrong, our pains and anxieties, with deep repentance for our sins and a firm resolution not to commit them again, our confidence will be rewarded as Christ promised: «*All who believe in Him will have eternal life*».

In order to show you how great must be our confidence in Christ, let me remind you of the time that the Apostles were crossing the lake after the miracle of the multiplication of the loaves. Jesus had told his disciples to get into a boat and cross to the other side of the lake opposite Bethsaida, while He dismissed the crowd. *«And after he had taken leave of them, he went into the hills to pray. And when evening came, the boat was out on the sea, and he was alone on the land. And he saw that they were distressed in rowing, for the wind was against them. And about the fourth watch of the night he came to them, walking on the sea. He meant to pass by them, but when they saw him walking on the sea they thought it was a ghost, and cried out; for they all saw him, and were terrified. But immediately he spoke to them and said, "Take heart, it is I; have no fear." And he got into the boat with them and the wind ceased. And they were utterly astounded, for they did not understand about the loaves, but their hearts were hardened. And when they had crossed over, they came to land at Gennesaret, and moored to the shore. And when they got out of the boat, immediately the people recognized him, and ran about the whole neighbourhood and began to bring sick people on their pallets to any place where they heard he was. And wherever he came, in villages, cities, or country, they laid the sick in the markt places, and besought him that they might touch even the fringe of his garment; and as many as touched it were made well.»* (Mk 6, 46-56).

This episode in the life of Jesus Christ teaches us the kind of confidence we must have, both by the behaviour of the apostles battling with the waves of the lake, and by the attitude of the people of Gennesaret who brought their sick to Jesus to be healed. The Evangelist tells us that all those who touched even the fringe of his garment were made well, because they touched Him with faith and confidence. This is the condition that must be fulfilled if we are to obtain grace: we must approach Christ with faith, trusting in his goodness and his love.

What Jesus said then to the apostles applies to us today as well: *«Take heart; it is I; have no fear».* In the midst of the storms of life, it can sometimes seem to us – as it seemed to the Apostles – that everything is a nightmare, making us afraid. But, if we know how to raise our eyes to Christ, we shall see Him close to us, and we shall have the happiness of hearing the harmonious sound of his voice deep within our heart re-assuring us: *«It is I; have no fear!»*

But if we are to hear this voice and understand it, our spirit must not be «*hardened*»; and the Evangelist tells us that the hearts of the Apostles were hardened, which is why they did not understand the words of Jesus. Hence, our spirit must be free from excessive attachment to the things of earth, to the vanities which cause us to turn aside to the ways of frivolity, the extremes of fashion which give bad example and scandalise others, inciting them to sin. If, however, we follow our evil inclinations, coveting things that do not belong to us nor can legitimately do so, indulging in envy, jealousy, and temptations to revenge against justice and charity, etc., then these things will make us blind and deaf to such an extent that we will neither see nor hear, nor will we be able to understand, the words of Jesus Christ, and in this way our faith and confidence will be eroded.

In the course of Jesus' farewell discourse during the Last Supper, the Apostle St John records for us a number of passages which inspire in us the same confidence. The Master had just finished washing the feet of the Apostles, after which He sat down again at the table and explained the meaning of what He had done, urging them to humility and charity. He then foretold the betrayal of Judas and when the latter had gone out to accomplish his perfidious purposes, Jesus said to his disciples: «*Let not your hearts be troubled; believe in God, believe also in me. In my Father's house are many rooms; if it were not so, would I have told you (...) that where I am you may be also.*» (Jn 14, 1-3).

He then went on to speak very intimately with his Apostles about his forthcoming death, saying to them: «*The hour is coming, indeed it has come, when you will be scattered, every man to his home, and will leave me alone; yet I am not alone, for the Father is with me. I have said this to you, that in me you may have peace. In the world you have tribulation; but be of good cheer, I have overcome the world.*» (Jn 16, 32-33).

Here, Jesus assures us that there is a place in Heaven for us if we choose to follow his way, the way that He has mapped out for us by his word and his example, the Way which is He himself: «*I am the way, and the truth, and the life; no one comes to the Father, but by me. (...) He who has seen me has seen the Father.*» (Jn 14, 6, 9). Hence, our way is Christ. He is our Way by his Word, by his teaching and by his life. We must therefore identify ourselves with Christ in order to reproduce in ourselves the life of Christ and see Christ in the Father, as He has told us: «*I and the Father are one*». (Jn 10,30).

It is this identification of our life with the life of Christ, victim of expiation for our sins, that provides the basis for our confidence and in which it grows strong. For we know that it is through our union with Christ and through his merits that we shall be saved; also that we shall become pleasing to the Father to the extent to which we reproduce in ourselves the sentiments of his Son, Jesus Christ, so that the Father sees in us the face of his Word. This is the way that we must follow if we are to reach the place that Jesus has prepared in Heaven for us.

The great sentiments of Jesus which we are called upon to imitate include his total dependence on the Father and his utter submission to the Father's will, so much so that He could assure us that his own word was the word of his Father: «*For I have not spoken on my own authority; the Father who sent me has himself given me commandment what to say and what to speak. And I know that his commandment is eternal life. What I say, therefore, I say as the Father has bidden me.*» (Jn 12, 49-50). Begotten eternally of the Father, the Word received everything from Him. Rightly, then, can He assure us that everything He has said to us was said to Him by his Father, and that everything He has communicated to us has come from the Father.

All we have to do is to follow this word of life with faith; to follow it with faith, and also with the simplicity of a child which, aware of its own helplessness, abandons itself in the arms of its father, where it rests and sleeps securely, because it knows that its father will carry it safely, protect it and lay it down to rest; and if it should happen to offend its father by disobeying one of his commands, it knows its father's heart and trusts in his love, and so runs to meet him, confessing its fault, confident of his forgiveness, and with the same confidence as before, throws itself into his arms. In God's eyes, we are all children. He is the Father of the great human family: He rocks us all in the cradle of his Providence, and leads us all in the ways of love. Let us not wander from this way, nor tear ourselves away from his fatherly arms! Then our hope will remain rooted in God, in his Word, in his fatherly Love, in his saving Hand. Like children in their father's arms, confident of his infinite mercy, we shall know that our confidence will not be misplaced.

Ave Maria!

6

The Call to love God

The fourth Call of the Message

I love You.

If only I were a Seraphim to tell you what love really is!

«*God is love*» – St John the Apostle tells us – and as such He loves with an eternal love, in other words, from all eternity. We see this eternal presence of ours to God and in God foretold in a text of Sacred Scripture which refers directly to divine Wisdom – which was of course prior to creation as it is spread throughout creation – but which Holy Church has no difficulty in applying to Our Lady: «*The Lord created me at the beginning of his work, the first of his acts of old. Ages ago I was set up, at the first, before the beginning of the earth. When there were no depths I was brought forth, when there were no springs abounding with water. Before the mountains had been shaped, before the hills, I was brought forth; before he had made the earth with its fields, or the first of the dust of the world. When he established the heavens, I was there, when he drew a circle on the face of the deep, when he made firm the skies above, when he established the fountains of the deep, when he assigned to the sea its limit, so that the waters might not transgress his command, when he marked out the foundations of the earth, then I was beside him*» (Prov 8, 22-30).

There can be no doubt that, of all creatures, Our Lady is the one who has been most loved by God. Nevertheless, from all eternity, we have all been equally present in the mind of God, and part of his creative design. Moreover, He created all other things for love of each one of us, because we have always been present to Him and loved by Him. We have an eternal debt of love to pay to God, a debt which can only be repaid as the centuries follow one another, though it can never be fully repaid because the love of God came first, and continually increases in intensity. Hence, no one and nothing is as deserving as God is of a return of our love.

We must therefore look upon the precept God has given us to «*love Him*» as yet another proof of his love; it is a sign that He accepts our love, our gratitude, our humble return of love for Love. We are very small before the immensity of God, but we give Him what we have: *our love!* It is a bit like what happens with children who, cradled in the arms of the father from whom they receive everything, repay him with a hug and a kiss, symbols of their love. And the father smiles happily and is satisfied, because the child has given him a return of love.

We show, and prove, our love for God by the love we bestow on our brothers and sisters, because, like ourselves, they too are children of God, loved and redeemed by Him in Jesus Christ. If we really want to show our love to the father of a family, we shall find no more effective way of doing so than by giving gifts to his children. It is in this sense that Jesus, in the Gospel, tells us that He regards as done to Himself whatever we do to one of the least of our brothers and sisters, the reason being that this brother or sister is as much his brother or sister as we ourselves are, children of one and the same Father who is in Heaven, created in his image and likeness and destined to share in the eternal life of God: «*So God created man in his own image, in the image of God he created him; male and female he created them.*» (Gen 1, 27).

The work of creation is a work of love. God created us out of love. Like a father, He guides our steps along the paths of life. He gave us his laws, his teaching, which are the guide we are to follow: «*You shall therefore love the Lord your God, and keep his charge, his statutes, his ordinances, and his commandments always. And consider this day (...) the discipline of the Lord your God, his greatness, his mighty hand and his outstreched arm,(...). You shall therefore lay up these words of mine in your heart and in your soul; and you shall bind them as a sign upon your hand, and they shall be as frontlets between your eyes. And you shall teach them to your children, talking of them when you are sitting in your house, and when you are walking by the way, and when you lie down, and when you rise. And you shall write them upon the doorposts of your house and upon your gates.*» (Dt 11,1-2. 18-20).

All that God says to us in this passage is a manifestation of the love He has for us, in the same way as a father gives instructions to his children so that they may not wander from the path they are to follow.

On the days following his triumphant entry into Jerusalem, Jesus was besieged with tricky questions and problems put to him by the Pharisees and Sadducees. Now «*And one of the scribes came up and heard them disputing with one another, and seeing that he answered them well, asked him,*

"Which commandment is the first of all? Jesus answered, "The first is, 'Hear, O Israel: The Lord our God, the Lord is one; and you shall love the Lord your God with all your heart, and with all your soul, and with all your mind, and with all your strength. The second is this, 'You shall love your neighbour as yourself.' There is no other commandment greater than these." And the scribe said to him, "You are right, Teacher; you have truly said that he is one, and there is no other but he; and to love him with all the heart, and with all the understanding, and with all the strength, and to love one's neighbour as oneself, is much more than whole burnt offerings and sacrifices." And Jesus saw that he answered wisely, he said to him, "Your are not far from the kingdom of God." » (Mk 12, 28-34). Thus, the Kingdom of God is the Kingdom of Love: to love, and to serve out of love.

But this love must be understood in the sense of respect for purity, for the chastity required by one's state in life, for fidelity to God and to others, the keeping of any promises, oaths and vows we have made. Failure to live up to any of these points is an act of infidelity and thus a lack of the love we owe to God and to our neighbour.

We all want to be loved, esteemed, held dear, appreciated and deemed of some account. This is a desire that God has engraved in the human heart, because He created us out of love in order to love. Charity is the virtue that abides eternally in Heaven, where we shall sing the canticle of Love. And it is to enable us to get there that God, in giving us his Law, placed right at the beginning the commandment to love Him, because it is this love which will cause us to fulfil all the other precepts.

It was love that moved God to create us, to redeem us by sending his Son, who offered Himself as a victim of expiation to be paid on our behalf, in order to make reparation for our sins. If God had not loved us, we would not exist; we should have remained in nothingness. Hence, it is our duty, in gratitude, in appreciation, in justice and in equity, to love God above all things, to repay Love with love, to *pay for love with love* as we Portuguese say. Moreover, it is an act of justice to love the One who loved us so much and from Whom we have received everything that is good. But our love must be sincere, cheerful and self-sacrificing.

Take the case of a good son who loves his father and does everything that he knows will please him. Even if he has to deny himself in doing so, he will do so cheerfully because it pleases him to see his father happy; on the other hand, his father's pleasure will in turn benefit the son because the father, being pleased with his son, will take him in his arms, heap good things on him and do everything for him. Our love for God must also be like that of husband and wife. When their love is genuine, the wife willingly sacrifices herself in order to see her husband happy, and the husband sacrifices himself for his wife so that she, too, may be happy. It is the familiar mutual exchange of love, which requires immolation, gift and surrender. And the fruit of this exchange is peace, joy and well-being.

Our love, too, must also be self-sacrificing. To begin with, we must avoid whatever might cause us to sin grievously against God or our neighbour; in other words we must not disobey God's law in any grave matter. Then, we must also deny ourselves anything that might cause us to offend God or our neighbour in less serious matters, in other words by venial sin.

The love which will lead us to do this must contain within itself the strength that will enable us to overcome our evil instincts which incline us to evil, those temptations to pride, envy, covetousness, revenge, vanity and sensuality, etc. Only by means of this battle with ourselves shall we manage to keep to the straight path of our love for God and our neighbour, as it is our duty to do, as Jesus Christ himself tells us in the Gospel: «*From the days of John the Baptist until now the kingdom of heaven has suffered violence, and men of violence take it by force.*» (Mt 11, 12). In other words, the Kingdom of Heaven is won by those who deny themselves, doing violence to themselves in order to overcome themselves, to conquer their evil inclinations, the temptations of the world, the devil and the flesh, in order to keep strictly to the path of justice, truth and love.

This is the effort that we must impose on ourselves, and it is this that gives value to our love for God and for our neighbour. All those who love, deny themselves for the one they love. This is precisely what Jesus Christ did for us. He sacrificed himself and gave himself up to death in order to give life to us. What more, then, are we doing if, for his sake, we sacrifice our fancies, our evil inclinations, our exaggerated vanity, our self-indulgence, our pride, our ambitions?

But what am I doing by speaking of our sacrificing ourselves for Him? The truth is that the sacrifice is for our own benefit, since by means of it we win the Kingdom of Heaven, and we secure peace and joy on earth. We all want to live in peace and joy, to have a happy life, but we do not realise that we are looking for it in places where it is not to be found. Our Lord tells us: «*Blessed are the meek, for they shall inherit the earth. Blessed are the peacemak-*

ers, for they shall be called sons of God. Blessed are those who are persecuted for righteousness' sake, for theirs is the kingdom of heaven.» (Mt 5, 5; 9-10).

The peacemakers, who suffer meekly, are the ones who are blessed in this life because they are at peace with their neighbour and enjoy their friendship; they are at peace with their own consciences, because they have denied themselves whatever was necessary in order to avoid offending God or their neighbour and to do good. This is where true love is to be found. It is that overflowing love for God which flows out of our heart onto our neighbour in such a burst of faith and generosity that we see the face of Jesus Christ in each human being – whether he or she shares our own faith or not, whether he or she is a good person or is enmeshed in sin – and in Christ we love them as our brothers and sisters, children of the same God and Father who created us all and calls us all to share in the inheritance of Heaven. Hence, our love must extend to everyone. It is to this that we are called by the Message that God sent by means of his Angel.

In order that our faith, our adoration, our hope and our love can be true and pleasing to God, they must reach out to our brothers and sisters through our prayer, our good example, our words and our deeds. We must endeavour to help them and to draw them, in order to lead them to God by the right ways of truth, justice, peace and love. I say 'of justice' because this virtue must not be understood only in terms of punishment, for it is as much a question of justice to reward the good as to punish the wicked. For instance, it is as much a question of justice to give a good mark to a student who throughout the course has made every effort to study and has answered well in the examination, as it is to give a low mark to one who did not make an effort during the course, who replied badly at the examination, or who behaved badly. In the same way, it is equally just to pay and to 'reward' those who work well and serve others, as it is not to pay those who, through laziness, do not wish either to work or to serve. This is so because the law of work applies to us all. We are all obliged to work and to serve one another, each according to his or her own aptitudes, position in life, culture, placing at the service of others the gifts we ourselves have received from God. The farmer who cultivates the land is not inferior to the professor who teaches the farmer's children in school, because the former sustains the latter by the product of his toil, and both serve, each one working for the benefit of the other.

«In the sweat of your face you shall eat bread» This law obliges us all to work in order to serve one another as brothers and sisters, children of the same Father who is God and who created us all for the same destiny: the Kingdom of Heaven. This is how Jesus Christ told us to live: *«But you are not to be called rabbi, for you have one teacher, and you are all brethren. And call no man your father on earth, for you have one Father, who is in heaven. Neither be called masters, for you have one master, the Christ. He who is greatest among you shall be your servant; whoever exalts himself will be humbled, and whoever humbles himself will be exalted.»* (Mt 23, 8-12). These words reveal how our whole lives and all our activities are to be lived and performed as a service to God in the person of our brothers and sisters.

Thus, when we love and serve one another as brothers and sisters, children of the same Father who created us all for the same destiny, namely, to possess supernatural life, we must always bear in mind this ultimate destiny, supernatural life, which is the one we need to store up for ourselves and possess in as high a degree as possible, as it is the only one that lasts for ever. It is for this that we make sacrifices, that we pray and work: so that all our brothers and sisters may turn aside from their false ways and tread the one true path which is Christ, as He himself tells us: *«I am the Way, the Truth and the Life»* (Jn 14, 6).

In the same way, and still in connection with the words of Christ quoted above, we must see in all fatherhood and human wisdom, the fatherhood and wisdom of God from Whom is derived, as from its source, all other fatherhood and wisdom. It is for this reason that we call 'father' the one who represents God to us and whom God makes use of to give us life; and we call 'master' the one who teaches us in the name of God. In this way, we see God in everyone, and in everyone we recognise the image of God, and are certain that we are all children and servants of the same God.

This is the true way that Christ taught us: the way of truth, the way of life, hope and peace. In order to follow it, we must turn our backs on the way of falsehood, illusion and fantasy that holds the world in thrall. Why would we want to live in a world of illusions? To be deceived by false companions, false promises, false ideas, which get hold of people and drive them into evil and misfortune? To allow ourselves to be misled by our own fantasies and evil inclinations which cause us to look for happiness where it does not exist? To be deceived by a desire for honour, riches, being given the first place, without reflecting that all this leads at the very least to the humiliation of nothingness at all? One day, Jesus complained of the blindness of so many in the world when He said: «*They do all their deeds to be seen by men;(...) and they love the place of honour at feasts and the best seats in the synagogues, and salutations in the market places, and being called rabbi by men.*» (Mt 23, 5-7). When this life is over, what will be left of all this?

And what will happen to all those souls and bodies on the day of the resurrection? They had no faith, they had no hope, they did not have a pure love of God and of their neighbour for the love of God. The Apostle St Paul speaks very plainly about all this: «*Do you not know that the unrighteous will not inherit the kingdom of God? Do not be deceived; neither the immoral, nor idolaters, nor adulterers, nor homosexuals, nor thieves, nor the greedy, nor drunkards, nor revilers, nor robbers will inherit the kingdom of God.*» (1 Cor 6, 9-10). Here we see the fate awaiting those who persist in following these false paths, who refuse to turn back and amend their lives, to repent of their sins and do penance for them, in order to embark, instead, on the paths of faith, hope and charity, which is the pure love of God and of our neighbour for the love of God.

This is the way that leads to life. And, in this way of life which we are to follow, the light is Christ, as He himself has told us: «*I am the light of the world; he who follows me will not walk in darkness, but will have the light of life*» (Jn 8, 12). This light shines on our steps, by the word, the life and the example of Christ. All we need is to want to follow Him. The incentive to do so is already there, as well as his invitation to us to do so, in the words: «*If anyone thirst, let him come to me and drink. He who believes in me, as the scripture has said 'Out of his heart shall flow rivers of living water.'*» And the Evangelist explains: «*Now this he said about the Spirit, which those who believed in him were to receive.*» (Jn 7, 37-39).

This water that the Lord mentions is a symbol of the Holy Spirit because the Spirit is the life in us, or rather, it is by the Spirit of God that supernatural life is born and wells up in us. It was of this same gift of the Spirit that Jesus was thinking when He revealed to the Samaritan woman that He possessed a water that was better than the one she had come to the well to draw: «*Everyone who drinks of this water will thirst again, but whoever drinks of the water that I shall give him will never thirst; the water that I shall give him will become in him a spring of water welling up to eternal life*» (Jn 4, 13-14). It is the water of grace which we have to plunge into, and also receive into ourselves so that it can then gush out from us to refresh the parched souls of our brothers and sisters and lead them to the fruits of eternal life.

And this, so that the faith in our souls may not weaken, nor the hope waver, nor the charity become extinguished, but may rather grow and be increasingly the bond of our intimate union with God and with our neighbour by our mutual understanding, help and pardon, so that peace, joy and love may reign among all, in accordance with Christ's words: «*As the Father has loved me, so have I loved you; abide in my love. If you keep my commandments, you will abide in my love, just as I have kept my Father's commandments and abide in his love. These things I have spoken to you, that my joy may be in you, and that your joy may be full. This is my commandment, that you love one another as I have loved you.*» (Jn 15, 9-12).

Ave Maria!

7

The Call to Forgiveness

The fifth Call of the Message

I ask Your pardon

Immediately after the call to charity, the Message speaks to us of forgiveness, urging us to ask God's pardon for our brothers and sisters and also for ourselves; for those who do not believe and for those who do; for those who do not adore and for those who bow down in worship before God; for those who do not hope and for those who have every confidence; for those who do not love and for those who practise charity.

The fact is that we all need to obtain God's pardon: for our lack of faith, which is often so fragile, for our hope which is often so weak, for our charity which is often so cold and insensitive, and for our adoration, which is often so languid. We ask pardon for those who do not believe, for those who do not adore, for those who do not hope and for those who do not love; and very often we ourselves are among this number!

For this reason, in what we call the Lord's Prayer, Jesus Christ taught us to ask: «*Forgive us our trespasses as we forgive those who trespass against us*» (Mt 6, 12). As we see, we cannot obtain God's pardon unless we ourselves first forgive our brothers and sisters. It follows that we must not harbour resentment, ill-will, dislike, and still less a desire to avenge any offence, whether great or small, that one or other of our neighbours may have committed against us. Our forgiveness must be generous, complete and self-sacrificing, in the sense of overcoming ourselves. It will be necessary to silence within us the cry of revolt, to calm excited nerves, to keep a firm grasp on the reins of our own temper and keep a lid on the heat of our wounded self-love which, whether rightly or wrongly, feels bruised and irritated.

It is in just such circumstances that we are called upon to forgive our neighbour when he or she comes to ask our pardon: «*So then, if you are bringing your offering to the altar, and there remember that your brother has something against you, leave your offering there before the altar go and be* reconciled with your brother first, and then come back and present your offering. Come to terms with your opponent» (Mt 5, 23-25).

These words of Jesus show us that God wants both forgiveness and reconciliation, and it is only thus that our offering, our prayer and our sacrifice will be pleasing to God and accepted by Him. Our forgiveness must be generous, sincere and from the heart, and also clearly manifested so that God can forgive us, too, in the same way. This is what our Divine Master teaches us: « Yes, if you forgive others their failings, your heavenly Father will forgive you yours; but if you do not forgive others, your Father will not forgive your failings either.» (Mt.6, 14-15). In view of these words of Jesus, our forgiveness of our neighbour is indispensable if we ourselves are to receive pardon from God. Hence it is that the Message instructs us to ask God's pardon for our brothers and sisters and for ourselves.

God is merciful and is always ready to forgive us, as soon as He sees in us our own repentance and desire of amendment, that is, when He sees that we are sorry, that we have changed our way of life, turning away from the path of sin to embark on the path of grace. The Lord said to Saint Mary Magdalen: «Your sins are forgiven. (..) Your faith has saved you. Go in peace». Then addressing Himself to the Pharisee who had strong suspicions as to what kind of woman she was, and reservations about the kindness and understanding with which Jesus had welcomed her, Jesus said: «Her sins, which are many, are forgiven, for she loved much» (Lk 7, 47). The Lord saw in Magdalen's eyes the tears that were coursing down her cheeks; He saw in her hair and in the ointment with which she anointed Him her contempt for the vanities of this world and her resolve to change her way of life; He saw in her heart the pain and sorrow with the resolution to amend her life ... so He said to her: «Woman, your sins are forgiven».

When she saw Jesus, Magdalen believed in Him and loved Him. It was this faith and this love that caused her to hate sin, to weep over and despise the vanities of the world, and to change her way of life. And the Lord was pleased with all this, saying: «Many sins have been forgiven her for she loved much. Your faith has saved you. Go in peace». It is faith and love which will cause us, too, to hate our sins, to be sorry for them and to change our way of life, so that God may say to us as He said to Mary Magdalen: «Your sins have been forgiven».

To the woman taken in adultery, Jesus said: « "Has no one condemned you?" She said, "No one, Lord."» (Jn 8, 10-11). The Lord saw in the woman's heart her sorrow and her desire to change her way of life; hence He promises not to condemn her and grants her forgiveness, on condition, however, that she does not sin again: *«Go and do not sin again»*.

It was from the same point of view that Jesus addressed the people who were content with seeming to be good in the eyes of others without bothering whether they were or not in the eyes of God who, through his messengers, was constantly calling on them to repent and change their way of life. Turning to them, He spoke to them about the many others who, like the woman taken in adultery, repent, change their way of life and do penance: *«The harlots go into the kingdom of God before you.»* (Mt 21, 31).

It is true that the Jews were accustomed to offer sacrifices to God for their sins, offering up animals as victims; but they did not understand the precept of charity, above all in relation to the poor and the outcast, orphans and widows, whom they often left without justice or help, while for themselves they begged Heaven for help and justice. God's reply, however, was as follows: *«Your love is like a morning cloud, like the dew that goes early away. (...) my judgment goes forth as the light. For I desire steadfast love not sacrifice, the knowledge of God, rather than burnt offerings.»* (Hos 6, 4-6). Indeed, how can an external sacrifice be pleasing to God unless we offer Him the interior sacrifice of forgiveness granted to others? It is because that act of virtue is so little understood that Jesus tells us in the Gospel: *«Go and learn what this means, 'I desire mercy, and not sacrifice.'»* (Mt 9, 13). We really need to learn this: to understand fully that it is mercy and the forgiveness of others that must well up out of our hearts as the fruit of the love we owe to God and to our neighbour for the love of God, as love wells up out of the heart of God for us.

One day, St Peter asked Jesus how many times he was to forgive his brother: *«As many as seven times? Jesus said to him, "I do not say to you seven times, but seventy times seven."»* (Mt 18, 21-22). In other words, we must always forgive.

Ave Maria!

8

The Call to Prayer

The sixth Call of the Message

Pray, pray very much!

As you already know, this call was made during the second apparition of the Angel.

The three children were sitting on the side of the well in the grounds attached to my parents' house. The heavenly Messenger appeared and said to them: «*What are you doing?*» Then, without waiting for a reply, he went on: *Pray, pray very much! The Hearts of Jesus and Mary have designs of mercy on you. Offer prayers and sacrifices constantly to the Most High. (...) Make of everything you can a sacrifice, and offer it to God as an act of reparation for the sins by which He is offended, and in supplication for the conversion of sinners. You will thus draw down peace upon your country. I am its Angel Guardian, the Angel of Portugal. Above all, accept and bear with submission the suffering which the Lord will send you*».

Supernatural revelations are ordinarily accompanied by a special grace which clarifies their meaning. In fact, however, at that time, the three children were very far indeed from understanding its full meaning, as we can understand it today and transmit it to souls, as it is God's will that I should, and it is for this that He continues to keep me here at his disposal.

At the time, the children could not begin to imagine that this call to prayer was not only for them, but for the whole of humanity. Today, I look upon this call as a pointer to the way marked out by God for his creatures since the beginning of creation.

In fact, in both the Old and the New Testament, which contain the Word of God, we find the path God mapped out for humanity very clearly marked. Unfortunately, however, human beings have, on the whole, disregarded the end for which they were created. They ignore the existence of God their Creator; they do not know the holy name of God, Whom they have never called Father; and they do not know the way they are to follow in order to be happy one day in their Father's House.

Thus the greater part of humanity is the victim of ignorance, seeks happiness where it is not to be found, and sinks ever deeper into misfortune and unhappiness. Let us take a brief look at the world we live in! What do we see? What picture appears before our eyes? Wars, hatred, ambition, kidnappings, robberies, vengeance, fraud, murder, immorality, etc. And, in punishment for all these sins: accidents, sickness, disasters, famine, and every kind of pain and suffering beneath which humanity groans and weeps.

Men who consider themselves wise and powerful continue to plan more wars, death, wretchedness and misery, more shedding of blood into the sea of blood in which whole peoples are already drowning – the very people whom those so-called wise men ought to be helping to live and to help themselves.

And all for what purpose? In order to drag humanity down and destroy it in waves of hatred, ambition, revenge, immorality... and to lose themselves into the bargain. Yes, because before long they, too, will be turning to ashes in the tomb! Where, today, are their predecessors who fought and lived in the very same way? In many cases, it is not even known in what way they met their deaths. And where will their souls be for all eternity?

Their bodies have, of course, returned to the earth from which they were taken, as it is written: «*You are dust, and to dust you shall return*» (Gen 3, 19). And the souls which gave life to those bodies for a time? They too have returned to the place from which they came – the eternal Being which is God. In fact, the soul, which is spiritual, was created by God in the likeness of God: «*The Lord God formed man of dust from the ground, and breathed into his nostrils the breath of life; and man became a living being*» (Gen 2, 7). It was this breath of life from the lips of God which gave life to our soul, creating it in the likeness of God, immortal.

Ever since Adam sinned by disobeying God's orders, all his descendants have incurred the pain of bodily death. Our soul, however, continues to live; it returns to God, if it is in a state of grace; if, on the other hand, it is in a state of sin, this very sin drives it away from God and carries it off to eternal punishment.

On the day of the general resurrection, we shall all rise again to be reunited with our souls and go to share the same eternal destiny which body and soul together have deserved: either eternal happiness with God, or the unhappiness of eternal punishment. Jesus Himself told us this when speaking about the work that the Father had entrusted to the Son of Man: *«Do not marvel at this; for the hour is coming when all who are in the tombs will hear his voice»* (Jn 5, 28) (the voice of the Son of Man) *«and come forth, those who have done good, to the resurrection of life, and those who have done evil, to the resurrection of judgment.»* (Jn 5, 29).

This being the case, it is most important that we should win eternal happiness for ourselves because, whereas our life on earth is transitory, eternal life is unchanging and unending. What, then, are we to do? Consider these words of St Paul: *«The first man was from the earth, a man of dust; the second man is from heaven. As was the man of dust, so are those who are of the dust; and as is the man of heaven, so are those who are of heaven. Just as we have borne the image of the man of dust, we shall also bear the image of the man of heaven.»* (1 Cor 15, 47-49). This heavenly image of which the Apostle speaks and which we must endeavour to reproduce in ourselves, is Jesus Christ; we must reproduce Him in ourselves by faith and charity so that, on the day of our departure to eternity, the Father may see in us the features of Christ and welcome us as his children into his Kingdom; and also so that, in the resurrection from the dead, our body may share in the happiness of the spirit.

A little later, in the same Letter, St Paul says concerning the last day: *«Lo! I tell you a mystery. We shall not all sleep, but we shall all be changed, in a moment, in the twinkling of an eye, at the last trumpet. For the trumpet will sound, and the dead will be raised imperishable, and we shall be changed.»* (1 Cor 15, 51-52). So we have to make sure that this transformation will take place in us, in accordance with God's grace which, in his mercy, will be granted to us in return for our own effort of humble fidelity; and not according to the misfortune of whatever sin we may have incurred. Let us not think that all this is a kind of Utopia; it is a proven reality. If our incredulity were to lead us into such an error, we are lost. Truth does not cease to exist simply because unbelievers deny it! What was true yesterday remains true today and will still be true tomorrow, because *«Jesus Christ is the same yesterday and today and for ever.»* (Heb 13, 8).

All of this shows our great need for prayer, for drawing close to God in prayer. It is by prayer that we secure pardon for our own sins, the strength and the grace to resist the temptations of the world, the devil and the flesh. We are very weak; without this strength we could never win through. Hence,

Jesus urged his Apostles: «*Watch and pray that you may not enter into temptation; the spirit indeed is willing, but the flesh is weak.*» (Mt 26, 41).

It is for this reason that the Message renews the Lord's words: «*Pray, pray very much!*». This call to prayer is a repetition of the call to prayer so often repeated to us by God and which Jesus Christ left to his Apostles as well as to ourselves: «*Watch and pray*».

Various passages in Sacred Scripture show us Jesus Christ giving us an example or urging us to pray; and He not only urges us to pray, but He taught us how to pray, as in this passage from the Gospel of St Luke: «*He was praying in a certain place, and when he ceased, one of his disciples said to him, "Lord, teach us to pray, as John taught his disciples." And he said to them, "When you pray, say: "Father, hallowed be thy name. Thy kingdom come..."*» (Lk 11, 1-2). Thus it was from his own lips that we learnt the Our Father, the most beautiful of all the prayers we address to God, and one in which Jesus Christ teaches us to address God by the lovely name of Father.

This name opens up for us the mystery of the Divine Fatherhood and confirms us in the truth that we are all children of the same God; this truth, confirmed by Jesus Christ, that God is our Father, fills us with confidence and strengthens us in love, because who has ever loved us as God does? Hence, our prayer must be the point of meeting between the love of the child reaching out to the heart of the Father and the Father's love stooping down to the child, listening to what it has to say, paying heed to its requests, its words of praise and thanksgiving, and answering its prayers.

There are many ways of praying, or of meeting God in prayer. Which is the best? The best for each person is the way that helps that particular person to meet God and remain in intimate contact with Him, heart to heart, thrilling with love for the Father with the heart of Jesus Christ, assuming the same longings and sentiments as Jesus Christ himself, becoming one with Christ as He wished us to do and prayed in this sense to the Father: «*I do not pray for these only, but also for those who believe in me through their word (...); even as thou, Father, art in me, and I in thee, that they also may be in us, so that the world may believe that thou hast sent me*» (Jn 17, 20-21).

In this sublime prayer of Christ's, we perceive God's plans for us: to be one with Him by our union with Christ: «*As you, Father, are in me and I in thee, that they also may be in us*». But this union with God can only be achieved through prayer; it is in prayer that we meet God, and it is in this meeting that He communicates to us his grace, his gifts, his love and his pardon.

We see that, in his prayer, Jesus Christ also asked on our behalf: «*I do not pray for these only, but also for those who through their word will come to believe in Me*». And we have the happiness of being among those who, through the word of the Apostles which was transmitted to us by their successors, believe in the Lord, which is what Christ also asked the Father on our behalf. I feel so happy when I think that I was present to Him when He addressed this prayer to the Father; that He was thinking about me and presented me to the Father as the child of his love!

He thought of me, He thought of you, He thought of the countless multitude of his brothers and sisters. And in order for our own prayer to be imbued with the same yearnings and sentiments as Jesus' own prayer, it must be united to his prayer for all those who will come to believe in Him and will be saved by his merits.

Let us go back to what I was saying about the various ways of praying. Our prayer can be predominantly «*vocal*», that is addressed to God in words, either those that well up spontaneously from our heart or using existing formulas such as, for example, the Our Father, the Hail Mary, the Glory be to the Father, the Creed and many other such prayers that are used in the Sacred Liturgy.

This is the most common way of praying, and it is also the most accessible to the ordinary faithful. Moreover, it has been recommended to us by Jesus Christ himself: «*Pray then like this: Our Father who art in heaven, hallowed be thy name. Thy kingdom come, thy will be done, on earth as it is in heaven. Give us our daily bread, and forgive us our debts, as we also have forgiven our debtors; and lead us not into temptation, but deliver us from evil.*» (Mt 6, 9-13). This is the most sublime form of vocal prayer, because it was taught to us by the Son of God himself. So we must pray it with renewed devotion, confidence, humility and love.

Then there is another kind of prayer which we must offer to God together with our vocal prayer: it is the «*prayer of our work*», of the performance of all the duties in our state in life in a spirit of humble submission to God, because it was He who imposed on us the law of work. We must do it with love and fidelity to God and to our neighbour; in this way, our everyday occupations, however seemingly insignificant, when offered to God will be a prayer of praise, thanksgiving, repentance and petition.

Like Tobit, to whom the angel said: «*And so, when you and your daughter-in-law Sarah prayed, I brought a reminder of your prayer before the Holy One; and when you buried the dead, I was likewise present with you. When you did not hesitate to rise and leave your dinner in order to go and lay out the dead, your good deed was not hidden from me, but I was with you.*» (Tb 12, 12-13)

This passage of Sacred Scripture tells us how we are to use the time that God gives us in our lives: part of it must be devoted to prayer, another part to performing the duties of our state in life and the rest in doing good to others for the love of God. There are twenty-four hours in every day; we are doing nothing special if we set aside a few minutes of each day for our encounter with God.

In carrying out our everyday tasks, we must endeavour to be aware of God's presence: call to mind that God and our Angel Guardian are close to us, see what we are doing, and in what frame of mind we are doing it. Hence, we must sanctify our work, our rest, our meals, our wholesome entertainments, as if they were an on-going prayer. Knowing that God is present, it is enough to call Him to mind and from time to time say a few words to Him: whether of love – *I love you, Lord!* – or of thanksgiving – *Thank you, Lord for all your benefits—*, or of petition – *Lord, help me to be faithful to You; forgive me my sins, my ingratitude, my coldness, my failure to understand, my backsliding* – or of praise – *I bless you, Lord, for your greatness, for your goodness, for your wisdom, for your power, for your mercy, for your justice, for your love*. This intimate and familiar converse with God transforms our work and our daily occupations into a true and abiding life of prayer, making us more pleasing to God and bringing down upon us extra special graces and blessings.

And we can't say that we have no time for this kind of prayer, because it is precisely the time that we are using in order to do our work. Like a wife working alongside her husband, chatting quietly and intimately with him, telling him how much she appreciates all he does for the family, praising his knowledge and experience, encouraging him in his work, asking him for his help and advice, telling him about her worries and desires. Or like children who show their father everything, tell their father everything, and expect everything from him. Like a mother bringing up her children, who always has something to say to them even when they, either because they are very small, or because they are not paying attention, cannot understand her. God, however, always understands what we say, always listens to us, always sees us and always pays attention to us.

Then there is mental prayer, which is popularly spoken of as «meditation». It consists in placing ourselves in the presence of God in order to reflect on one or other of the revealed Mysteries, some episode in the life of Our Lord, some point of doctrine, the Law of God, or even about one or other of the virtues which we find in Jesus Christ, in Our Lady or in the Saints, as an example for us.

This prayer is very advantageous if we make it well. In order to do so, we have to talk to God about the subject on which we are meditating; look at ourselves in order to see what we lack in order to grow in the virtue corresponding to the subject on which we are meditating, as, for example, an increase in faith, humility, charity, or a spirit of sacrifice, in order to overcome our repugnances and difficulties, our idiosyncrasies and defects, our temptations. And all this is accomplished in an intimate conversation with the Lord: discussing everything with Him, confident that it is He who will give us the light, grace and strength that will enable us to remain faithful to the end and achieve the ideal of supernatural life that we have set before ourselves and that God wills and expects of us.

Then there is the prayer which is habitually called «contemplation». This consists in an even closer intimacy with God; in which those practising it enter more deeply into the presence of God within them, abandoning themselves more intimately to the work of the grace, light, and love of God within them.

Wrapped in a supernatural atmosphere, the soul allows itself to be imbued, raised up, and transformed by the action of God within it, purifying and absorbing it; it finds itself purified, transformed and uplifted by a divine action which it feels, but does not know how. God can certainly grant this grace to a person without any effort on the person's part, but ordinarily the Lord waits for the soul to reach this point by being faithful to the paths of vocal and mental prayer, because it is by this way that the soul is purified and lets go of the things of earth in order to entrust itself to God alone.

Very few indeed are the souls that reach this point because very few indeed are the ones who let go completely of the materialism of life, of the ambitions born of self-love, covetousness, pride and marks of respect. And even if these things do not reach the point of being actually sinful, they nevertheless sprinkle the soul with the dust of earth and prevent it from rising to the higher regions of the supernatural.

Hence they will never savour the intimate delights of divine love, because God can only grant these to souls when they are anxious to receive his graces, ready to listen to his voice and follow in his ways. There is nothing on earth which can be compared to the happiness experienced by a soul in this intimate union with God. Unfortunately, we are not able to appreciate these gifts or the true value of such riches, nor do we know how to live this gift. For this, too, we require a special gift from God which we do not deserve, but which He grants to us in his mercy and out of the great love He has for us.

In conclusion, prayer is necessary for all, and we must all pray, whether our prayer is vocal, mental or contemplative.

In addition to urging us to pray, Jesus Christ left us marvellous examples of the life of prayer. Thus, in the Gospel of St Luke, in order to demonstrate for us the need to pray always and without losing heart, He tells us the parable of the unjust judge. Immediately afterwards, we have the parable of the Pharisee and the publican in the temple: while the Pharisee was priding himself on his good works, the publican was humbly making his prayer, and asking God's forgiveness: «*God be merciful to me a sinner!' I tell you, this man went down to his house justified rather than the other; for every one who exalts himself will be humbled, but he who humbles himself will be exalted.*» (Lk 18, 13-14). Because we are all sinners, we all need to pray with humility and perseverance.

In this, too, our divine Saviour gave us an example, because He took upon Himself our sins and prayed on our behalf. Thus, before beginning his public life, He spent forty days and forty nights in the desert, praying and fasting in order to do penance for us. He wished in this way to set us an example, but also to offer adequate reparation to his Father for our sins and make his apostolate fruitful, preparing Himself for it by the power of prayer and penance.

Sacred Scripture tells us that Jesus Christ frequently went to the Temple and to the synagogues in order to take part in the collective prayer of the People of God. On one such occasion, when He saw the traders in the temple in Jerusalem, the profanation made Him angry and He drove them all out of the temple, saying: «*It is written, 'My house shall be called a house of prayer'; but you make it a den of robbers.'*» (Mt 21, 13). Undoubtedly, what is said here about the temple in Jerusalem applies equally to our churches which are consecrated to God as houses of prayer. Shrines, churches and chapels in the parishes, seminaries, and religious houses must be houses of prayer where the people of God can gather around Christ in order to unite themselves with Him in addressing to the Father their praise thanksgiving and supplication, so that in union with Christ they may offer to the Father their work and their sufferings, their day-to-day crosses and their sacrifices for the salvation of their brethren.

Our temples must be respected, because they are houses of God. Christ, true God and true Man, is there present in the Tabernacle at the disposition of his people, so that He can welcome them into his presence, talk to them, help them and feed them: «*I am the bread of life. (...) if any one eats of this bread, he will live for ever*» (Jn 6, 48.51)

Churches are the houses of our Father in Heaven. In the same way as children gather round their father to hear his words, to listen to his teaching and to act on his advice, so the People of God gathers together with Christ in the house of their Father, in order to listen to his Word, tell Him of their needs, receive his graces and sing his praises.

I am talking to you now about collective prayer, in which we must all take part. We go to church to pray, to unite our own prayer with that of our brothers and sisters. This is what happens when we assemble together for the celebration of the Eucharist, to adore the Blessed Sacrament, to pray the Rosary and for other communal devotions.

Then let us not forget that there is also each one's private prayer. All children look for a time when they can be alone with their father in order to explain to him their problems, and ask his help and advice. Now God is our true Father; hence we must try to spend time alone with Him in order to address to Him our petitions, our thanksgiving, our declarations of fidelity and love; in order, also, to present to Him our difficulties, receive his help, his advice, his light, grace, and comfort.

It is in this prayer, lived in intimate conversation with Christ, that we must prepare ourselves to carry out the mission which God wishes to entrust to us, because it is in this encounter that God gives us his light, his strength and his grace, together with the gifts of the Holy Spirit. Only thus shall we be true apostles to our brothers and sisters, transmitting to them the word of Christ.

However, in addition to these temples built by the hand of man, we have other temples which are no less real, where we must pray and offer to God our sacrifices: I mean our soul, our heart, our conscience. God is there! The most Holy Trinity dwells there! If we are in a state of grace, we are temples of God: «*If a man loves me, he will keep my word, and my Father will love him, and we will come to him and make our home with him.*» (Jn 14, 23).

We have thus come to the mystery of God dwelling within us, which comes about not only through the real presence of Jesus Christ, when we receive Him in Holy Communion, under the consecrated species of bread and wine, in which He is present and gives Himself to us with his body, blood, soul and divinity, alive and real as He is in heaven, from which He descends to our soul, identifying Himself with us by a union of complete self-giving. Besides this, God dwells in us by the real presence of the three Divine Persons, who transform our soul into a living and abiding temple where He dwells unless, by sin, we make ourselves unworthy of his divine presence.

This is what St Paul tells us: «*Do you not know that you are God's temple and that God's Spirit dwells in you? If any one destroys God's temple, God will destroy him. For God's temple is holy, and that temple you are.*» (1 Cor 3, 16-17). The Apostle is here reminding us of those who, by sin, profane the temple of God, which is the soul, making themselves unworthy to have the divine Presence within them. We are called to be holy, that is, not to offend God by sin, by deliberately transgressing his Law in serious matters, or even in lesser matters.

A little further on in the same letter of St Paul's, we read: «*The body is not meant for immorality, but for the Lord, and the Lord for the body. And God raised the Lord and will also raise us up by his power. Do you not know that your bodies are members of Christ? (...) He who is united to the Lord becomes one spirit with him. Shun immorality. (...) Do you not know that your body is a temple of the Holy Spirit within you, which you have from God? You are not your own; you were bought with a price. So glorify God in your Body.*» (1 Co 6, 13-20). Perhaps we do not fully appreciate the inestimable treasure we carry within us and it is for this reason that at times we live so carelessly.

Our faith has grown dim, and so its light ceases to illuminate our footsteps: thus our life becomes slack, our prayer without fervour, and our intimate union with God gets forgotten and fades away. In order to respond to this call to prayer which God addresses to us by means of the Message, we must intensify our life of faith, so that it will lead us to practise the degree of renunciation required to avoid offending God and so remain in his grace.

We are well aware that our wills are weak and how much we need the strength of grace to enable us to overcome the temptations which assail us, the dangers surrounding us and the tendencies which incline us to evil. That is why Jesus Christ taught us to pray to the Father, saying: «*Lead us not into temptation*». (Mt 6, 13).

And, as Jesus Christ has told us that without Him we can do nothing (Jn 15, 5), let us take a strong grip on prayer through which God will grant us the grace that we need to understand his commandments, know how to carry them out and so win for ourselves the help of his Fatherly love: «*Ask, and it will be given you; seek, and you will find; knock, and it will be opened to you. For every one who asks receives, and he who seeks finds, and to him who knocks it will be opened. (...) If you then, who are evil, know how to give good gifts to your children, how much more will your Father who is in heaven give good things to those who ask him!*» (Mt 7, 7-8. 11).

This is the promise that inspires our confidence in prayer and assures us of its efficacy.

Ave Maria!

9

The Call to Sacrifice

The seventh Call of the Message

«Offer prayers and sacrifices constantly to the Most High»

This call to sacrifice, which God now addresses to us, is something which we find in many pages of Sacred Scripture. It may seem superfluous to repeat it again here; but it will not be in vain, because we are all so forgetful and lackadaisical about fulfilling this great duty.

In the Old Testament, the priests used to offer sacrifices of animals, which they presented as propitiatory victims for themselves and for the people. But these victims were but fore-runners, images, of the sacrifice of Christ who was to be the one true victim offered to God for the sins of all human beings. This sacrifice of Christ, who came to put an end to the images, was to be perpetuated in place of the sacrifices of the Old Covenant. And we have it renewed on the altar every day in the celebration of the Eucharist, which is an unbloody repetition of the sacrifice of the Cross.

But this is not enough because, as St Paul tells us (Col 1, 24), we must complete in ourselves what is lacking in the Passion of Christ, because we are members of his Mystical Body. Now, when one member of the body is suffering, all the other members suffer with it, and when one member has to be removed, all the other members of the body are affected by this 'sacrifice'; if one member is seriously diseased, even though the disease is restricted to one part of the body, the whole body suffers and dies. The same happens in the spiritual life. We are all ill, we all have many defects and sins; hence we all have a duty to make sacrifices, in union with Christ, the innocent victim, in reparation for our own sins and for those of our brothers and sisters, because we are all members of the one and the same Mystical Body of the Lord.

The Message calls on us to *«make of everything you can a sacrifice and offer it to God as an act of reparation for the sins by which He is offended and in supplication for the conversion of sinners».* (Words of the Angel). They may be sacrifices of spiritual, intellectual, moral, physical or material things; depending on the particular moment, we shall have the opportunity of offering first one and then another. What is important is that we should be ready to take advantage of every opportunity that presents itself; in particular, that we should be ready to make sacrifices when this is required of us in order to fulfil our duty to God, to our neighbour and to ourselves. All the more so if such a sacrifice is necessary in order to avoid transgressing one of the commandments of God's Law; in these circumstances, the sacrifice we must impose on ourselves is obligatory, because we have an obligation to offer up whatever is necessary in order to avoid committing sin. Our eternal salvation depends on it, as Jesus Christ tells us in the Gospel: «*If any man would come after me, let him deny himself and take up his cross daily and follow me. For whoever would save his life will lose it; and whoever loses his life for my sake, he will save it. For what does it profit a man if he gains the whole world and loses or forfeits himself?*» (Lk 9, 23-25). From what Our Lord says to us here, we see that we must be prepared to die rather than commit a grave sin which might cause us to lose eternal life. Now the same is true, and all the more so, if obeying God's law demands of us sacrifices of something of less value than our own lives.

Renouncing anything which might cause us to sin is the way to salvation. It is for this reason that the Lord warns us that «*whoever would save his life, will lose it*», in other words, anyone who wishes to satisfy their disordered appetites, live a sinful life, tread the broad path of sin, without repenting or making amends, will lose eternal life. How can we not ask ourselves, with Jesus « *What does it profit us if we gain the whole world, and lose or forfeit ourselves?*»

In the same way, Jesus warns us: «*He who does not take his cross and follow me is not worthy of me*» (Mt 10, 38). Yes! How can anyone be a friend of God and worthy of eternal life if they do not deny themselves whatever is necessary in order to walk in the way of his commandments, renouncing illicit pleasures, the whims of pride, vanity, covetousness, avarice, excessive self-indulgence, failure to practice charity and justice towards others, shrugging off the yoke of the daily cross or carrying it reluctantly without bringing it into line and uniting it with the Cross of Christ ?

At times it will be the cross of our daily work: «*You will eat your bread in the sweat of your brow*» was the burden God imposed on Adam as a penance for his sin. At other times, it will be the difficulties of life which occur at every step we take, and which we must accept with serenity, patience and resignation. At yet other times, it will be the humiliations which happen all of a sudden and which we must accept, acknowledging whatever is imperfect within us and resolving to amend ourselves with confidence in God, who always helps souls who mean well to raise themselves up to a better and more perfect life. *«Make of everything you can a sacrifice – the Message tells us – and offer it to God as an act of reparation for the sins by which He is offended and in supplication for the conversion of sinners».*

God here gives us yet another reason for making sacrifices: *To make reparation for the sins by which He is offended, your own sins and those of others.* Whenever we offend a person, we must make reparation to them, insofar as we can, for whatever upset or damage we may have caused them; that is why we are accustomed to say sorry, to apologise, and so on. Now, it is all the more necessary for us to do this in relation to God. It was for this reason that Jesus Christ taught us in the Lord's Prayer to ask for forgiveness: *«Our Father who art in heaven, (...) forgive us our debts, as we also have forgiven our debtors»* (Mt 6, 9; 12) and immediately afterwards we say: *«And lead us not into temptation, but deliver us from evil.»* (Mt 6, 13). The fact is that the best reparation we can offer to God is to combine with our petition for forgiveness a firm resolution not to offend Him again. That is why we ask for forgiveness, help and protection.

Notice that Jesus taught us to use the plural in asking for forgiveness; in other words to ask it for ourselves and for our brothers and sisters: *forgive us; deliver us; lead us not into temptation!* This is the Call of the Message: *To make sacrifices as an act of reparation and in supplication for the conversion of our brothers and sisters who have wandered off on false and erroneous paths.* Yes, to pray and make sacrifices so that our whole life may be a holocaust offered to God on the arms of our day-to-day cross, in union with the Cross of Christ, for the salvation of souls, co-operating with Him in his redemptive work as members of his Mystical Body, the Church, which works, prays and suffers in intimate union with its Head for the redemption of humanity.

As we live our daily lives, we come across all sorts of sacrifices which we can and must offer to God. The sacrifice of gluttony, which in many cases is obligatory. To abstain from alcoholic drinks taken in excess, as these darken our judgement, interfere with our reason and degrade our dignity, leaving whoever overindulges in them prostrate on the ground before God and honest men. How many families are made unhappy on account of this sin. Why not offer to God the sacrifice of not drinking, sharing, instead, with the poor whatever might otherwise have been wasted in sinful excess and have caused so much suffering, when so many of our brothers and sisters have not enough to buy clothes for themselves.

Such a sacrifice, which is demanded by the moderation with which we must serve ourselves from the table of creation, was one that God required, at the very beginning, from the first two human beings. Sacred Scripture tells us: «*And the Lord God planted a garden in Eden, in the east; and there he put the man whom he had formed. And out of the ground the Lord God made to grow every tree that is pleasant to the sight and good for food, (...) And the Lord commanded the man saying, "You may freely eat of every tree of the garden but the tree of knowledge of good and evil you shall not eat, for in the day that you eat of it you shall die."*» (Gn 2, 8-9. 16-17). Adam and Eve were free to eat the fruit of so many trees that they did not need the fruit from the tree of the knowledge of good and evil; moreover, it was seriously harmful to them, which is why God forestalled it and forbade them to eat from it. The best thing they could have done would have been to obey God's command and offer Him the sacrifice of not touching that fruit.

In this, as in so many other circumstances in life, we have to practise the virtue of temperance, which requires us to mortify the appetite of gluttony. God, like the good Father that He is, has placed such a wide variety of good and delightful things in the world which his children may, and must, use as their food and even take delight in, but always in accordance with the Law of God and without forgetting to practice the self-denial of moderation which we must offer to God in thanksgiving for so many benefits, and also for the benefit of our brothers and sisters in need.

I am not saying that God asks of all of us, as He asks of some of His elect, to strip ourselves of everything, give it to the poor and then follow Him in a complete abandonment of the goods of the earth; what He does ask is that we should all strip ourselves of any excessive love for such goods. Let us recall the conversation between Jesus Christ and the young man who had sought Him out in order to ask Him: «*Teacher, what good deed must I do, to have eternal life?" And he said to him, "Why do you ask me about what is good? One there is who is good. If you would enter life, keep the commandments. He said to him, "Which?" And Jesus said, "You shall not kill, You shall not commit adultery, You shall not steal, You shall not bear false witness, Honour your father and mother, and, You shall love your neighbour as your-*

self." The young man said to him, "All these I have observed; what do I still lack? Jesus said to him, "If you would be perfect, go, sell what you possess and give to the poor, and you will have treasure in heaven; and come follow me." When the young man heard this he went away sorrowful; for he had great possessions. And Jesus said to his disciples, "Truly, I say to you, it will be hard for a rich man to enter the kingdom of heaven. Again I tell you, it is easier for a camel to go through the eye of a needle than for a rich man to enter the kingdom of God."» (Mt 19, 16-24).

According to what I have heard from a number of commentators, Jesus Christ was referring in this statement to rich people who are avaricious and whose only concern is to amass more riches, and who, in order to do so, avoid spending money and refuse to share their surplus with those in need. The Lord teaches us the same lesson when, in connection with the Last Judgement, He describes the reasons for the terrible condemnation meted out to those standing on his left hand: «*Depart from me, you cursed, into the eternal fire prepared for the devil and his angels; for I was hungry and you gave me no food, I was thirsty and you gave me no drink, I was a stranger and you did not welcome me, naked and you did not clothe me, sick and in prison and you did not visit me." (...) "Truly I say to you, as you did it not to one of the least of these, you did it not to me". And they will go away into eternal punishment, but the righteous into eternal life.*» (Mt 25, 41-43. 45-46).

We are reminded of all this when God asks us in the Message of Fatima: *Make sacrifices;* and make use of whatever you have that you do not need or cannot use to help your brothers and sisters who have not enough and are dying of hunger or cold. This is the renunciation and the sacrifice that God asks of us: if we do not sacrifice ourselves in this life, we shall find ourselves being sacrificed in eternal life and not only because we did wrong, but also because we failed to do good: «*For I was hungry and you gave me no food, I was naked and you did not clothe me." (...) as you did it not to one of the least of these, you did it not to me." And they will go away into eternal punishment, but the righteous into eternal life.*»

In order to attain salvation, it is not enough to do no wrong; we all also have a duty to practice virtue in doing good.

Then there is another series of little sacrifices that we can and, to a certain extent must, offer to God. The fact that they are small in themselves does not make them any less pleasing to God, and also very meritorious and advantageous to ourselves, because by means of them we prove the delicacy of our fidelity, and our love for God and for our neighbour. Making such little sacrifices enriches us with grace, strengthens us in faith and charity, ennobles us before God and our neighbour, and frees us from the temptation to egoism, covetousness, envy and self-indulgence.

It is generosity in ordinary little things that are constantly happening; it is making perfect the present moment. Hence:

1) To make our prayer with faith and attention, avoiding distractions as far as possible; praying respectfully, remembering that we are speaking to God; praying with confidence and love, because we are in the presence of Someone who we know loves us and wants to help us, like a father who takes his small son's hand in order to help him to walk: in God's eyes we are always small fragile children who are weak in the practice of virtue, who are constantly tripping and falling, which is why we need our Father to give us his hand to help keep us on our feet and walking in the ways of holiness.

Whether we make our prayer in church, at home, during a journey, out in the fields or walking along the street, God is everywhere and is listening to our petitions, our praise and thanksgiving. This is what Jesus Christ has taught us in his reply to the Samaritan woman who put this question to Him: «*Our fathers worshipped on this mountain; and you say that in Jerusalem is the place where men ought to worship"... Jesus said to her, "Woman, believe me, the hour is coming when neither on this mountain nor in Jerusalem will you worship the Father. You worship what you do not know; we worship what we know (...). But the hour is coming, and now is, when the true worshippers will worship the Father in spirit and truth, for such the Father seeks to worship him. God is spirit, and those who worship him must worship in spirit and truth.*» (Jn 4, 19-24).

God wants us to pray with truth, recognising what we are, our poverty, our nothingness before God; realising what it is we are asking for and promising with sincerity, ready to keep our promises. Let our praise and thanksgiving to God express the truth that is in our heart, in a spirit of faith, love and confidence; God is not content with fine words that are foolish and meaningless, or with formulas designed to win applause from creatures. No, our prayer must be humble and accompanied by a spirit of sacrifice.

Many times, it will be necessary to sacrifice a little of our time for relaxation; perhaps getting up a little earlier in order to go to church and attend Mass; or at night, before going to bed, to set aside some time in which to recite the Rosary, making the sacrifice of turning off the radio or television in order to do so. It is the renunciation of our own likes and fancies that God requires of us; and, as has already been said, if we do not want to deny ourselves in this life, we shall find ourselves being sacrificed in the life to come, because if we cannot hope for salvation through our innocence, only by prayer and penance shall we be saved.

2) To offer to God the sacrifice of some little act of self-denial in the matter of *food*, but not to the extent of impairing the physical strength we need in order to do our work. Thus, for example, to choose a fruit, a dessert, a drink that we don't particularly like rather than one that we do; to endure thirst for a while and then slake it, but with a drink that we don't particularly like; to abstain from alcohol, or at least avoid drinking it to excess.

When we are serving ourselves at table, not to take the best bit. But if we cannot avoid doing so without drawing attention to ourselves, to take it with simplicity and without scruple, thanking God for spoiling us, because we must not think that God, good Father that He is, is only pleased with us when He sees us practising self-denial. God created good things for his children, and likes to see us making use of them, without abusing them, and then fulfilling our duty of working to deserve them, and making use of them with gratitude and love for the One who heaps his gifts upon us.

3) The sacrifice that we can and must make in the matter of *clothing*: putting up with a little cold or heat without complaining; if we are in a room with other people, let them close or open the doors and windows as they wish. Dress decently and modestly, without becoming enslaved to the latest fashion, and refrain from adopting it whenever it is not in accordance with those two virtues, so that we ourselves may not be, by our way of dressing, a cause of sin for others, bearing in mind that we are responsible for the sins that others commit because of us.

Hence, we must dress in accordance with Christian morals, personal dignity and solidarity with others, offering to God the sacrifice of exaggerated vanity. As regards the question of vanity, to know how to offer to God the sacrifice of dispensing with exaggerated external adornment with jewels, which we can well do without, and the money from the sale of which we can use to help our brothers and sisters in need. Instead of wearing clothes made of a rich and expensive material, let us be content with something much simpler and less costly, thus economising in order to be able to help our brothers and sisters who have nothing to cover themselves with.

4) To endure uncomplainingly whatever little annoyances we may encounter on our path: sometimes, it may be a disagreeable, irritating or unpleasant word; at others, it may be an ironic smile, a look of disdain, a contradiction; or we are passed over or set aside as of no account; yet again, it may be a misunderstanding, a reproof, a rejection, when we are passed over, forgotten, an act of ingratitude, etc.

Thus, it is necessary to know how to endure all things, offering our sacrifice to God and letting things drop: to let all these things pass as if we were blind, deaf and dumb, so that we may in fact see better, speak with greater certainty and hear the voice of God. Let others seem to have their way; I say "seem" because in reality the one who prevails is the one who knows how to keep silent for the love of God. Cheerfully to allow others to occupy the first places, whatever is best for them, let them enjoy and take credit for the fruit of our labours, of our sacrifices, of our activities, of our ability, of things that have been taken from us, I would even say of our virtue, as if it belonged to them, and let us content ourselves with being humble and self-sacrificing for the love of God and of our neighbour.

To endure with a good grace the company of those we do not like or whom we find disagreeable, of those who go against us, upset us and torment us with indiscreet or even unkind questions; let us repay them with a smile, a little kind deed done for them, a favour, forgiving and loving, with our eyes fixed on God.

This denial of ourselves is often the most difficult for our human nature, but it is also the one most pleasing to God and meritorious for ourselves.

5) Then there are *exterior penances and sacrifices*, some obligatory, the others voluntary.

Obligatory penances are, for example, the fast and abstinence imposed by the Church. But we can and we must go beyond this limit, which is in fact very little as compared with the need we all have to do penance for our own sins and for those of others.

There are certain instruments of penance which have been used by many Saints, such as disciplines, hair shirts, etc. Such penances are undertaken in union with Christ scourged at the pillar, bound with cords, crowned with thorns. If Christ suffered thus for us, it is more than just that we should do something for Him and for his redemptive work.

Another practice is to pray, in a spirit of penance, with one's arms outstretched in the form of a cross, in union with Christ crucified, or to pray prostrate with one's forehead touching the ground, thus abasing ourselves before God Whom we have dared to offend, we who are nothing in his presence.

Although such penances are not obligatory, they are necessary in many cases; for example, to help overcome fiery natures which cause people to sin, or the violent temptations of the world, the devil, pride and the flesh.

Jesus Christ, who was divine, could not sin, yet He gave us a splendid example of a life of penance. Before beginning his public life, He spent forty days in the desert, praying and fasting. The Gospels tell us that throughout his public life, Jesus frequently withdrew from the crowd in order to pray to the Father in a place apart. And before delivering Himself to death, He spent a long time in prayer in the Garden of Gethsemane.

And do we, poor weak creatures that we are, not need to pray? We do indeed. It is in prayer that we meet God; it is in this meeting with God that He gives us the grace and strength we need in order to deny ourselves by offering up whatever it is that is required of us: *«Enter by the narrow gate; for the gate is wide and the way is easy, that leads to destruction, and those who enter by it are many. For the gate is narrow and the way is hard, that leads to life, and those who find it are few.»* (Mt 7, 13-14). Here Jesus Christ points out to us our great need for self-denial because, without a spirit of renunciation, we shall not enter into eternal life.

«Offer prayers and sacrifices constantly to the Most High».

Ave Maria!

10

Call to share in the Eucharist

The eighth Call of the Message

«Take and drink the Body and Blood of Jesus Christ, horribly outraged by ungrateful men. Make reparation for their crimes and console your God».

This call which the Message addresses to us is very explicit in the Gospel, but very many people misunderstand it, have forgotten it, ignore it, turn their backs on it and, saddest of all, revile it.

When Jesus Christ revealed his intention of remaining with us in the Eucharist in order to be our spiritual food, our strength and our life, the Pharisees were scandalised and did not believe. But Our Lord insisted: *«I am the bread of life. (...) if anyone eats of this bread, he will live for ever; and the bread which I shall give for the life of the world is my flesh. (...) unless you eat the flesh of the Son of man and drink his blood, you have no life in you.»* (Jn 6, 48-51. 53-54). It is clear from these words that if we do not receive the food of Holy Communion, we shall not have within us the life of grace, the supernatural life that depends on our union with Christ through receiving his Body and Blood in Communion. It was for this that He remained in the Eucharist, in order to be our spiritual food, our daily bread which sustains the supernatural life within us.

But in order to be able to receive this Bread, we have to be in the grace of God, as St Paul warns us: *«For I received from the Lord what I also delivered to you, that the Lord Jesus on the night when he was betrayed took bread, and when he had given thanks, he broke it, and said, "This is my body which is for you. Do this in remembrance of me". In the same way also the cup, after supper, saying, "This cup is the new covenant in my blood. Do this, as often as you drink it, in remembrance of me." For as often as you eat this bread and drink the cup, you proclaim the Lord's death until he comes. Whoever, therefore, eats the bread or drinks the cup of the Lord in an unworthy manner will be guilty of profaning the body and blood of the Lord. Let a man examine himself, and so eat of the bread and drink the cup. For any one who eats and drinks without discerning the body eats and drinks judgment upon himself.»* (1 Cor 11, 23-29).

The Apostle's warning is for all of us. Before approaching the Table of the Eucharist, we must examine our conscience and if we find that we have committed some serious fault, we must first purify ourselves by confessing our sins in the Sacrament of Penance, with true repentance and a firm resolve not to sin again. Without these two conditions, our confession will not produce its full effect, even if the priest gives us absolution in the name of God. God sees our confession and confirms the pardon granted to us in his Name by the priest, to the extent to which He sees in our heart our repentance for having offended Him and the resolution we have made not to offend Him again.

Jesus entrusted the power to forgive sins to his Apostles when, after the resurrection, He appeared to them in the Upper Room and said: «*"Peace be with you. As the Father has sent me, even so I send you."And when he had said this, he breathed on them, and said to them, "Receive the Holy Spirit. If you forgive the sins of any, they are forgiven; if you retain the sins of any, they are retained."*» (Jn 20, 21-23).

On another occasion, Jesus said to St Peter, whom He had chosen as the Head of his Church: «*I will give you the keys of the kingdom of heaven, and whatever you bind on earth shall be bound in heaven, and whatever you loose on earth shall be loosed in heaven.*» (Mt 16, 19). Thus the Supreme Head of the Church founded by Jesus Christ was given the authority to decide how our sins were to be forgiven. And since the Head of the Church has decreed that this is to be by means of a humble and sincere confession, made with contrition and a firm purpose of amendment, this is the means which we must use in order to obtain pardon for our sins.

Only after we have prepared ourselves in this way may we receive the Body and Blood of Jesus Christ, confident that this sacrament is for us a source of life, strength and grace, which makes us pleasing in the eyes of God, who sees in us his only-begotten Son, united with us through this complete union and abandonment of his very Self to us out of love.

This is how St Matthew describes the way in which Jesus entrusted Himself to us with his own hands: «*Now as they were eating, Jesus took bread, and blessed, and broke it, and gave it to the disciples and said, "Take, eat; this is my body. And he took a cup, and when he had given thanks he gave it to them, saying, "Drink of it, all of you; for this is my blood of the covenant, which is poured out for many for the forgiveness of sins.*» (Mt 26, 26-28).

We see that Jesus Christ assures us of his real Presence, body and soul, living as He is in Heaven, wherever the consecrated bread and wine are preserved. He says: «*This is*». He did not say: 'This was', nor 'This may be' nor yet 'This will be'. What He said was: «*This is*». In every moment, everywhere, the consecrated bread and wine are the Body and Blood of Jesus Christ, and continue to be so for as long as this bread and this wine are preserved. The words of Jesus Christ, true God and true Man, make this clear; and the Word of God accomplishes what it signifies.

The living Jesus is present in the Eucharist. I say the *living* Jesus because He rose from the dead by his divine power never to die again, and He remains for ever with the Father and the Holy Spirit. In truth, the Son of God has power over death and life: «*For this reason the Father loves me, because I lay down my life, that I may take it again. No ones takes it from me, but I lay it down of my own accord. I have the power to lay it down, and I have the power to take it again; this charge I have received from my Father.*» (Jn 10, 17-18). Thus, Jesus Christ raised from the dead is our life and our resurrection: those who are to live with Him will be raised with Christ as He has promised: «*I am the bread of life; he who comes to me shall not hunger, and he who believes in me shall never thirst. (...) For this is the will of my Father, that every one who sees the Son and believes in him should have eternal life; and I will raise him up at the last day.*» (Jn 6, 35. 40).

It is by faith that we see Jesus Christ: we know that He is the Word of God; we believe in his Word, in his Church; we want to follow the path He has mapped out for us so that through Him we can come to the Father; and, through Him, we shall be raised up on the last day. Yes, if we are nourished with the bread from his Table and we drink from his Chalice, we shall have his Life in us. We become one with Him by participation in his Body and Blood in the Eucharist.

But Christ present on our altars is not only the food of life; He is also the expiatory victim, offering Himself there to the Father for our sins. In fact, the Mass is the unbloody renewal of the sacrifice of the Cross; it is Christ offered as a victim for our sins, under the species of bread and wine. The Cross, on which He gave his life for us, is the greatest proof of his love; and He chose to give us with his own hands the living memorial of this manifestation of his love, by instituting the Eucharist during the Last Supper that He shared with his Apostles: «*Now as they were eating, Jesus took bread, and blessed, and broke it, and gave it to the disciples and said, "Take,* eat; *this is my body. And he took a cup, and when he had given thanks he gave it to them, saying, "Drink of it, all of you; for this is my blood of the covenant, which is poured out for many for the forgiveness of sins."* (Mt 26, 26-28).

Jesus gives us his Body and then his Blood which, He says, is «poured out for many». The word «many» as used here does not exclude «some», as if Jesus had not died for all; but, as I have heard many commentators saying, that word is to be understood in the sense in which it was used in the language of that people: «many» being the opposite of «one», that is, one who dies instead of many. It was in this sense that the high priest, Caiphas, justified the necessity of the death of Jesus: «*You do not understand that it is expedient for you that one man should die for the people, and that the whole nation should not perish.*» (Jn 11, 50).

Christ truly shed his Blood for the whole of humanity, for all, without excluding anyone. But it is also true that not everyone is interested, or makes the effort to welcome into their lives Jesus Christ, the price of their ransom, thereby excluding themselves from the Redemption. How can we not think of the very many who do not know, or who do not wish to be nourished by his Body and Blood? What will happen to them? «*Truly, truly, I say to you, unless you eat the flesh of the Son of man and drink his blood, you have no life in you.*» (Jn 6,53). This is the reply that Jesus gave us in connection with those who do not wish to avail themselves worthily of the gift that He offers us, namely, the gift of his Body and Blood, really and truly present in the Sacrament of the Eucharist.

Enclosed within our tabernacles, offered on our altars, our Saviour continues to offer Himself to the Father as a victim for the remission of the sins of all human beings, in the hope that many generous people will wish to be united to Him, to become one with Him by sharing in the same sacrifice, so that with Him they can offer themselves to the Father as victims in expiation for the sins of the world. In this way, Christ offers Himself as a victim, in Himself but also in the members of his Mystical Body which is the Church. It is the call of the Message: *offer to the Most Holy Trinity the merits of Christ the Victim in reparation for the sins with which He himself is offended,* as the Angel taught the three children to pray: *Most Holy Trinity, Father, Son and Holy Spirit, I adore You profoundly, and I offer You the most precious Body, Blood, Soul and Divinity of Jesus Christ, present in all the tabernacles of the world, in reparation for the insults, sacrileges and indifference with which He himself is offended. And, through the infinite merits of his most Sacred Heart and the Immaculate Heart of Mary, I beg of You the conversion of poor sinners»* (Message of the Angel).

And what are these sins? They are the insults and sacrileges, the indifference and ingratitude of those who receive Him unworthily, of those who insult Him, of those who persecute Him, of those who do not know Him, and of those who, knowing Him, turn their backs on Him and do not love Him. It is the coldness and hardness of other Judases, who place their hand with Him in the dish, after which they go off and betray Him in exchange for their own condemnation, thus rendering fruitless in relation to themselves the fruits of the Redemption which Christ achieved and offered to the Father.

In prayerful silence in the solitude of our churches, He continues to offer Himself unceasingly to the Father as a victim on our behalf; forgotten, despised, ill-treated, humble and poor, He remains a prisoner in our tabernacles. And the Message continues to call on us to offer to the Most Holy Trinity the Victim on our altars in reparation for all the sins by which He is offended.

And our own contribution? It is our humble prayer, our poor little acts of self-denial which we must unite with the prayer and sacrifice of Jesus Christ and of the Immaculate Heart of Mary in reparation, and for the salvation of our brothers and sisters who have wandered away from the one true path that leads to Life.

At this point, I ask myself: Why is it that, since the merits and prayer of Jesus Christ are sufficient to make reparation for and to save the world, the Message invokes the merits of the Immaculate Heart of Mary and calls on us, too, to pray, to make sacrifices, to offer reparation?

I have to say that I do not know! Nor do I know what explanation the theologians of the Church would give me if I were to ask them. But I have meditated on, and thought about this question. I open the Gospel and I see that from the very beginning Jesus Christ united to his redemptive work the Immaculate Heart of Her whom He chose to be his Mother.

The work of our redemption began at the moment when the Word descended from Heaven in order to assume a human body in the womb of Mary. From that moment, and for the next nine months, the blood of Christ was the blood of Mary, taken from her Immaculate Heart; the Heart of Christ was beating in unison with the Heart of Mary.

114

And we can think that the aspirations of the Heart of Mary were completely identified with the aspirations of the Heart of Christ. Mary's ideal had become the same as that of Christ Himself, and the love in the Heart of Mary was the love in the Heart of Christ for the Father and for all human beings; to begin with, the entire work of redemption passed through the Immaculate Heart of Mary, through the bond of her close intimate union with the divine Word.

Since the Father entrusted his Son to Mary, enclosing Him for nine months within her chaste virginal womb – and *«All this took place to fulfil what the Lord had spoken by the prophet: "Behold, a virgin shall conceive and bear a son, and his name shall be called Emmanuel" (which means, God with us).»* (Mt 1, 22-23; Is 7,14). – and since Mary of her own free will opened herself entirely to whatever God willed to accomplish in her – *«Behold, I am the handmaid of the Lord; let it be to me according to your word.»* (Lk 1,38) is what she said to the angel – in view of all this and by God's disposition, Mary became, with Christ, the co-Redemptrix of the human race.

It is the body received from Mary that, in Christ, becomes a victim offered up for the salvation of mankind; it is the blood received from Mary that circulates in Christ's veins and which pours out from his divine Heart; it is this same body and this same blood, received from Mary, that are given to us, under the appearances of bread and wine, as our daily food, to strengthen within us the life of grace, and so continue in us, members of the Mystical Body of Christ, his redemptive work for the salvation of each and all to the extent to which each one clings to Christ and co-operates with Christ.

Thus, having led us to offer to the Most Holy Trinity the merits of Jesus Christ and those of the Immaculate Heart of Mary, who is the Mother of Christ and of his Mystical Body, the Message then goes on to ask us to contribute also the prayers and sacrifices of all of us who are members of that one same Body of Christ received from Mary, made divine in the Word, offered on the Cross, present in the Eucharist, constantly growing in the members of the Church.

Since she is the Mother of Christ and of his Mystical Body, the Immaculate Heart of Mary is in some sense the Heart of the Church: and it is here in the heart of the Church that She, always united with Christ, watches over the members of the Church, granting them her maternal protection. Better than anyone, Mary fulfils Christ's injunction: *«Hitherto you have asked nothing in my name; ask, and you will receive, that your joy may be full.*» (Jn 16, 24). It is in the name of Christ, her Son, that Mary intercedes for us with the Father. And it is in the name of Christ, present in the Eucharist and united with us in Holy Communion, that we unite our humble prayers with those of Mary so that She can address them to the Father in Jesus Christ, her Son.

Hence it is that over and over again we beseech Her: «*Holy Mary, Mother of God, pray for us, sinners, now and at the hour of our death. Amen.*»

Ave Maria!

11

The Call to intimacy with the Most Holy Trinity

The ninth Call of the Message

«Most Holy Trinity, Father, Son and Holy Spirit, I adore you profoundly».

Here the Message presents to our faith and our adoration the mystery of the one God in three Persons: Father, Son and Holy Spirit; it presents to us the mystery of the Most Holy Trinity, one God and three distinct Persons.

We are dealing here with a mystery that has been revealed to us and which only in Heaven will we be able to comprehend perfectly. We believe in it, because God revealed it to us, and we know that our limited understanding is very far removed indeed from the power and the wisdom of God.

In the work of creation, which issued from the creative power of God, we see so many marvellous things concerning which we also do not understand how they came about, so we can look upon them as a figure of the Mystery that is placed before us by God for our consideration.

Thus, for example, each individual is a single person, but in this person there are so many separate things: some of a natural order, others of a supernatural order. We are a body, matter formed by God from the slime of the earth, and this body is kept in being from the products of that same earth from which the body was made and to which it will return.

Already the life of our body is the soul, a spiritual being, created by God in his image and likeness, as we are told in Sacred Scripture: «*So God created man in his own image, in the image of God he created him; male and female he created them*» (Gn 1, 27), after which it explains that «*The Lord God formed man of dust from the ground, and breathed into his nostrils the breath of life; and man became a living being.*» (Gen 2, 7). Hence, our soul is a spiritual being created by the breath of God: it is immortal. For as long as it remains united to our body, we are a living being, but when the body completely ceases to be able to co-operate with the action of the soul, the soul leaves it and flies back to the Being which, being its breath, had created it; it flies back to God who, being its centre of gravity, attracts it. The body, abandoned by the soul, remains lifeless and descends into the earth from which it had been taken.

The soul takes with it the gifts it had received from God: understanding, memory, will, etc. And even if the body continues to possess all its natural organs in good condition, it can no longer see, speak, move, understand or work things out. Before, it was a being which thought, had life; now it is inert, motionless, liable to decompose and disappear in the dust of the tomb.

If we ask ourselves how it is that all these things come together in a single person – a material body that dies; a spiritual soul possessing immortal life, because it shares in the life of God; understanding, the ability to think, memory, and will – we have to confess that we do not know, we do not understand how all this is possible. We do not understand what happens in ourselves, what there is within us, nor what we are; and we are what others do not see, what we ourselves are unaware of, in brief we are what God knows very well. Hence, we are accustomed to say, and to say truly: only God knows what we are.

I once heard a specialist, who had just finished examining a patient, saying: «We doctors have studied a great deal, and medicine has made great progress. Nevertheless, there are many mysteries in the human body which we have not yet managed to unveil». What the doctor said about the human body we can apply to the whole of creation: in everything God has placed a mystery which is not within the range of our limited understanding. And the reason for this is that human understanding constitutes only a tiny fraction of the divine Intelligence.

For us, the whole of nature presents itself to us as if wrapped in mystery, and it also appears to be a revelation of the mystery of God in three Persons – Father, Son and Holy Spirit – and one true God.

If we pick a piece of fruit, an orange for example, we remove the skin which is thrown away, we take out the seeds, which can be sown and grow into other trees, and we are left with the individual sections, which we eat. Thus in a single whole – an orange – we have three separate things which have three separate purposes. And we find the same thing in other types of fruit.

If we look at a rose tree, we see the stock which links it to the ground and from which it draws the nourishment that sustains it; it has green leaves which wither and die in the autumn, and it is covered with lovely roses which we cut and which delight our eyes and our sense of smell. The fact is that the whole of nature was created to speak to us of God, and reveal to us the greatness of the mystery of one God *in three Persons*. If, throughout nature, we find little groups of separate things within the one whole, things which we separate and call by different names, then why should we be astonished to find three distinct Persons – *Father, Son and Holy Spirit* – in the one God? If we choose to listen, all created things speak to us of God the Creator.

But it is above all Sacred Scripture that speaks to us of, and reveals to us in different places, this mystery of the Most Holy Trinity as, for instance, when St Luke describes to us the mystery of the incarnation of the Word: «*The Holy Spirit will come upon you, and the power of the Most High will overshadow you; therefore the child to be born will be called holy, the Son of God*» (Lk 1, 35). All three divine Persons are mentioned in this passage: the *Holy Spirit* who comes down upon the Virgin; the *Most High* (Whom Jesus Christ, the «Son of the Most High» called *Father*) who begets the Word; and the *Son* who is to be born and, as the Angel said, «will be called the Son of God».

Begotten by the Father from all eternity, Jesus Christ is conceived and born, in time, of the Virgin Mary. As man, He began to exist at the moment He became flesh in the womb of his Virgin Mother; as God He was always in existence together with the Father and the Holy Spirit. St John tells us: «*In the beginning was the Word, and the Word was with God, and the Word was God. He was in the beginning with God. (...) And the Word became flesh and dwelt among us*» (Jn 1, 1-2; 14).

On various occasions, in the Gospel, Jesus Christ speaks of all three – the Father, the Son and the Holy Spirit – and He refers to Himself as the Son: «*Whatever you ask in my name, I will do it, that the Father may be glorified in the Son. (...) But the Counsellor, the Holy Spirit, whom the Father will send in my name, he will teach you all things, and bring to your remembrance all that I have said to you*» (Jn 14, 13; 26). In another place, He says: «*The Father loves the Son, and has given all things into his hand.*» (Jn 3, 35), and a little further on «*For as the Father raises the dead and gives them life, so also the Son gives life to whom he will*» (Jn 5, 21).

So we have only one God, but in three distinct Persons: *Father, Son and Holy Spirit*.

The Holy Spirit comes to us as a Teacher, to teach us and remind us of all that Jesus Christ has revealed: *«He will teach you all things, and bring to your remembrance all that I have said to you»*. The Spirit does this either directly by means of the gifts which He himself communicates to the soul, or indirectly, by making use of human means, chief among which are the Church, our Mother and Mistress which, among the principal missions entrusted to it to accomplish on earth, has that of reminding us authoritatively and faithfully of all that Jesus Christ said and did.

In addition to this, as we are told in the Gospel, it will also be given to us to know and dwell with the Holy Spirit, who has come to dwell with us and to be in us: *«I will pray to the Father, and he will give you another Counsellor, to be with you for ever, even the Spirit of truth, whom the world cannot receive, because it neither sees him nor knows him; you know him, for he dwells with you, and will be in you.»* (Jn 14, 16-17). The reference here is to a knowledge by faith which the world, of course, does not possess. The possibility of knowing the Holy Spirit is a marvellous grace which He gives to us: *«Whom you know, for He dwells with you and is in you»*.

Yes! It is an immense grace to be able to know God by means of our faith; to know the revelation of God and about the love He has shown us in all his works; to know Him in the human sciences, in the arts, in the various forces of nature or in the things that surround us: all these things are a manifestation of God, because He reveals Himself in his works. Here we could apply in some sense the invitation that Jesus addressed to his disciples to see in the works accomplished the One who had accomplished them in Him: *«Or else believe me for the sake of the works themselves.»* (Jn 14, 11). To be able to know God, even in the limited manner which is proper to our capacity, is a great grace of inestimable value! To be able to know God, as the Father who created us, as Man and God who redeemed us, as the Spirit who guides us in the ways of truth and love: *«When the Spirit of truth comes, he will guide you into all truth»* (Jn 16, 13).

Now, in a certain sense, the whole truth is love, because, as St John tells us, God is Love. Thus, to love is to possess the greatest gift of God, because it is to possess God Himself. *«If a man loves me, he will keep my word, and my Father will love him and we will come to him and make our home with him.»* (Jn 14, 23). It is to possess God and be ourselves immersed in God; it is the love of God in us, communicated by the presence of the three divine Persons, which will transport us to live immersed in the ocean of supernatural life, always following the path pointed out for us by the light of the word of God. And it is thus that the love of God is manifested in us, transforming us and identifying us with the three divine Persons through our complete union with Jesus Christ: «*In that day you will know that I am in my Father, and you in me, and I in you. He who has my commandments and keeps them, he it is who loves me; and he who loves me will be loved by my Father, and I will love him and manifest myself to him*» (Jn 14, 20-21).

Hence, it is love that transforms us into living temples of the Most Holy Trinity, because God is love and communicates to us the life of his love, which is the life of God in us – «*I will reveal Myself to him*» – it is the life of Christ in us, as He prayed to the Father: «*O righteous Father, the world has not known thee; and these know that thou hast sent me. I made known to them thy name, and I will make it known, that the love with which thou hast loved me may be in them, and I in them.*» (Jn 17, 25-26).

The materialistic world does not know God, does not understand the spiritual life of the indwelling of the Most Holy Trinity in us. And not only does it not understand it. It actually despises it and even persecutes it; but it persecutes it because it does not know it, and is unaware of the countless treasures and intimate riches which are contained in it. Knowing this, Jesus Christ wished to put us on our guard, saying: «*If the world hates you, know that it has hated me before it hated you. If you were of the world, the world would love its own; but because you are not of the world, I chose you out of the world, therefore the world hates you. Remember the word that I said to you, 'A servant is not greater than his master'*» (Jn 15, 18-20).

The world seduces and deceives, and Christ cannot reveal Himself to those who allow themselves to be caught in the deceitful illusions of the world. Hence, those who abandon themselves to materialism do not understand the language used by Jesus Christ who is the Word of God; they have been called, since we were all called to follow the divine Law, but they have not been chosen, because they did not wish to hear the voice of God, that is, the teaching of Christ who is the Word of God, the only One «*who has words of eternal life*». (Jn 6, 68). They have blocked off their own entrance to eternal life. Hence, in the prayer that He addressed to the Father during the Last Supper, Jesus said: «*Father, the hour has come; glorify thy Son that the Son may glorify thee, since thou hast given him power over all flesh, to give eternal life to all whom thou hast given him. And this is eternal life, that*

they know thee the only true God, and Jesus Christ whom thou hast sent. (...)
I have manifested thy name to the men whom thou gavest me out of the world;
thine they were, and thou gavest them to me, and they have kept thy word.»
(Jn 17, 1-6).

In the first place, we see that Jesus Christ tells us quite clearly that eternal life consists in knowing God and the Son sent by the Father. And that is how it is: knowledge of God leads us to love Him, love creates union and union transmits to us the supernatural life of God. Next, let us look at how our Saviour prays to the Father for those whom He has chosen from the world, because they were his; and they are his because they listen to his Word: *thine they were, and thou gavest them to me, and they have kept thy word.*»

It is true that keeping the word of God involves self-denial and renunciation, but it is also true that it is precisely in this self-denial and renunciation that we prove our love to God: «*If any man would come after me, let him deny himself and take up his cross and follow me*» (Mk 8, 34).

The world, on the other hand, promises an easy life and pleasure, and surrounds us with many enticing temptations, but they are false and are born of ignorance because the world, or rather those who follow the maxims of the world, do not know the value of the good thing they are rejecting and losing when they turn their backs on God. They are all in search of happiness, but they do not find it, because they are looking for it where it is not to be found, and so, since they are on the wrong road, the further they go along it the further they go from happiness.

God is the only Being where happiness is to be found, for which, moreover, we were created. But God is not to be found in the satisfaction of the sensual pleasures of the flesh and of the senses, nor of the passions of pride, self-esteem, covetousness, etc. God is to be found in pure souls, in humble hearts and upright consciences, free from attachment to the things of the earth, such as honours, pleasures, riches, etc. People of this kind identify themselves with God, and the life of God in them; and He communicates to them an ever increasing share in his gifts.

It was for this that Christ prayed to the Father: «*Holy Father, keep them in thy name, which thou hast given me, (...) that they may have my joy fulfilled in themselves.(...) Sanctify them in the truth; thy word is truth (...) And for their sake I consecrate myself, that they also may be consecrated in truth. I do not pray for these only, but also for those who believe in me through their word,* that they may all be one; even as thou, Father, art in me, and I in thee, that they also may be in us, so that the world may believe that thou hast sent me. The glory which thou hast given me I have given to them, that they may be one even as we are one, I in them and thou in me, that they may become perfectly one, so that the world may know that thou hast sent me and hast loved them even as thou hast loved me.» (Jn 17, 11-23).

We see that Jesus asks the Father that we may be united with the Most Holy Trinity: «As thou, Father, art in me, and I in thee, that they also may be in us». It is this which is our supernatural life, because to be in God is to live the life of God: God present in us, and ourselves immersed in God. This life of intimate union with God has at times been presented as something difficult and sad, whereas in fact it is simple, joyful and happy, as Jesus Christ himself tells us: «So that they may have my joy fulfilled in themselves». The joy of doing God's will, of being pleasing to God, keeping and observing his Word: «They have kept thy word. Now they know that everything that thou hast given me is from thee; for I have given them the words which thou gavest me, and they have received them» (Jn 17, 6-8). We believe in God, we receive his word and we have within us the fullness of divine joy. We are, as St Paul says, temples of God «Do you not know that you are God's temple and that God's Spirit dwells in you?» (1 Cor 3, 16).

In the Gospel, we are told that we have been specially chosen by Christ: «You did not choose me, but I chose you and appointed you that you should go and bear fruit and that your fruit should abide» (Jn 15, 16). Now, to be chosen by Christ is unquestionably to be chosen by God for the life that never fades, for the love that never dies, for happiness that never comes to an end. Whatever God takes for Himself and identifies with Himself becomes one with God through its intimate union with Christ: «In that day you will know that I am in my Father, and you in me and I in you.» (Jn 14, 20). We see the same thing stated in the Letter to the Ephesians: «You were sealed with the promised Holy Spirit, who is the guarantee of our inheritance until we acquire possession of it, to the praise of his glory.» (Eph 1, 13-14).

Thus it is through our union with Christ that the life of God in us grows and develops, transforming us into living temples of God, as Jesus has told us: «I will not leave you desolate; I will come to you. Yet a little while, and the world will see me no more, but you will see me; because I live, you will live also.» (Jn 14, 18-19). Yes, we live because the life of God in us makes us immortal.

In the Apocalypse, St John tells us that he saw no temple in the City of God, «*for its temple is the Lord God the Almighty and the Lamb. And the city has no need of sun or moon to shine upon it, for the glory of God is its light, and its lamp is the Lamb.*» (Rev 21, 22-23). The Lamb is Christ; the light of Christ is our life, and we live immersed in this light, and thus we are a praise for the glory of God, we walk in the light of his glory and through it we are transformed into a temple of God. «*In whom the whole structure is joined together and grows into a holy temple in the Lord; in whom you also are built into it for a dwelling place of God in the Spirit.*» (Eph 2, 21-22).

We are temples of God, and God is our dwelling place; we walk in the light of the glory of God, we were chosen by God, and God called us and knows us by our name:«*The shepherd (...) calls his own sheep by name (...) and the sheep follow him, for they know his voice.(...) I am the good shepherd; I know my own and my own know me, as the Father knows me and I know the Father; and I lay down my life for the sheep.*» (Jn 10, 2-4; 14-15). It was for this that He came into the world: «*I came that they may have life, and have it abundantly (...) I give them eternal life, and they shall never perish, and no one shall snatch them out of the Father's hand. I and the Father are one.*» (Jn 10, 10b; 11ª; 28-29) (And where the Father is, there is the Son and the Holy Spirit). «*I and the Father are one*».

Our greatness is immense: we were chosen by God, we are kept by God, we are sanctified by the presence of God for the praise of his glory, we are living tabernacles where the Most Holy Trinity dwells, we are the House of God and the Gate of Heaven!

O Holy Trinity, whom I adore, whom I love, whose eternal praises I am to sing! In me you are light, you are grace, you are love! Plunge me into Yourself and I plunge deeply into the love of your Being.

Ave Maria!

12

The Call to the daily recitation of the Rosary

The tenth Call of the Message

This call was made for the first time on 13th May, 1917, when the three little children from Aljustrel were pasturing their sheep in the field known as the Cova da Iria.

As was their custom, the three children ate their lunch shortly after noon, and then prayed. Then, to amuse themselves, they began to build a small wall of loose stones around a bush known as a «moita» from which people were accustomed to make sweeping brushes, hence the children's desire to protect it so that the animals would not gnaw at it. They did this because, when they found such bushes in good condition, they liked to let them grow in order to make brushes from them later on, and these they would bring to their mother when they returned home at night.

When they did this, it was a joy to see their parents' delight with their gift and with their caresses, so that each one did their best to find whatever would give them the greatest joy and pleasure. Poor, yes! But happy, because happiness comes not from riches nor from what can often be dangerous entertainments but from love. In truth, to love and to deny oneself for the sake of love is what brings happiness, joy, peace and well-being to families.

Well, as I was saying, the children were playing and amusing themselves when they were suddenly surprised to see a flash of light, which they thought must be lightning. It was a fine clear spring day, and the sun was shining, but the children were so small that they did not know how to interpret the look of the sky. Accustomed as they were to seeing flashes of lightning immediately after it had thundered, their only thought was to urge on the flock in order to return home before they got caught in a storm.

When they had gone a few steps down the slope they saw another flash of light, which they took to be a second flash of lightning, and this made them hurry even faster and urge the flock on even more. A few steps further on, about half way down the slope, they stopped in surprise when they saw a lovely Lady of light on a small holm oak. They were not afraid, because the supernatural does not arouse fear; causing instead a pleasant surprise of absorbing fascination.

The lovely Lady opened her lips as if about to speak and said to the children: «*Do not be afraid. I will do you no harm*».

I think that these words of Our Lady – *Do not be afraid* – did not refer to any actual fear we might have had of Her, because She knew well we were not frightened of Her. The words must have referred to the fear that had caused us to hurry away from the supposed thunderstorm in which we thought we were going to get caught.

It has also been said that Francisco picked up a few stones to throw at the Apparition. I don't think this can be true. There must have been some confusion or misunderstanding about the stones that shepherds often throw around the flock when they want to get the sheep to come together and move faster.

Once the silence had been broken, and encouraged by the trust that the lovely Lady inspired in us, I asked: «*Where are you from?*» «*I am from Heaven*» She replied. «*And what do you want of me?*» I asked. She replied: «*I have come to ask you to come here on the 13th day of the month for six months in succession, at this same hour. Later on, I will tell you who I am and what I want. Afterwards, I will return here yet a seventh time*».

When I heard this reply, the thought that I was talking to someone who had come from Heaven gave me courage and I asked whether I, too, would have the good fortune to go to Heaven, whereupon the Lady replied: «*Yes, you will.*» «*And Jacinta?*» I asked. «*She will go too.*» She replied. «*And Francisco?*» I persisted. She replied: «*He will go too, but he must say many Rosaries*».

I think that this special injunction to Francisco is for all of us. It is not that saying many Rosaries, as such, is an indispensable condition for going to Heaven, but that we must pray much. Naturally, to say the Rosary every day was the most accessible form of prayer for those children, as it is today for the great majority of people, and there is no doubt that it will be difficult for someone to be saved if they never pray.

We know how weak we are, that we slip back and fall. Without the help of grace, we shall not be able to pick ourselves up or overcome temptations. We can only acquire the strength we need, the strength that comes to us from grace when our soul meets with God in prayer. It was Jesus

Christ Himself who told us this and urged it on his Apostles shortly before He gave Himself up to death for us: «*Watch and pray that you may not enter into temptation; the spirit indeed is willing, but the flesh is weak.*» (Mt 26, 41). And He gave us an example, preparing Himself by his prayer in Gethsemane for his sacrifice and his death. In addition to this, among other things in the Our Father, He taught us to pray: «And lead us not into temptation, but deliver us from evil.» (Mt 6, 13).

Now to return to the Apparition of Our Lady. I remember that I then asked her about a girl I knew who had died shortly before that; the reply Our Lady gave confirms that there is a Purgatory, and is at the same time yet another proof of the need we have to pray.

Sacred Scripture tells us that St Peter went up to Jesus one day and asked Him: «*Lord, how often shall my brother sin against me, and I forgive him? As many as seven times? Jesus said to him, "I do not say to you seven times, but seventy times seven.."*»

Then He went on: "*Therefore the kingdom of heaven may be compared to a king who wished to settle accounts with his servants. When he began the reckoning, one was brought to him who owed him ten thousand talents; and as he could not pay, his lord ordered him to be sold with his wife and children and all that he had, and payment to be made. So the servant fell on his knees, imploring him, "Lord, have patience with me, and I will pay you everything". And out of pity for him the lord of that servant released him and forgave him the debt.*

But that same servant, as he went out, came upon one of his fellow serv-ants who owed him a hundred denarii; and seizing him by the throat he said, 'Pay what you owe.' So his fellow servant fell down and besought him, 'Have patience with me, and I will pay you. He refused and went and put him in prison till he should pay the debt. When his fellow servants saw what had taken place, they were greatly distressed, and they went and reported to their lord all that had taken place. Then his lord summoned him and said to him, 'You wicked servant! I forgave you all that debt, because you besought me; and should not you have had mercy on your fellow servant, as I had mercy on you? And in anger his lord delivered him to the jailers, till he should pay his debt. So also my heavenly Father will do to every one of you, if you do not forgive your brother from your heart.» (Mt 18, 21-35).

This servant who was in danger of condemnation on account of the debt that he had incurred, threw himself at his master's feet begging for mercy and to be given time to pay his debts: «*Have patience with me and I will pay you everything*». Now, in this possibility of being given more time in which to pay what is lacking, we can see an image of Purgatory: a time of waiting to purify ourselves from any minor faults that we have not confessed, and of making any reparation we still owe for our sins because, while we were still living in this world, we had not done enough penance for them.

To begin with, the servant in the parable begged for complete forgiveness for everything, and this he was granted. But he then sinned again by his cruelty to his fellow servant, with the result that he ended up having to do penance and to pay all he owed to his master. This is what will happen to us, as Jesus Christ showed us by the conclusion of his story. The same thing will happen to us if, in addition to the forgiveness for our sins which we ask for and receive in the Sacrament of Reconciliation, we have not also made suitable reparation for them, including always the obligation on us to be merciful to others, as the Lord has been merciful to us.

Jesus taught us to ask for this, too, in the Our Father: «*Our Father, (...) forgive us our debts, as we also have forgiven our debtors*» (Mt 6, 12). Here it is clear that, in order to obtain forgiveness for our sins, we must ask for it from God, and that the extent to which forgiveness will be granted to us will be the same as the extent to which we have forgiven others for any wrongs they may have done to us. «*Forgive and you shall be forgiven*», as Jesus explains after teaching us the Lord's Prayer: «*For if you forgive men their trespasses, your heavenly Father also will forgive you; but if you do not forgive men their trespasses, neither will your Father forgive your trespasses*» (Mt 6, 14-15).

The belief in the possibility of making expiation for sin after death also underlies an event described in the second Book of the Maccabees: «*As Esdris and his men had been fighting for a long time and were weary, Judas called upon the Lord to show himself their ally and leader in the battle. In the language of their fathers he raised the battle cry, with hymns; then he charged against Gorgias' men when they were not expecting it, and put them to flight*. Then Judas assembled his army and went to the city of Adullam. As the seventh day was coming on, they purified themselves according to the custom, and they kept the sabbath there. *On the next day, as by that time it had become necessary, Judas and his men went to take up the bodies of the fallen and to bring them back to lie with their kinsmen in the sepulchres of their* fathers. Then under the tunic of every one of the dead they found sacred tokens of the idols of Jamnia, which the law forbids the Jews to wear. And it became clear to all that this was why these men had fallen. So they all blessed the ways of the Lord, the righteous Judge, who reveals the things that are hidden; and they turned to prayer, beseeching that the sin which had been committed might be wholly blotted out. And the noble Judas exhorted the people to keep themselves free from sin, for they had seen with their own eyes what had happened because of the sin of those who had fallen. He also took up a collection, man by man, to the amount of two thousand drachmas of silver, and sent it to Jerusalem to provide for a sin offering. In doing this he acted very well and honourably, taking account of the resurrection. For if he were not expecting that those who had fallen would rise again, it would have been superfluous and foolish to pray for the dead. But if he was looking to the splendid reward that is laid up for those who fall asleep in godliness, it was a holy and pious thought. Therefore he made atonement for the dead, that they might be delivered from their sin.» (2 Mac 12, 36-46).

This passage from Sacred Scripture helps us to understand better this truth of our faith concerning Purgatory as a place of expiation where the souls of those who die in grace are purified of all stain of sin before being admitted to eternal happiness with God.

Hence, Our Lady's reply to the question I asked her about that girl – Amelia – was as follows: «*She will be in purgatory until the end of the world*». This may seem a lot to us, but the mercy of God is always great. By our sins we have gravely offended Him and have deserved Hell! In spite of this, He forgives us and grants us time to pay for them and, by means of reparation and purification, to be saved. Moreover, He accepts the prayers and sacrifices that others offer to Him for the benefit of those who are in this place of expiation.

Our Lady then asked the three children the following question: «*Are you willing to offer yourselves to God and bear all the sufferings He wills to send you, as an act of reparation for the sins by which He is offended, and of supplication for the conversion of sinners?*» To which I replied in the name of all three: «*Yes, we are willing!*»

At the time, this reply was given spontaneously and in ignorance, because I had not the remotest idea what it really meant nor what its full implications were. But I never regretted it; on the contrary I renew it every day, asking God for the grace and strength that I need to keep it faithfully until the end.

This question of Our Lady's reminds me of the one Jesus put to the two sons of Zebedee, when they asked Him to grant them the two first seats in the Kingdom of Heaven: «*But Jesus answered, "You do not know what you are asking. Are you able to drink the cup that I am to drink?" They said to him, "We are able."* (Mt 20, 22).

In order to attain salvation, we all have to drink of the chalice of self-sacrifice, renouncing our own illicit desires, our evil inclinations, our own exaggerated desire for comfort; while at the same time we must embrace whatever sacrifices life asks of us, whether material and physical, or moral, social and spiritual.

This kind of self-denial comes to everyone, even to those who do not have the happiness of possessing the gift of faith. They, too, are confronted by the need to make sacrifices, because the whole of humanity is marked by the sign of the redeeming cross of Christ, even when they are not aware of it, or do not wish to take advantage of it. We all have to carry that part of the cross of Christ which falls to us in the work of Redemption, because the cross weighs on account of sin, or rather, sin brings with it the weight of the cross.

In fact, it was in order to cleanse us from the stain of sin that Jesus Christ took upon Himself the weight of the Cross. But if this act of Christ is to be of benefit to us, each of us must take up his or her own cross with faith and love and carry it after Christ and in union with Christ; in other words, there is a need for sacrifice, accepted and offered to God with Christ for our own sins and for those of our brothers and sisters. It is in this sense that the Message asks us all, because it is addressed to all: «*Are you willing to offer yourselves to God and bear all the sufferings He wills to send you, as an act of reparation for the sins by which He is offended, and of supplication for the conversion of sinners?*»

But, for a fragile nature, weakened by sin as ours is, the constant, generous and meritorious bearing of self-sacrifice is not possible without the special help of the grace of God, who upholds and strengthens us. This is why Our Lady replied to the children's humble little «*Yes*» with a promise of the help of grace: «*Then you are going to have much to suffer, but the grace of God will be your comfort*».

What a beacon of light these words of Our Lady are for us! In fact, we know our own weakness and we know that, of ourselves, we are not capable of producing the fruits of eternal life but only when united to Christ, as He tells us in the Gospel: «*He who abides in me, and I in him, he it is that bears much fruit, for apart from me you can do nothing.*» (Jn 15, 5). This is why our Mother in Heaven promises the consolation of God's grace: consolation, in the sense of strength to assist our weakness; consolation, in the sense of grace which comes to console us, animate, help and support us. And it is this certainty that generates the confidence which we must have in God.

Putting up with any sacrifices that are asked of us in our day-to-day lives becomes a slow martyrdom which purifies us and raises us up to the level of the supernatural, through the encounter of our soul with God, in the atmosphere of the presence of the Most Holy Trinity within us. We have here an incomparable spiritual richness! Anyone who has understood this lives in Light; in this Light, which is not from the sun nor from the stars, but comes to us from the source from which every other light springs and receives its being. It is a living Light, which both sees and penetrates as it enlightens, and causes us to see what it wishes to show to us. It is the living Light of God.

Hence, when the three little children saw themselves bathed in this Light, without understanding quite what they were saying, they were led to repeat: «*O most Holy Trinity, I adore You! My God, my God, I love You in the most Blessed Sacrament!*» It was a supernatural impulse that accomplished in them what of themselves they were incapable of doing. It led them to believe in the real presence of God in the Eucharist. It is the gift of faith that God grants to our soul with the Sacrament of Baptism.

And Our Lady ended her Message on that 13th May 1917 with the words: «*Pray the Rosary every day, in order to obtain peace for the world, and the end of the war*».

Why should Our Lady have told us to say the Rosary every day rather than telling us to go to Mass every day ?

This is a question that I have been asked many times, and it is one which I should like to reply to here. I cannot be absolutely certain of the answer, as Our Lady did not explain, and it never occurred to me to ask. Hence, I say only what I think, and what I have come to understand about it all. In fact, I willingly leave all interpretation of the meaning of the Message to Holy Church, because it pertains to the Church to do so; hence, I humbly and willingly submit myself to whatever It may wish to say or to correct, amend or declare.

As regards the question referred to above, I think that God is Father; and as Father He adapts Himself to the needs and possibilities of his children. Now, if God, through Our Lady, had asked us to go to Mass and receive Holy Communion every day, there would undoubtedly have been a great many people who would have said, quite rightly, that this was not possible. Some, on account of the distance separating them from the nearest church where Mass was celebrated; others on account of the circumstances of their lives, their state in life, their job, the state of their health, etc. On the other hand, to pray the Rosary is something everybody can do, rich and poor, wise and ignorant, great and small.

All people of good will can, and must, say the Rosary every day. Why? In order to put ourselves into contact with God, to thank Him for his benefits and ask Him for the graces we need. It is the prayer which places us in familiar contact with God, like the son that goes to his father to thank him for the gifts he has received, to talk to him about his special concerns, to receive his guidance, his help, his support and his blessing.

Since we all need to pray, God asks of us, as a kind of daily instalment, a prayer which is within our reach: the Rosary, which can be recited either in common or in private, either in Church in the presence of the Blessed Sacrament or at home, either with the rest of the family or alone, either when travelling or while walking quietly in the fields. A mother of a family can say the Rosary while she rocks her baby's cradle or does the housework. Our day has twenty four hours in it. It is not asking a great deal to set aside a quarter of an hour for the spiritual life, for our intimate and familiar converse with God.

On the other hand, I believe that, after the liturgical prayer of the Holy Sacrifice of the Mass, the praying of the Rosary, in view of the origin and sublime nature of the prayers used in it, and of the mysteries of the Redemption which we recall and on which we meditate during each decade, is the most pleasing prayer that we can offer to God, and one which is most advantageous to our own souls. If such were not the case, Our Lady would not have asked for it so insistently.

When I speak of saying the five or fifteen mysteries of the Rosary, I do not want to give the impression that God requires us to count the number of times that we address our supplications, our praise or our thanksgiving to Him. God certainly does not expect this of us: in Him everything is present! But we need to count, in order to have a clear and vivid idea of what we are doing, and to know positively whether or not we have completed what we had planned to offer to God each day, in order to preserve and enhance our relationship of intimacy with God and, by this means, preserve and enhance in ourselves our faith, hope and charity.

I would add that even those people who are able to assist at Mass every day should not, for this reason, neglect to say their daily Rosary. Obviously, the time they devote to saying the Rosary is not the same as that during which they are assisting at Mass. For such people, praying the Rosary can be looked upon as a way of preparing themselves to participate better in the Eucharist, or as an act of thanksgiving after it.

I don't know, but from the little knowledge that I have from my contact with people in general, I see that there are very few truly contemplative souls who preserve and maintain within themselves a relationship of intimate familiarity with God which prepares them for the worthy reception of Christ in the Eucharist. Thus, vocal prayer is necessary for them too, meditated, pondered and reflected upon as much as possible, as the Rosary should be.

There are many fine prayers that can be used as a means of preparing to receive Christ in the Eucharist, and of maintaining our intimate relationship with God. But I do not think that we shall find one more suited to people in general than the praying of the five or fifteen mysteries of the Rosary. For example, the prayer of the Liturgy of the Hours is marvellous, but I do not think it is accessible to all, nor that some of the psalms that one recites will be readily understood by all. It requires a certain degree of instruction and preparation which cannot be expected of all.

Perhaps for all these reasons, and others that we are unaware of, God, who is our Father and understands better than we do the needs of His children, chose to stoop to the simple ordinary level of all of us in asking for the daily recitation of the Rosary, in order to smooth for us the way to Him.

Finally, bearing in mind all that the Magisterium of the Church has said to us over the years about the praying of the Rosary – I shall remind you of some of these things further on – and what God, through the Message, has asked us for so insistently, we can conclude that the Rosary is the form of vocal prayer which is most suited to people in general, which we must appreciate, and which we must make every effort never to abandon. God and Our Lady know better than anyone else what is most appropriate for us and what we most need. Moreover, it will be a powerful means of helping us to preserve our faith, hope and charity.

Even for those people who do not know how, or who are not able to recollect themselves sufficiently to meditate, the simple act of taking the rosary in their hands in order to pray is already to become mindful of God, and the mention in each decade of a mystery of the life of Christ recalls Him to their minds; this in turn will light in their souls the gentle light of faith which supports the still smouldering wick, preventing it from extinguishing itself altogether.

On the other hand, those who give up saying the Rosary and who do not go to daily Mass, have nothing to sustain them, and so end up by losing themselves in the materialism of earthly life.

Thus the Rosary is the prayer which God, through his Church and Our Lady, has recommended most insistently to us all, as a road to and gateway of salvation: «*Pray the Rosary every day*» (Our Lady, 13th May 1917).

Ave Maria!

13

The Call to devotion to the Immaculate Heart of Mary

The eleventh Call of the Message

«Jesus wants... to establish in the world devotion to my Immaculate Heart».

To establish in the world devotion to the Immaculate Heart of Mary means to bring people to a full consecration through conversion, self-dedication, intimate esteem, veneration and love. Thus, it is in this spirit of consecration and conversion that God wishes to establish in the world devotion to the Immaculate Heart of Mary.

We all know that a mother's heart represents love in the bosom of a family. In fact, it is love which makes the mother bend over her baby's cradle, sacrifice herself for it, give herself, rush to the defence of her child. All children trust in the heart of their mother, and we all know that we have in her a place of special affection. The same applies to the Virgin Mary. Thus the Message says: *«My Immaculate Heart will be your refuge and the way that will lead you to God»*. Hence, the Heart of Mary is the refuge and the way to God for all his children.

This refuge and this way were proclaimed to all humanity immediately after the fall of our first parents. To the devil, who had tempted the first human beings, and had induced them to disobey the divine order they had been given, the Lord said: *«I will put enmity between you and the woman, and between your seed and her seed; he shall bruise your head, and you shall bruise his heel.»* (Gen 3, 15). The 'new generation' that God foretold would be born of this woman, will triumph in the battle against the progeny of Satan, to the point of crushing its head. Mary is the Mother of this new generation, as if she were a new tree of life, planted by God in the garden of the world so that all her children can partake of her fruit.

It is from the heart of their mother that children receive their natural life, their first breath, their life-giving blood, the beating of their heart, as if the mother were the spring of a clock impelling movement to two pendulums. When we see how dependent the child is on its mother in those early months of its formation in the womb, we could almost say that the heart of the mother is the heart of the child. And we can say the same of Mary, when She carried the Son of the Eternal Father in her womb. Hence, it follows that the Heart of Mary is, in some sense, the heart of all that other generation, the first fruit of which is Christ, the Word of God.

And it is from this fruit that that other generation of this Immaculate Heart is to be fed, as Jesus said: «*I am the bread of life. He who eats my flesh and drinks my blood abides in me, and I in him. As (...) I live because of the Father, so he who eats me will live because of me.*» (Jn 6, 48; 56-57). And to live thus because of Christ is also to live because of Mary, since Jesus had received his Body and Blood from Mary.

It was in this Heart that the Father placed his Son, as if in the first Tabernacle. Mary was the first pyx that held Him, and it was the blood of her Immaculate Heart which communicated to the Son of God his life and his human nature, from which we all, in turn, receive «*grace upon grace*» (Jn 1, 16).

This is that new generation born from this wonderful mother: Christ in Himself and in his Mystical Body. And Mary is the Mother of this progeny chosen by God to crush the head of the infernal serpent.

Thus we see that devotion to the Immaculate Heart of Mary must be established in the world by means of a true consecration, through conversion and self-giving. In the same way, through the consecration, the bread and wine are converted into the Body and Blood of Christ, which were drawn with his very life from the Heart of Mary.

Hence it is that this Immaculate Heart must be for us a refuge and the way that leads us to God.

We thus constitute the retinue of the new generation created by God, drawing our supernatural life from the same life-giving source, the Immaculate Heart of Mary, who is the Mother of Christ and of his Mystical Body. Thus we are truly brothers and sisters of Christ, as He himself said: «*My mother and my brethren are those who hear the word of God and do it.*» (Lk 8, 21).

This word of God is the bond which links all the children in the Heart of the Mother; there we hear the echo of the word of the Father, because God enclosed his eternal Word in the Heart of Mary; and it is from this Word that life comes to us: «*If any one thirst, let him come to me and drink. He who believes in me, as the scripture has said, 'Out of his heart shall flow rivers of living water.*» (Jn 7, 37-38). In fact, we read in the Book of Isaiah:

«*For I will pour water on the thirsty land, and streams on the dry ground; I will pour my Spirit upon your descendants, and my blessing on your offspring*» (Is 44, 3).

This blessed and watered land is the Immaculate Heart of Mary, and God wants our devotion to take root there, because it was for this very purpose that God placed so much love within the heart of the Mother of all human beings, who consecrates and converts her progeny into the Body and Blood of Christ, her First-born, Son of God, the Word of the Father: «*In him was life, and the life was the light of men. (...) And the Word became flesh and dwelt among us, full of grace and truth; we have beheld his glory, glory as of the only Son from the Father.*» (Jn 1,4.14).

God began the work of our redemption in the Heart of Mary, given that it was through her *«fiat»* that the redemption began to come about: «And Mary said, *"Behold, I am the handmaid of the Lord; let it be to me according to your word,"* (Lk 1, 38). «*And the Word became flesh and dwelt among us*» (Jn 1, 14). Thus, in the closest union possible between two human beings, Christ began, with Mary, the work of our salvation. The Christ's heart-beats are those of the heart of Mary, the prayer of Christ is the prayer of Mary, the joys of Christ are the joys of Mary; it was from Mary that Christ received the Body and Blood that are to be poured out and offered up for the salvation of the world. Hence, Mary, made one with Christ, is the co-Redemptrix of the human race. With Christ in her womb, with Jesus Christ in her arms, with Christ at Nazareth and in his public life; with Jesus Christ she climbed the hill of Calvary, she suffered and agonised with Him, receiving into her Immaculate Heart the last sufferings of Christ, his last words, his last agony and the last drops of his Blood, in order to offer them to the Father.

And Mary remained on earth in order to help her other children to complete the redeeming work of Christ, preserving it in her heart as a wellspring of grace – *Ave gratia plena* – in order to pass on to us the fruits of the life, passion and death of Jesus Christ, her Son.

Ave Maria!

14

The Call to reflect on eternal life

The twelfth Call of the Message

We all have a desire to preserve our temporal life, which passes with the days, the years, work, joys, sorrows and suffering. But how little we concern ourselves with eternal life! And yet, this is the only life that is truly decisive and that lasts for ever.

When God created human beings, He destined them for eternal life by sharing in his divine life. Hence, «*God created man in his own image, in the image of God he created him; male and female he created them*» (Gn 1,27), and then went on to explain that «*The Lord God formed man of dust from the ground, and breathed into his nostrils the breath of life; and man became a living being.*» (Gen 2, 7). We see here that the human body was taken from the dust of the earth, but human beings received life itself from the very Being of God, from the creative breath of His lips. Hence, our soul is a spiritual being which participates in the life of God and is immortal. When the body becomes totally incapable of co-operating with the action of the soul, the soul leaves it and flies to its centre of attraction, which is God.

But our participation in eternal life must be decided between two very different realities: Heaven or Hell.

In the Call to devotion to the Immaculate Heart of Mary, we saw how there are two distinct progenies which are at loggerheads with each other: the progeny of Satan, which leads people into the way of sin, and the progeny of the Immaculate Heart of Mary who, as the Mother of the children of God, leads them in the way of truth, justice and love, since *God is Love*, and all His children are known by the way they love. And whereas the children of God climb by the way of love to the possession of eternal happiness in the Kingdom of God, the children of Satan are dragged down by the vileness of sin into the abyss of eternal punishment.

There are unbelievers in the world who deny these realities, but this does not make them any the less real; nor does these people's incredulity deliver them from the pains of hell if their lives of sin should lead them to it.

There are many passages in Sacred Scripture that speak to us about hell and its torments, and about those who go there. Thus, at the Last Judgement, those who have not performed the works of mercy will be told: «*Depart from me, you cursed, into the eternal fire prepared for the devil and his angels (...)*" *And they will go away into eternal punishment, but the righteous into eternal life*» (Mt 25, 41, 46).

When warning his disciples against the temptation to pride because of the success of the mission they had accomplished, Jesus said: «*I saw Satan fall like lightning from heaven.*» (Lk 10, 18). And when He was giving them his instructions for the conduct of their apostolate, He said: «*Do not fear those who kill the body but cannot kill the soul; rather fear him who can destroy both soul and body in hell*» (Mt 10, 28). Speaking of the final resurrection, Jesus ended the parable of the net that was cast into the sea and enclosed all kinds of fish, which the fisherman then had to sort out, by saying: «*So it will be at the close of the age. The angels will come out and separate the evil from the righteous, and throw them into the furnace of fire; there men will weep and gnash their teeth.*» (Mt 13, 49-50).

And the following words of Jesus, too, leave no room for doubt:«*If your hand causes you to sin, cut it off; it is better for you to enter life maimed than with two hands go to hell, to unquenchable fire. (...) And if your eye causes you to sin, pluck it out; it is better for you to enter the kingdom of God with one eye than with two eyes to be thrown into hell, where their worm does not die, and the fire is not quenched.*» (Mk 9, 43-48). In these passages, Jesus speaks of the fire of hell and of eternal condemnation; and He says the same thing in other parts of the Gospel which it would take too long to copy out here.

The last passage quoted does not mean that God really intends us to tear out our eyes or to cut off our hands and feet, but that we are to tear out, or cut off, the temptations, evil inclinations, passions and vices which drag us along the path of sin and might, for this reason, be the cause of our eternal damnation.

In the Old Testament, we find texts that, when read today in the light of the faith of the Church, constitute the first dawning of divine revelation concerning the truths that they teach, as, for example, this question of the existence of hell. This is true of the following passage from Isaiah, describing the fate of those who refused to obey the Law of God: «*The hand of the Lord is with his servants, and his indignation is against his enemies. (...) And* they shall go forth and look on the dead bodies of the men that have rebelled against me; for their worm shall not die, their fire shall not be quenched, and they shall be an abhorrence to all flesh.» (Is 66, 14, 24).

And in the Book of Wisdom, the Holy Spirit describes as follows the lamentations of those who have condemned themselves on seeing the salvation of the just: «*Then the righteous man will stand with great confidence in the presence of those who have afflicted him, and those who make light of his labours. When they see him, they will be shaken with dreadful fear, and they will be amazed at his unexpected salvation. They will speak to one another in repentance, and in anguish of spirit they will groan, and say, "This is the man whom we once had in derision and made a byword of reproach – we fools! We thought that his life was madness and that his end was without honour. Why has he been numbered among the sons of God? And why is his lot among the saints? So it was we who strayed from the way of truth, and the light of righteousness did not shine on us, and the sun did not rise upon us. We took our fill of the paths of lawlessness and destruction, and we journeyed through trackless deserts, but the way of the Lord we have not known. What has our arrogance profited us? And what good has our boasted wealth brought us?*

"All those things have vanished like a shadow, and like a rumour that passes by; like a ship that sails through the billowy water, and when it has passed no trace can be found, nor track of its keel in the waves; (...) So we also, as soon as we were born, ceased to be, and we had no sign of virtue to show, but were consumed in our wickedness."

(...) But the righteous live for ever, and their reward is with the Lord; the Most High takes care of them. Therefore they will receive a glorious crown and a beautiful diadem from the hand of the Lord, because with his right hand he will cover them, and with his arm he will shield them. (...) He will take holiness as an invincible shield, (...) Lawlessness will lay waste the whole earth, and evil doing will overturn the thrones of rulers.» (Ws 5, 1-23).

And we could go on transcribing similar passages from Sacred Scripture where God speaks to us of the existence of an eternal life, either of bliss or of condemnation, according as our deeds deserve. The word of God affirming this truth is sufficient for us who have faith, because we know that his word is true.

In Fatima He sent us his Message as further proof of these truths, bringing them to our minds so that we do not allow ourselves to be deceived by the false teaching of unbelievers who deny them, and of those who have left the true path, who distort them. With this end in view, the Message assures us that hell does truly exist and that the souls of poor sinners do in fact go there: *«You have seen hell* (the Message said to the three little shepherds from Aljustrel*) where the souls of poor sinners go. To save them, God wishes to establish in the world devotion to my Immaculate Heart. If what I say to you is done, many souls will be saved and there will be peace»* (Our Lady. 13th July 1917).

Moreover, after showing the children the horrible vision of hell, the Message once again points to devotion to the Immaculate Heart of Mary as the way of salvation: *«To save them, God wishes to establish in the world devotion to my Immaculate Heart. If what I say to you is done, many souls will be saved and there will be peace».* Peace with one's own conscience, peace with God, peace in our homes, peace within families, peace with one's neighbours and peace between the nations.

This is the peace that the world ardently longs for, and from which it is so far removed because it does not listen to, or follow, the word of God! Hence the words of the Message: *«If what I say to you is done ...».* And what is it that Our Lady says to us ?

We shall continue to see what it is She says in the description of the Calls of the Message. For the moment, let me remind you of a passage from the Gospel of St John, in which we find what we might call *«Mary's commandment».*

There was a marriage being celebrated in Cana in Galilee, at which Jesus Christ, his Mother and his disciples were present. At a certain moment, Mary noticed that the wine was running short and she told her Son about the awkwardness of the situation which would cause embarrassment to the young couple. She then said to the waiters: *«Do whatever He tells you».* They obeyed and the Lord changed the water into wine (Jn 2, 1-10). We could regard this as Mary's commandment: *«Do whatever He tells you».* Follow the Word of God, which is Jesus Christ, his Word!

This commandment comes from a Mother who is ever anxious to lead her children into the arms of their Father, because only there will they be able to find the way of Truth that leads to Life. She herself is a Mother, because she followed this way, that of the Word of the Father: *«Be it done unto me according to your word»* was her reply to the Angel when he conveyed to her the word of God (Lk 1, 38). And this faith of hers in the word of God was praised by her cousin Elizabeth: *«Blessed is she who believed that* there would be a fulfilment of what was spoken to her from the Lord.» (Lk 1, 45) And all this is confirmed by the following words of Jesus: «*For whoever does the will of my Father in heaven is my brother, and sister, and mother.*» (Mt 12, 50).

It was thus that the servants deserved to see the miracle of the changing of the water into wine; they did what Mary told them to do and they obeyed the word of Jesus. This is the way of salvation: to hear the word of God and keep it.

Ave Maria!

15

The Call to the Apostolate

The thirteenth Call of the Message

«Pray, pray very much and make sacrifices for sinners; for many souls go to hell because there is no one to make sacrifices and to pray for them» (Our Lady, 19th August, 1917).

In this passage, the Message asks us to undertake an apostolate on behalf of our brothers and sisters. The apostolate is a continuation of the mission of Christ on earth; we must be co-workers with Christ in his work of Redemption, in the salvation of souls. There is the *apostolate of prayer* which must be the basis of every other apostolate, if it is to be effective and fruitful; there is the *apostolate of self-denial:* undertaken by those who make sacrifices, denying themselves for the good of their brothers and sisters; and there is the *apostolate of charity*, which is the life of Christ reproduced in us by our dedication of ourselves to God in the service of others.

Thus, to begin with, we have the apostolate of prayer, praying in union with Christ for the salvation of our brothers and sisters. Jesus Christ continues to pray on earth in the Sacrament of the altar, where He offers himself continuously to the Father in propitiation for the salvation of all. It is by our union with Christ in the Eucharist that our prayer is raised to God for the salvation of our brothers and sisters.

Shortly before He gave Himself up to death, Jesus Christ said to his disciples: *«Abide in me, and I in you (...) for apart from me you can do nothing.»* (Jn 15, 4; 5). These words mean that it is by our prayer that our apostolate is to bear fruit. Without prayer, we can do nothing! In his prayer to the Father, Jesus said: *«I do not pray for these only, but also for those who believe in me through their word, that they all may be one; even as thou, Father, art in me, and I in thee, they also may be in us, so that the world may believe that thou hast sent me.»* (Jn 17, 20-21). The Lord insists on our union with Him, so that our apostolate may bear fruit and the world may believe that He was sent by the Father. This insistence is the expression of the yearning for our salvation that wells up from his divine heart: a yearning for us to remain united amongst ourselves and with Him so that his redemptive work may bear fruit for all: «*I pray (...) for those who, through their word, will believe in me*». And Jesus concluded his priestly prayer by asking the Father that we might share in his own life: «*Father, I desire that they also, whom thou hast given me, may be with me, where I am, (...) I made known to them thy name, and I will make it known, that the love with which thou hast loved me may be in them, and I in them*» (Jn 17, 24; 26). Love is the link binding us to Christ; it is love that gives value to our prayer and makes it fruitful for the salvation of our brothers and sisters.

The first step in our apostolate, and the necessary condition for it to bear fruit, is thus our union with Christ through prayer. Both vocal prayer, which places us in the presence of Christ, and the prayer of sacrifice when we unite ourselves with Christ, and also the prayer of love whereby we abandon ourselves with Christ to the Father for the conversion of all.

Jesus Christ has given us the example. Before beginning his own apostolate in his public life, He withdrew to the desert in order to pray and do penance there, and fast for forty days: «*And Jesus full of the Holy Spirit, returned from the Jordan, and was led by the Spirit for forty days in the wilderness, (...) And he ate nothing in those days*» (Lk 4, 1-2). Moreover, the Evangelists frequently record that He would escape from the bustle of the crowds who were following Him and withdraw to pray in solitude.

On one of these occasions, when He re-joined his disciples, He found them unable to cast a devil out of a boy who was possessed. When, later on, they wanted to know why they had been unable to expel that demon, the Lord replied: «*This kind cannot be driven out by anything but prayer and fasting*» (Mk 9, 29). This kind of persistent demon makes me think of temptations to pride, which are the most serious and difficult to overcome, both in ourselves and in others, because they blind us and prevent us from seeing the precipice down which we are slipping. As the Lord said, in such circumstances both prayer and penance are needed, because only through them can we rediscover the virtue of humility which prompts us to ask God for his strength and grace.

When the sentence of extermination was hanging over the People of Israel for having offended God by the sin of idolatry, Moses went up the mountain to meet God and implore Him to pardon his people. God heard Moses' prayer and spared his people, punishing only those who had been guilty: «*Whoever has sinned against me, him will I blot out of my book. But now go, lead the people to the place of which I have spoken to you; behold, my angel shall go before you.»* (Ex 32, 33-34). Here we see the Lord, who is ever good and merciful, co-operating with those who work together with Him; it is a model of the apostolate which is based on prayer, and which springs from direct contact with God.

Moses is the apostle of the People of Israel, but before giving instructions to the people, he speaks with God and receives from God what he is to communicate to the people. Hence, God helps him, promising to send an angel to go before him.

Without this life of prayer and contact with God, every apostolate is fruitless, because it is God who must make effective what we do, what we say, and the efforts we make. Hence, the Message tells us: *«Pray and make sacrifices»* so that, through your prayers, your words, your example, your acts of self-denial, your work and your charity, you will be able to help your brothers and sisters to get up again if they have fallen, to return to the right path if they have strayed away from it, and to draw close to God if they are estranged from Him. You will also be able to help them to overcome the difficulties, dangers and temptations that surround, seduce and pull them down. Very often, people are overcome and fall because they have no one at their side willing to pray and to make sacrifices for them, stretching out a hand to them, and helping them to follow a better path.

In this field of the apostolate, we all have a mission to accomplish which has been entrusted to us by God. We are all responsible for our neighbour. By Baptism we share in the priesthood of Christ our Saviour, and we are also incorporated into his Mystical Body, with a specific place and specific duties to perform. Human beings were not created to be strangers to one another, to ignore one another eternally, but rather to be companions to one another, brothers and sisters who love and help one another, and gather together around their Father who provides for their daily needs for food and clothing; from Him each one receives the same blessing and all are heading for the same destination, their Father's House.

The true apostolate consists in this union of the children with their Father in Heaven; it is this union which is the grace and the gate of salvation; if not, let us see what Christ's priestly prayer says to us: *«Holy Father, keep them in thy name, which thou hast given me, that they may be one, even as we are one. While I was with them, I kept them in thy name, which thou hast given me; I have guarded them, and none of them is lost but the son of perdition.»* (Jn 17, 11-12). These words of Jesus should help us not to grow discouraged when we encounter in our path those 'sons of perdition' who resist grace, the tenacity of our charity, of our efforts and sacrifices and prayers. They are the children of that other progeny whom Satan turns aside into the ways of perdition.

This is in accordance with what God said to Moses: «*Whoever has sinned against me, him will I blot out of my book. But now you go, lead the people to the place of which I have spoken to you; behold, my angel shall go before you.*» (Ex 32, 33-34). Because some persist in their evil ways, the Lord, who is ever merciful, does not cause the rest to perish, but orders Moses to continue his apostolate and to lead his people in the ways of the Lord. Each one is responsible for his own acts, so that the one who sinned and persists in his or her sin, is to be blotted out from the Book of Life, but not the brother or sister who repented and chose to be led by the Lord.

Yes, our God is truly merciful! And we, too, must be merciful, created as we have been in his image and likeness. This is why Jesus Christ said: «*I desire mercy, and not sacrifice*» (Mt 12,7), quoting the words of the prophet Hosea, who describes the feelings of the heart of God as follows: «*For I desire steadfast love and not sacrifice, the knowledge of God, rather than burnt offerings.*» (Hos 6, 6). Here we have the *apostolate of forgiveness,* whereby we are to bring our brothers and sisters to the knowledge of God. Let them find in us sentiments of forgiveness which will be for them a reflection of the mercy of God.

Let us reflect that God has made the granting of his pardon to us dependent on the degree to which we ourselves forgive those who have wronged us in some way: «*For if you forgive men their trespasses, your heavenly Father also will forgive you; but if you do not forgive men their trespasses, neither will your Father forgive your trespasses.*» (Mt 6, 14-15). This obligation on us to forgive others requires us to overcome temptations of pride which lead to revenge. This law had already been proclaimed by God in the Old Testament: «*You shall not take vengeance or bear any grudge against the sons of your own people, but you shall love your neighbour as yourself: I am the Lord.*» (Lev 19, 18). As God here ordains, we have to resist the temptation to revenge, contempt or indifference, by the *apostolate of charity* which will lead us to forgive, to pay back evil with good, and to pray for those who persecute us. We have to imitate Jesus Christ who, on the cross, asked his Father to forgive those who had insulted, maltreated and crucified Him: «*Father, forgive them; for they know not what they do*» (Lk 23, 34).

And the Lord's own words leave no room for doubt: «*And whenever you stand praying, forgive, if you have anything against any one; so that your Father also who is in heaven may forgive you your trespasses.*» (Mk 11, 25-26). In another place the Lord says to us: «*Love your enemies, do good to those who hate you, bless those who curse you, pray for those who abuse you.*» (Lk 6, 27-28). This pardon is the fruit of the charity which burns in the heart of Christ and which must animate our apostolate to our brothers and sisters: «*I came to cast fire upon the earth; and would that it were already kindled!*» (Lk 12, 49).

However, this call of the Message includes another characteristic which should also mark our apostolate. When Our Lady was asked what was to be done with the offerings that the people had begun to leave at the place of the Apparitions in fulfilment of their promises, She replied: *"Have two litters made. One is to be carried by you and Jacinta and two other girls dressed in white; the other one is to be carried by Francisco and three other boys. The money from the litters is for the "festa" of Our Lady of the Rosary, and what is left over will help towards the construction of a chapel that is to be built here."* (Our Lady, 19th August, 1917).

The litters that the Message refers to here are not litters for carrying images but those used for carrying in procession the offerings made by the people to the Lord. In fact, the people were accustomed to thank God for His gifts by offering Him some of the fruits of their harvest, in accordance with each one's means. These offerings were collected by stewards who placed them in litters which were carried processionally on big feast days. After the High Mass, they were carried in procession and offered to God in thanksgiving for the grace received and as a contribution to church expenses.

Our Lady clearly revealed, by her answer, how pleasing to God this simple act of thanksgiving was, since we must show our gratitude to God and we also have a duty to take part in, and contribute to, the cost of the public honour that is paid to Him.

A word, now, about the gesture that the Message asks us to make, that of joining with our brothers and sisters in bringing to Him our offerings, our thanksgiving, our prayers and our sacrifices: this constitutes an act of collaboration which animates and gives life to the apostolate, making us apostles of one another.

Some of the customs that the people of Fatima had at that time were reminiscent of those described in the Bible. I think that the people of that time, most of whom could neither read nor write, knew little or nothing about bible history, apart from a few facts which a few people in the area, who did know how to read, were able to read about in summaries of Sacred History. At least, that is how it was with me. Only many years later was I able to read the Holy Bible, and only then did I discover the most intimate meaning of the Message and its connection with the Word of God.

Continuing our examination of this particular aspect of the apostolate, and making use of the similarities between incidents in bible history and the customs of the people of Fatima at that time, let us recall the following instructions given by the Lord to his people:«*And the Lord said to Moses, "On the tenth day of this seventh month is the day of atonement; it shall be for you a time of holy convocation, and you shall afflict yourselves and present an offering by fire to the Lord. And you shall do no work on this same day; for it is a day of atonement, to make atonement for you before the Lord your God. For whoever is not afflicted on this same day shall be cut off from his people. And whoever does any work on this same day, that person I will destroy from among his people. You shall do no work: it is a statute for ever throughout your generations in all your dwellings."*» (Lv 23, 26-31).

It is not difficult to see in this «tenth day of the seventh month» Sundays and Holydays which the Church requires us to consecrate to the Lord. On these days we are obliged to observe that law of the Lord; they are days on which we are to worship God, offering Him our prayers and our sacrifices.

On another occasion, God said to Moses: «*And the Lord said to Moses, "Thus you shall say to the people of Israel:" (...) An altar of earth you shall make for me and sacrifice on it your burnt offerings and your peace offerings, your sheep and your oxen; in every place where I cause my name to be remembered I will come to bless you*» (Ex 20, 22; 24). I do not know what interpretation the Church's theologians give to this passage from Sacred Scripture. I myself find it enchanting because it shows us the tenderness of the fatherly love of God. And since we ourselves are, in Christ, descended from the Chosen People, to us too, today, these words of the Lord are addressed: «*where I cause my name to be remembered I will come to bless you*». God seems to deal with us like a father who listens to the prattling of his baby son and, as soon as the baby pronounces his name, he runs towards him, picks him up in his arms, fondling and caressing him.

In this passage, God also shows us how pleasing to Him are our offerings and sacrifices, when they are offered in thanksgiving for his benefits and in reparation for our own sins and those of others. God is the same today as then, hence what He asked of his people then, He asks of us today, even though the object and the form of the offering may have changed with the passage of time.

A few years ago, the Archbishop of Cízico said to me in conversation: «Do you know, Sister, the meaning of those litters which Our Lady told you to have made with the gifts that the people used to leave in the Cova da Iria? They were a prophecy of the litters used for the Pilgrim Virgin as she goes around the world, and the litter for the statue in the Chapel of the Apparitions». I entirely agree with this interpretation because, in the mind of God, the same fact can have various meanings, and these journeys of Our Lady's image are yet another facet of the apostolate of the Message which She came to earth to bring, and which is travelling all over the world in search of people to bring them to God.

Thus is fulfilled her prophecy: «*For behold, henceforth all generations will call me blessed; for he who is mighty has done great things for me, and holy is his name. And his mercy is on those who fear him from generation to generation*» (Lk 1, 48-50)

Ave Maria!

16

The Call to persevere in virtue

The fourteenth Call of the Message

«*Continue to pray the Rosary in order to obtain the end of the war*» (Our Lady, 13th September, 1917).

The Message asks us to continue to pray the Rosary, which is the form of prayer most accessible to everyone, great and small, rich and poor, wise and ignorant. Everyone of good will can say the Rosary every day.

But why does the Message ask us to continue to say the Rosary every day? Because prayer is the basis of the spiritual life. If we give up praying, we deprive ourselves of that supernatural life which comes to us from the meeting of our soul with God, a meeting which comes about in prayer. Look at what Jesus says to us: «*Ask, and it will be given you; seek, and you will find; knock, and it will be opened to you. For every one who asks receives, and he who seeks finds, and to him who knocks it will be opened.*» (Mt 7, 7-8). Prayer is to seek and meet with God. We need to seek God in order to meet Him, and we have His promise: «*Whoever seeks finds*». It is not that God is far from us; we are the ones who distance ourselves from God and lose the sense of his presence. It is for this reason that the Message urges us to persevere in prayer, or, in the words of the Message, to «*continue to pray to obtain the end of the war*».

Clearly, at the time, the Message was referring to the [first] world war which was afflicting so many people just then. But the word *war* also stands for many other wars going on all round us and which we must help to bring to an end by our prayer and self-sacrifice. I think, too, of the wars waged against us by *the enemies of our eternal salvation:* the devil, the world and our own carnal nature.

There are people, nowadays, who actually deny that devils exist; but they most certainly do. Devils are angels who were created by God to serve and praise Him. The chief of these Angels, known as «Lucifer» got puffed up with pride, and wanted to be equal to God. He dragged down with him a multitude of other angels who followed his example. St John tells us in the Book of the Apocalypse: «*Now war arose in heaven, Michael and his angels fighting against the dragon; and the dragon and his angels fought, but they were defeated and there was no longer any place for them in heaven. And the great dragon was thrown down, that ancient serpent, who is called the Devil and Satan, the deceiver of the whole world – he was thrown down to the earth, and his angels were thrown down with him.»* (Rev 12, 7-9).

Later in the same book we read: «*I saw another angel coming down from heaven, having great authority; and the earth was made bright with his splendour. And he called out in a mighty voice, "Fallen, fallen is Babylon the great! It has become a dwelling place of demons, a haunt of every foul and hateful bird; for all nations have drunk the wine of her impure passion, and the kings of the earth have committed fornication with her, and the merchants of the earth have grown rich with the wealth of her wantonness.»* (Rv 18, 1-3)

And later, he writes: «*Then I saw an angel coming down from heaven, holding in his hand the key of the bottomless pit and a great chain. And he seized the dragon, that ancient serpent, who is the Devil and Satan, and bound him (...) and threw him into the pit, and shut it and sealed it over him, that he should deceive the nations no more.»* (Rv 20, 1-3).

The prophet Isaiah composed a satire against the king of Babylon in terms that recall the fall of the angels:«*How you are fallen from heaven, O Day Star, son of Dawn! How you are cut down to the ground, you who laid the nations low! You said in your heart, 'I will ascend to heaven; above the stars of God I will set my throne on high; I will sit on the mount of assembly in the far north; I will ascend above the heights of the clouds, I will make myself like the Most High.' But you were brought down to Sheol, to the depths of the Pit.»* (Is 14, 12-15).

And in one of the visions in his book, the prophet Zechariah describes the devil as the accuser before God of the High Priest: «*Then he showed me Joshua the high priest standing before the angel of the Lord, and Satan standing at his right hand to accuse him. And the Lord said to Satan, "The Lord rebuke you, O Satan! The Lord who has chosen Jerusalem rebuke you! Is not this a brand plucked from the fire?"»* (Zech 3, 1-2). The Book of the Apocalypse, too, after describing the defeat of Satan and his expulsion from heaven, goes on: «*And I heard a loud voice in heaven, saying, "Now the salvation and the power and the kingdom of our God and the authority of his Christ have come, for the accuser of our brethren has been thrown down, who accuses them day and night before our God. And they have conquered him by the blood of the Lamb»* (Rev 12, 10-11).

In the course of his public life, Jesus drove out many demons. One day, in reply to the Pharisees, who were saying maliciously that He was driving out demons by the power of Beelzebub, Jesus said: «*And if Satan also is divided against himself, how will his kingdom stand? For you say that I cast out demons by Beelzebul, by whom do your sons cast them out? (...) But if it is by the finger of God that I cast out demons, then the kingdom of God has come upon you.*» (Lk 11, 18-20). Later, when He was both warning and fore-arming St Peter against the assaults and temptations of the devil, the Lord said to him: «*Simon, Simon, behold, Satan demanded to have you, that he might sift you like wheat, but I have prayed for you that your faith may not fail; and when you turned again, strengthen your brethren.*» (Lk 22, 31-32).

In one of his letters, St Peter himself writes: «*Be sober, be watchful. Your adversary the devil prowls around like a roaring lion, seeking some one to devour. Resist him, firm in your faith, knowing that the same experience of suffering is required of your brotherhood throughout the world. And after you have suffered a little while, the God of all grace, who has called you to his eternal glory in Christ, will himself restore, establish, and strengthen you. To him be the dominion for ever and ever. Amen.*» (1 Peter 5, 8-11).

All these passages of Sacred Scripture, and many others that it would take too long to transcribe here, prove to us that devils exist. We cannot doubt this truth revealed by God. The Message came to remind us of this truth and to restate it for us so that we would not let ourselves be deceived or taken in by false assertions. It asks us to continue to pray, and to be on our guard against being taken in by the suggestions of this enemy who, by every means in his power, endeavours to secure our eternal damnation. Jesus Christ said: «*Every one who commits sin is slave to sin*» (Jn 8, 34). The devil tries to drag us off into the path of sin, in order to make slaves of us, in time and in eternity.

But why did the devil turn into such a great enemy of both God and human beings? He became an enemy of God because he had been defeated by Him – this was a humiliation which his pride could not accept so, in his fury, he tries to avenge himself in every possible way. Driven by this pride, when he saw that God had created human beings with a nature inferior to his, but destined one day to go to heaven and enjoy the happiness that he himself had lost, the devil was filled with envy and decided to do every-thing in his power to cause human beings to be lost by inducing them to disobey God, disregard his orders and cease to believe in his word. That was how he deceived the first human beings.

Assuming the form of a serpent, he went to meet Eve, the first woman God had created, who was walking in the Garden of Eden, and asked her:«*"Did God say, 'You shall not eat of any tree of the garden'?" And the woman said to the serpent, "We may eat the fruit of the trees of the garden; but God said, 'You shall not eat of the fruit of the tree which is in the midst of the garden, neither shall you touch it, lest you die'." But the serpent said to the woman, "You will not die. For God knows that when you eat of it your eyes will be opened, and you will be like God, knowing good and evil." So when the woman saw that the tree was good for food, and that is what a delight to the eyes, and that the tree was to be desired to make one wise, she took of its fruit and ate; and she also gave some to her husband, and he ate. The the eyes of both were opened, and they knew that they were naked; and they sewed fig leaves together and made themselves aprons.*
And they heard the sound of the Lord walking in the garden in the cool of the day, and the man and his wife hid themselves from the presence of the Lord God among the trees of the garden. But the Lord called to the man, and said to him, "Where are you?" And he said, "I heard the sound of thee in the garden, and I was afraid, because I was naked; and I hid myself."» (Gen 3, 1-10).

In the sacred text, we see that the devil deceived the first two human beings. He told them that if they ate that fruit, they would become like God: *you will be like God!* The truth is that not only did they not become like God but they became much less than they had been before and, having become afraid of God – *I was afraid because I was naked and I hid* –, they wished to hide from His presence.

Why are they naked? Because, through their disobedience to God, they had lost the garment of grace: they saw themselves with no clothes on, stripped of the garment of grace that had covered them. This is what they achieved by allowing themselves to be seduced and tricked by the devil. This is how he works! It is for this reason that Jesus Christ warns us against him: «*He was a murderer from the beginning, and he has nothing to do with the truth, because there is no truth in him. When he lies, he speaks according to his own nature, for he is a liar and the father of lies.*» (Jn 8, 44)

But I believe that the devil's envy must have become even greater when he saw God promising a Redeemer to the human beings that he had seduced, whereas there was no redemption for him. And why would God have been so merciful to human beings? I am not absolutely sure, but I think the reason was that they fell through having been seduced and deceived by another, whereas the devil sinned out of his own malice.

God must have seen in human beings the possibility that they would repent and humbly ask pardon, but the devil's pride is so great that it admits of no repentance nor of the humility that might lead him to ask for forgiveness. Thus he saw himself defeated and condemned for ever, when God said to him: «*I will put enmity between you and the woman, and between your seed and her seed; he shall bruise your head, and you shall bruise his heel.*» (Gen 3, 15).

In addition to the temptations of the devil, we also have the temptations of the *world* which surrounds us, enticing and deceiving us. Many times we are both deluded and deceived by the voices of the world.

These are the temptations of the world which blind and darken the understanding. Hence when Jesus Christ prayed to his Father: «*I am praying for them; I am not praying for the world but for those who thou hast given me, for they are thine; (...) I have given them thy word; and the world has hated them because they are not of the world, even as I am not of the world. I do not pray that thou shouldst take them out of the world, but that thou shouldst keep them from the evil one.*» (Jn 17, 9.14-15). He had in mind those who, with hearts faithful to his word and grace, struggle to overcome these temptations.

They are not of the world because they follow the Word of God who is the truth, not allowing themselves to be deceived by the lying and deceitful maxims of the world. They belong to God, since the Father has entrusted them to Jesus Christ who, in turn, entrusts Himself to his Father for them, to consecrate them in the truth: «*They are not of the world even as I am not of the world. Sanctify them in the truth; thy word is truth. (...) And for their sake I consecrate myself, that they also may be consecrated in truth*» (Jn 17, 16-19).

To be consecrated in the truth is to dedicate oneself entirely to God, and to souls for the love of God; it is to persevere in the service and in the love of God and of one's neighbour; it is to keep going in the way mapped out for us by God – *in truth* – because the maxims of the world are lies and illusion. And that is why the world *hates us*, persecutes us and speaks calumny about us.

Like the devil, and instigated by the devils, the world surrounds us with envy, jealousy and hatred: «*If the world hates you, know that it has hated me before it hated you. If we were of the world, the world would love its own; but because you are not of the world, but I choose you out of the world, therefore the world hates you.*» (Jn 15, 18-19).

Let me repeat for you, in my own words, what the Message says: *Continue to pray, in order to achieve peace, to gain victory over temptations and persecutions.*

Within *ourselves*, too, there is another source of temptations; in order to overcome them we must *continue to pray,* and to struggle, because only thus shall we be able to persevere in the good path. Listen to what Jesus Christ says to us: «*Enter by the narrow gate; for the gate is wide and the way is easy, that leads to destruction, and those who enter by it are many. For the gate is narrow and the way is hard, that leads to life, and those who find it are few. Beware of false prophets, who come to you in sheep's clothing but inwardly are ravenous wolves. You will know them by their fruits.*» (Mt 7, 13-16)

The Lord says that there are many who follow the wide road that leads to perdition; and that only a few find the narrow road that leads to life. So let us be doubly watchful over our own tendencies towards an exaggerated freedom that sets aside the authority of those who represent God for us, thus setting us unwittingly, and foolishly, on the slippery downward path.

We want to be free, but we do not know how to use our freedom well. Hence, God has placed over us those who can point out to us the right path that we may, and must, freely follow. But our pride deceives us and does not allow us to see the good which we despise, nor the evil that we are doing. In such circumstances, the temptation is within ourselves, setting a trap for us without our realising it. It is what we call the concupiscence of the heart and of the feelings, which causes us to long for things that are not good for us. In order to recognise and overcome these temptations, we must do what the Message tells us: *continue to pray,* so that God will give us light, strength and grace.

Jesus also said: «*Beware of false prophets, who come to you in sheep's clothing but inwardly are ravenous wolves*». (Mt 7, 15). These false prophets are all those people surrounding us, trying to induce us to follow the wide road, to give free rein to our evil tendencies, caprices, vices and disordered passions, all of which are contrary to God's Law. They are the bad company that turns us aside from the right path of truth, justice and charity. They are all those false prophets who deny the truths revealed by God, endeavouring to introduce new and erroneous doctrines in support of the disordered lives that they themselves wish to lead.

The Lord gives us a rule by which to identify such people: «*You will know them by their fruits. (...) Every sound tree bears good fruit, but the bad tree bears evil fruit. (...) Every tree that does not bear good fruit is cut down and thrown into the fire. Thus you will know them by their fruits.*» (Mt 7, 16-20).

These warnings must put us on our guard against ourselves and the maxims of the world around us. How many times does one hear people say: «I do such and such because everybody does it»; «I dress like this because it is the fashion and everyone is dressed like this»; «I live like this, because that's how people live nowadays»; etc. Are we to allow ourselves to be condemned just because other people live like that? *Every tree that does not bear good fruit will be cut down and cast into the fire.* God tells us that He does not wish the death of the sinner but rather that he be converted and live (Ezek 18, 23). However, we should note the condition: *that he be converted.*

«*Continue to pray, in order to achieve peace*», which is the fruit of the victory achieved over all the temptations which drag us towards the paths opposed to the Law of God. Jesus Christ says quite clearly: «*Not every one who says to me, 'Lord, Lord,' shall enter the kingdom of heaven, but he who does the will of my Father who is in heaven*» (Mt 7, 21).

Thus it is that the Message tells us: *Continue to pray the Rosary in order to obtain the end of the war.*

Ave Maria!

17

The Call to stop offending God

The fifteenth Call of the Message

«Do not offend the Lord our God any more, because He is already so much offended» (Our Lady, 13th October, 1917).

The Call that the Message is making to us here reminds us once again of the need to observe the first of all the commandments of God's Law, in other words, the love of God. The precept to love God is the first of the commandments, not only on account of the unique greatness of the Object it contemplates, but also because it is this love which will lead us to fulfil faithfully all the other commandments.

Speaking to his people through Moses, God said: *«Hear, O Israel: The Lord our God is one Lord, and you shall love the Lord your God with all your heart, and with all your soul, and with all your might. And these words which I command you this day shall be upon your heart; and you shall teach them diligently to your children, and shall talk of them when you sit in your house, and when you walk by the way, and when you lie down and when you rise. And you shall bind them as a sign upon your hand, and they shall be as frontlets between your eyes. And you shall write them on the doorposts of your house and on your gates.»* (Deut 6, 4-9).

God's insistence that we should engrave the law of his Love in our hearts, that we should use it as a symbol on our arm and a frontlet before our eyes, that we should have it written on the doors and doorposts of our houses, is in order to ensure that it should always be present to us, that we should meditate on it night and day, and that we should teach it to our children, to our brothers and sisters and to all those around us. This love is to be a guide for our footsteps, a light for our aspirations and the object of our desire. It is to be the guide of our footsteps, that is, we must walk in the path of love.

One day, the Pharisees came to Jesus and one of them, who was a doctor of the law, asked him: *«"Teacher, which is the great commandment in the law?" And he said to him, "You shall love the Lord your God with all your heart, and with all your soul, and with all your mind. This is the great and* first commandment. *And a second is like it, You shall love your neighbour as yourself. On these two commandments depend all the law and the prophets.* "» (Mt 22, 34-40). This second commandment to which Jesus refers had been given to his people in these words: «*You shall not take vengeance or bear any grudge against the sons of your own people, but you shall love your neighbour as yourself: I am the Lord. You shall keep my statutes.*» (Lev 19, 18-19).

The essence of the Message – *Do not offend the Lord our God any more* – is contained in the observance of these two commandments. We all know that it is by sin that we offend God, when we fail to observe this commandment of love which we owe to Him, to our neighbour and to ourselves; yes, to ourselves, because we do serious harm to ourselves also, at times without thinking or feeling that we do.

We offend God because we transgress his precepts, all of which are a manifestation of his love for us. As in the case of the love of a father, who takes his son by the hand and points out to him the path he is to follow in order to attain happiness and inherit his father's property, if the son becomes unruly and rebellious, if he despises the things his father has taught him, obviously he hurts and offends his father in the most sensitive part of his heart, his love.

In the same way, when we despise or violate the commandments of God, we cause hurt and offence to that which is most magnificent in God, in the fatherly love with which He created us, enfolded us with loving care in all that surrounds us for our good and which He created for our good, the love with which He redeemed us from sin and opened to us the gates of Heaven, with which He will grant to us our inheritance in his Kingdom. Hence, every sin is an offence against God our Father and a rejection of His love, since we are preferring our sin to the love we owe to God and to possession of his Kingdom, knowing that by our sin we lose the right to it.

In this connection, read the stern words of the Apostle St Paul: «*For you were called to freedom, brethren; only do not use your freedom as an opportunity for the flesh, but through love be servants of one another. For the whole law is fulfilled in one word, "You shall love your neighbour as yourself." But if you bite and devour one another take heed that you are not consumed by one another. But I say, walk by the Spirit, and do not gratify the desires of the flesh. For the desires of the flesh are against the Spirit, and the desires of the Spirit are against the flesh; for these are opposed to each other, to prevent you from doing what you would. But if you are led by the Spirit you are not under the law.*

Now the works of the flesh are are plain: immorality, sorcery, enmity, strife, jealousy, anger, selfishness, dissension, party spirit, envy, drunkeness, carousing and the like. I warn you, as I warned you before, that those who do such things shall not inherit the kingdom of God. But the fruit of the spirit is love, joy, peace, patience, kindness, goodness, faithfulness, gentleness, self-control; against such there is no law. And those who belong to Christ Jesus have crucified the flesh with its passions and desires. If we live by the Spirit, let us also walk by the Spirit.» (Ga 5, 13-25).

These words that the Apostle has just addressed to us tell us what we must do in order to respond to the Call of the Message urging us: *«Do not offend God any more»!* Let us not offend against the love of God any more! And this love that we owe to Him must lead us to love others. No one can say that they love someone if they despise and maltreat his or her children, because parents naturally take as done to themselves what is done to their children. We can say the same of God's reaction to the love which we bestow on, or deny to, those around us: they are his children!

In the case of God and his children, there is another reason that obliges us to love them: they are our brothers and sisters! But, *«brother goes to law against brother, and that before unbelievers? To have lawsuits at all with one another is defeat for you. Why not rather suffer wrong? Why not rather be defrauded? But you yourselves wrong and defraud, and that even your own brethren. Do you not know that the unrighteous will not inherit the kingdom of God? Do not be deceived; neither the immoral, nor idolaters, nor adulterers, nor homosexuals, nor thieves, nor the greedy, nor drunkards, nor revilers, nor robbers will inherit the kingdom of God.»* (1 Cor 6, 6-10).

We must avoid sin in order not to offend God or lose the right to eternal life. Sin severs our relationship with God and poisons the place in our heart which we owe to others; it makes us unworthy of God's friendship and of sharing in his glory. That is why St Paul urges us: *«But let each one test his own work, and then his reason to boast will be in himself alone (if his works are good) and not in his neighbour. For each man will have to bear his own load. Let him who is taught the word share all good things with him who teaches. Do not be deceived; God is not mocked, for whatever a man sows, that he will also reap. For he who sows to his own flesh will from the flesh reap corruption; but he who sows to the Spirit will from the Spirit reap eternal life. And let us not grow weary in well doing, for in due season we shall reap, if we* do not lose heart. So then, as we have opportunity, let us do good to all men, and especially to those who are of the household of faith.» (Gal 6, 4-10).

Here we have clearly marked out for us the way we are to follow in order to live in accordance with the commandment of the love of God, and of our neighbour for the love of God. It is the way outlined, taught and lived by Jesus Christ; as St Paul says, let us not pay attention to any other teachers! «*As therefore you received Christ Jesus the Lord, so live in him, rooted and built up in him and established in the faith, just as you were taught abounding in thanksgiving. See to it that no one makes a prey of you by philosophy and empty deceit, according to human tradition, according to the elemental spirits of the universe, and not according to Christ. For in him the whole fulness of deity dwells bodily, and you have come to fulness of life in him, who is the head of all rule and authority.*» (Col 2, 6-10). This whole teaching of the Apostle is wonderful, casting beams of light ahead of us to guide our feet, strengthen our weakness and enlighten our faith and our understanding.

But we must not think that, in order to respond fully to the implications of the Message and of the precept of love, it is sufficient to avoid sin, in order not to offend God. This is undoubtedly the first step, but it is not enough. If we were to be cold, indifferent or neglectful in our attitude to our father, our mother or anyone to whom we are beholden in some way, it goes without saying that we are being unjust and ungrateful to this person, and so offending them. The same is true of God, who is more than a Father to us: we offend Him by our coldness, our forgetfulness, our indifference and our carelessness; we are behaving in an ungrateful way towards Him, like someone who does not recognise his or her principal Benefactor, the One to whom we owe most.

Let us look at Jesus Christ in the Gospel! The one great concern of his heart was to reveal to human beings the love of the Father, to love Him and to make Him loved, observing his precepts and his word. For this, He offers Himself to us as a model: «*As the Father has loved me, so have I loved you; abide in my love. If you keep my commandments, you will abide in my love, just as I have kept my Father's commandments and abide in his love. These things I have spoken to you, that my joy may be in you, and that your joy may be full. (...) for all that I have heard from my Father I have made known to you. (...) This I command you, to love one another.*» (Jn 15, 9-17) Jesus Christ's joy consists in the fact of having the Father's love within Him and of responding to it, and it is this joy that He wishes to share with us, allowing knowledge of the Father to overflow from his heart: «*I shall tell you plainly of the Father (...) for the Father himself loves you, because you have loved me and have believed that I came from the Father. I came from the Father and have come into the world; again, I am leaving the world and going to the Father.*» (Jn 16, 25-28).

In his priestly prayer to his Father, Jesus was able to say that He had fulfilled the mission entrusted to him: «*I glorified thee on earth, having accomplished the work which thou gavest me to do (...) I have manifested thy name to the men whom thou gavest me out of the world; thine they were, and thou gavest them to me, and they have kept thy word. Now they know that everything that thou hast given me is from thee; for I have given them the words which thou gavest me, and they have received them and know in truth that I came from thee; and they have believed that thou didst send me. I am praying for them (...) for they are thine; all mine are thine, and thine are mine, (...) Holy Father, keep them in thy name, which thou hast given me, that they may be one, even as we are one.* (Jn 17, 4-11).

Love is the bond which must bind us close to God and to our neighbour, identifying us with the Heart of Christ, plunging us into the Heart of God, so that our will is his, and our one yearning is be in full possession of his love.

Ave Maria!

18

The Call to the sanctification of the family

The sixteenth Call of the Message

God chose to conclude the Message in Fatima, in October 1917, with three further apparitions which I regard as three more calls placed before us for our consideration, so that we may keep them in mind during our earthly pilgrimage. While the people were gazing in astonishment at the sun which had gone pale in the light of the presence of God, the three children saw, beside the sun, three distinct and, to us, significant apparitions.

I do not know whether or not the Church's theologians and thinkers have attached any special significance or interpretation to these apparitions. They would certainly be able to do so in more precise language based on sacred doctrine. I am only speaking about them here in order to do what I have been asked to do, and within the limits imposed by my humble ignorance and poverty. Thus I propose to say quite simply what I think God wished to say to us with these three apparitions.

The first was the apparition of the Holy Family: Our Lady, and the Child Jesus in the arms of St Joseph, blessing the people.

In times such as the present, when the family often seems misunderstood in the form in which it was established by God, and is assailed by doctrines that are erroneous and contrary to the purposes for which the divine Creator instituted it, surely God wished to address to us a reminder of the purpose for which He established the family in the world ?

God entrusted to the family the sacred mission of co-operating with Him in the work of creation. This decision to associate his poor creatures with his creative work is a great demonstration of the fatherly goodness of God. It is as if He were making them sharers in His creative power; making use of his children in order to bring forth new lives, which will flower on earth but be destined for Heaven.

Thus the divine Creator wished to entrust to the family a sacred mission, that makes two beings become one in a union so close that it does not admit of separation. It is from this union that God wishes to produce other beings, as He generates flowers and fruit from the plants.

God established Matrimony as an indissoluble union. Once a couple have received the sacrament of Matrimony, the union between the two is definitive and cannot be broken; it is indissoluble as long as the couple remain alive. It was thus that God ordained it to be.

We read in the Book of Genesis: «*So God created man in his own image, in the image of God he created him; male and female he created them*» (Gen 1,27); two, yes, but these two are one: «*Therefore a man leaves his father and his mother and cleaves to his wife, and they become one flesh*» (Gen 2, 24). This is a law of God, which Jesus Christ confirmed and endorsed, in the face of human efforts, at that time, to pull in the opposite direction: «*Have you not read that he who made them from the beginning made them male and female, and said, "For this reason a man shall leave his father and mother and be joined to his wife, and the two shall become one. So they are no longer two but one. What therefore God has joined together, let no man put asunder.*» (Mt 19, 4-6).

This is the law of Matrimony: from the time that they have been joined together by the blessing of God, the two become one, and this union does not allow of separation – *What God has joined together, let no one put asunder.* They become one by the bond of love that led them to commit themselves to each other in the one ideal of co-operation with God in the work of creation, and this involves the sacrifice and immolation that the giving of oneself always implies; it involves, too, mutual understanding, forgiveness and pardon. It is thus that a home is built up, made holy and gives glory to God.

A home must be like a garden, where fresh rosebuds are opening, bringing to the world the freshness of innocence, a pure and trusting outlook on life, and the smile of innocent happy children. Only thus does God take pleasure in his creative work, blessing it and turning his fatherly gaze upon it. Any other way of behaving is to divert the work of God from its end, to alter the plans of God, failing to fulfil and carry out the mission that God has entrusted to the married couple.

Hence, in the Message of Fatima, God calls on us to turn our eyes to the Holy Family of Nazareth, into which He chose to be born, and to grow in grace and stature, in order to present to us a model to imitate, as our footsteps tread the path of our pilgrimage to Heaven.

The Evangelist St Luke, after describing for us how Jesus Christ, as a young boy, went up to the temple in Jerusalem where He got separated from his parents and where they found Him three days later, adds: «*And he went down with them and came to Nazareth, and was obedient to them; and his mother kept all these things in her heart.. And Jesus increased in wisdom and in stature, and in favour with God and man.*» (Lk 2, 51-52).

Parents who do not instil a knowledge of God and of his commandments into their children from an early age, teaching them to keep them in mind and to observe them, are failing to fulfil the mission entrusted to them by God. It is a law that God prescribed for his people: «*And these words which I command you this day shall be upon your heart; and you shall teach them diligently to your children, and shall talk of them when you sit in your house, and when you walk by the way, and when you lie down, and when you rise*» (Deut 6, 6-7). Parents who disregard this law of God make themselves responsible for the ignorance of their children and for any misdemeanours that may result from it. And, very often, it is this ignorance that is responsible for the disordered lives of the children who torment the declining years of their parents, and are themselves lost.

What has been said applies even when the children are entrusted to the care of competent teachers, because what remains most engraved in the hearts of children is what they have received in their father's arms and on their mother's lap. Nothing can dispense parents from this sublime mission: God has entrusted it to them and they are answerable to God for it.

Parents are the ones who must guide their children's first steps to the altar of God, teaching them to raise their innocent hands and to pray, helping them to discover how to find God on their way and to follow the echo of his voice. This is the most serious and important mission that has been entrusted by God to parents; and they must fulfil it so well that, throughout their lives, the memory of their parents will always arouse in their children the memory of God and of his teaching.

This is how St Paul encourages us to behave: «*Children, obey your parents in the Lord, for this is right. "Honour your father and mother" (this is the first commandment with a promise), "that it may be well with you and that you may live long on the earth." Fathers, do not provoke your children to anger but bring them up in the discipline and instruction of the Lord.*» (Eph 6, 1-4). And in the second Letter of St John, which was undoubtedly addressed to an ecclesial community, but which he sees personified in the person of a mother – *the elect lady and her children* – we find, from the pen of the Apostle, a eulogy that we wish could be applied to all fathers and mothers: «*I rejoiced greatly to find some of your children following the truth, just as we have been commanded by the Father. And now I beg you, lady, not as though I were writing you a new commandment, but the one we have had from the beginning, that we love one another.*» (2 Jn 4-5).

In families composed of parents and children, there are duties which the parents have to fulfil in relation to their children, and, vice versa, the children in relation to their parents. The Book of Sirach (Ecclesiasticus), after listing the many duties of children, concludes with this appeal to their submission and gentleness: «*My son, perform your tasks in meekness; then you will be loved by those who God accepts. The greater you are, the more you must humble yourself; so you will find favour in the sight of the Lord. For great is the might of the Lord; he is glorified by the humble.*» (Sir 3, 17-20). And the Apostle St Peter presses home the same idea: «*Likewise you that are younger be subject to the elders. Clothe yourselves, all of you, with humility toward one another, for "God opposes the proud, but gives grace to the humble." Humble yourselves therefore under the mighty hand of God, that in due time he may exalt you. Cast all your anxieties on him, for he cares about you. Be sober, be watchful.*» (1 Pet 5, 5-8).

These words are addressed to us all, but especially to the young people who have as yet no experience of life, which is why the Apostle urges them to be submissive, sober and vigilant, in order not to be taken in by the illusions of life, by the disordered appetites of nature, and the diabolical seductions of the world. Because – St Peter goes on – «*Your adversary the devil prowls around like a roaring lion, seeking some one to devour. Resist him, firm in your faith, knowing that the same experience of suffering is required of your brotherhood throughout the world. And after you have suffered a little while, the God of all grace, who has called you to his eternal glory in Christ, will himself restore, establish, and strengthen you.*» (1 Pet 5, 8-10).

Yes, firm in faith, in hope and in charity, we must all struggle to achieve victory over evil, and attain the peace, joy and blessedness of the house of our Father who is God; and we, all together, form his family.

The children must never forget or set to one side the respect, gratitude and help which they owe to their parents, who are for them the image of God. In fact, just as the parents sacrificed themselves in order to bring up, educate and establish their children in life, so the children, in their turn, have a duty to sacrifice themselves in order to give pleasure, joy and serenity to their parents, aiding and assisting them, if necessary, in such a way that everything is done out of true love and with one's eyes fixed on God: «*Whatever your task, work heartily, as serving the Lord and not men, knowing that from the Lord you will receive the inheritance as your reward; you are serving the Lord Christ.*» (Col 3, 23). And we shall enjoy his friendship, as He has told us: «*You are my friends if you do what I command you*» (Jn 15, 14) And what has He commanded us? «*This is my commandment, that you love one another as I have loved you.*» (Jn 15, 12).

This is how a family sanctifies itself, grows and prospers in that unity, fidelity, mutual understanding and forgiveness which generate peace, joy, mutual trust and love.

Ave Maria!

19

The Call to perfection in the Christian life

The seventeenth Call of the Message

In the second of the three further apparitions, Our Lord appeared as the *Perfect Man* and Our Lady as *Our Lady of Sorrows.*

What is the meaning of this apparition? I am not absolutely certain, but I say what I think and what God has enabled me to understand, by meditating on these events. It may be that Holy Church sees another meaning in them or has a different interpretation; if so, I would be fully in agreement. However, in expressing my own humble opinion, I say that this apparition is a call to the practice of the Christian life as Jesus and his Mother lived it here on earth and, by his example and his teaching, He taught us to follow in his footsteps.

Jesus did not come into the world as our Redeemer only, but also as our Teacher, to teach us the way that we are to follow in order to go to the Father: *«I am the way, and the truth, and the life; no one comes to the Father, but by me. If you had known me, you would have known my Father also»* (Jn 14, 6-7). Now, this Way and this Life call for knowledge of God and of his Son, whom He sent into the world as our Teacher and our Saviour. Hence, Christ said: *«If you had known me, you would have known my Father also (...) He who has seen me has seen the Father (...) Do you not believe that I am in the Father and the Father in me? The words that I say to you I do not speak on my own authority; but the Father who dwells in me does his works. Believe me that I am in the Father and the Father in me; or else believe me for the sake of the works themselves.»* (Jn 14, 7-11).

Jesus Christ left us the works He accomplished and that bear witness to Him as a proof of his divinity. Let us now take a brief look at these works so that they can confirm us in our conviction that He is truly our Teacher, the guide of our steps, and the example that we are to copy.

Jesus lived in the world as a perfect man who did his Father's will in all things. These were his words: *«All that the Father gives me will come to me; and he who comes to me I will not cast out. For I have come down from heaven not to do my own will, but the will of him who sent me; and this is the will of him who sent me, that I should lose nothing of all that he has given me, but raise it up at the last day. For this is the will of my Father, that every one who sees the Son and believes in him should have eternal life; and I will raise him up at the last day.»* (Jn 6, 37-40). Hence it was in order to do his Father's will that Jesus came into the world.

And the will that Jesus is to fulfil is that He should not lose any of those whom the Father has entrusted to Him, but that He should save them and raise them up on the last day. However, this resurrection requires our co-operation or, in other words, our faith: *«For this is the will of my Father, that every one who sees the Son and believes in him should have eternal life; and I will raise him up at the last day».* Yes, it requires our faith: we must believe in the Son so that He may raise us up on the last day. The first step in our Christian life is to live the life of faith; to believe in the Son and in the Father who sent Him, to believe in his word and abide by it. It was this that Jesus urged us to do: *«Come to me, all who labour and are heavy laden, and I will give you rest. Take my yoke upon you, and learn from me; for I am gentle and lowly in heart, and you will find rest for your souls. For my yoke is easy, and my burden light»* (Mt 11, 28-30)

When the time was drawing near for Him to give up his life for our redemption, Jesus, during the last supper that He took with his disciples, wanted to give them one more proof of his love and his profound humility. In accordance with a Jewish custom of the time – one day He himself had pointed out that it had not been followed in his own case: *«I entered your house, you gave me no water for my feet»* (Lk 7, 44) –, the Lord himself, contrary to all the customs and norms of the time, took a basin of water and washed his disciples' feet, wiping them with a towel which He had fastened round his waist. When He had finished, He sat down again at the table and said to them: *«You call me Teacher and Lord; you are right, for so I am. If I then, your Lord and Teacher, have washed your feet, you also ought to wash one another's feet. For I have given you an example, that you also should do as I have done to you.»* (Jn 13, 13-15). The fundamental basis of our faith is humility; Christ teaches this to us by his own example.

The Gospels tell us that after Jesus, as a young boy, had gone with his parents to the temple to pray, He returned with them to their home in Nazareth, *«and was subject to them»* (Lk 2, 51). That was how He spent the first thirty years of his life: there He passed his childhood and adolescence and there He grew to perfect manhood. As a child subject to his parents, or as a young apprentice preparing for life, «*And Jesus increased in wisdom and in stature, and in favour with God and man.*» (Lk 2, 52).

We see in this passage that Jesus studied, and showed signs of his growth in wisdom before men, even though some of the leaders of the Jews said that He had not been to school. The episode took place in Jerusalem, when Jesus went up into the temple and taught, «*The Jews marvelled at it, saying, "How is it that this man has learning, when he has never studied?" So Jesus answered them, "My teaching is not mine, but his who sent me"*» (Jn 7, 15-16).

Besides the mystery of the Trinitarian communion between the Father and the Son that these words express, they also enable us to say that schools are not the only places where one can study and learn; with the help and grace of God, every family must be a school where its members are instructed in the knowledge of the natural and supernatural life. More than once, Jesus declared that He had been taught by his Father in Heaven: «*The Father who sent me has himself given me commandment what to say and what to speak. And I know that his commandment is eternal life. What I say, therefore, I say as the Father has bidden me.*» (Jn 12, 49-50).

Jesus Christ learnt from the Father what He was to teach to us, and this is what He did: «*"he who sent me is true, and I declare to the world what I have heard from him."(...) "When you have lifted up the Son of man, then you will know that I am he, and that I do nothing on my own authority but speak thus as the Father taught me. And he who sent me is with me; he has not left me alone, for I always do what is pleasing to him."*» (Jn 8, 26-29). When we reflect that every father of a family represents God for his children, then the father, like God, must be the teacher of his children; but in order to do this, he must have the necessary grounding in the knowledge of natural and supernatural things.

Jesus Christ was also our model as a worker. He is a worker who, fulfilling the law of work, earns his living with the sweat of his brow, as God had ordered all human beings to do: «*in toil you shall eat of it all the days of your life. (...) In the sweat of your face you shall eat bread*» (Gen 3, 17; 19). Being a humble worker, Jesus was known as the son of the carpenter; this is what the people of Nazareth said of Him when they saw Him teaching in his synagogue: «*Where did this man get this wisdom and these mighty words? Is not this the carpenter's son?*» (Mt 13, 54-55). He is a worker who humbly works in his father's workshop; a modest, submissive young man, falling in with the opinions and the orders of his parents.

That home was one where there was joy, peace and well-being, because there was a supernatural spirit. United with one another, parents and Child prayed together, worked together, respected one another and loved one another. Hence, God was there in that house. He was present to them and bestowed on them his grace, his blessing and his Fatherly help. Let us recall the words of the Angel to Mary: «*Hail, full of grace, the Lord is with you!*» (Lk 1, 28).

When the day came that had been ordained by the Father for Him to begin his public life, Jesus Christ prepared Himself by baptism, penance and prayer. The accounts in the Gospels show us that everything was ready and waiting for Him: «*In the fifteenth year of the reign of Tiberius Caeser, Pontius Pilate being governor of Judea,(...) in the high-priesthood of Annas and Caiaphas, the word of God came to John the son of Zechariah in the wilderness; and he went into all the region about the Jordan, preaching the baptism of repentance for the forgiveness of sins.(...) As the people were in expectation, and all men questioned in their hearts concerning John, whether perhaps he were the Christ, John answered them all, "I baptize you with water; but he who is mightier than I is coming, the thong of whose sandals I am not worthy to untie; he will baptize you with the Holy Spirit and with fire.*» (Lk 3, 1-3. 15-16).

«*Then Jesus came from Galilee to the Jordan to John, to be baptized by him. John would have prevented him, saying, "I need to be baptized by you, and do you come to me?" But Jesus answered him, "Let it be so now; for thus it is fitting for us to fulfil all righteousness." Then he consented. And when Jesus was baptized, he went up immediately from the water (...) Then Jesus was led up by the Spirit into the wilderness (...). And he fasted forty days and forty nights, and afterwards he was hungry*» (Mt 3, 13-16; 4, 1-2).

Prayer and penance are the solid foundation on which Jesus Christ rests his sacred mission of Master; Doctor and Redeemer.

As Master, He clarifies and explains passages in the Sacred Scriptures that were obscure or had been misinterpreted, summing up his position as follows: «*Think not that I have come to abolish the law and the prophets; I have come not to abolish them but to fulfil them*» (Mt 5, 17). 'Fulfil the Scriptures', not in the sense of adding any norms and regulations that might have been missing, but carrying out to the full the essence of the Law:

charity. Thus, the Lord corrects a certain intransigence on the part of the Pharisees when He says to them: «Have you not read what David did, when he was hungry, and those *who were with him: how he entered the house of God and ate the bread of the Presence, which it was not lawful for him to eat nor for those who were with him, but only for priests? Or have you not read in the law how on the sabbath the priests in the temple profane the sabbath, and are guiltless? I tell you, something greater than the temple is here. And if you had known what this means, 'I desire mercy, and not sacrifice,' you would have not condemned the guiltless.»* (Mt 12, 3-7). We have here a lesson in charity and justice, showing us how to give pride of place to compassion and mercy for one's neighbour who is in need.

On another occasion, the Master teaches us and invites us to differentiate between the divine and the human in the rules of life. The Pharisees and the Scribes «*said, "Why do your disciples transgress the tradition of the elders? For they do not wash their hands when they eat." He answered them, "And why do you transgress the commandment of God for the sake of your tradition? For God commanded, 'Honour your father and your mother,' and, 'He who speaks evil of father or mother, let him surely die.' But you say, 'If any one tells his father or his mother, 'What you would have gained from me is given to God, he need not honour his father.' So, for the sake of your tradition, you have made void the word of God. You hypocrites! Well did Isaiah prophesy of you, when he said: 'This people honours me with their lips, but their heart is far from me: in vain do they worship me, teaching as doctrines the precepts of men." And he called the people to him and said to them, "Hear and understand: not what goes into the mouth defiles a man, but what comes out of the mouth, this defiles a man. (...) what comes out of the mouth proceeds from the heart, and ... out of the heart come evil thoughts, murder, adultery, fornication, theft, false witness, slander. These are what defiles a man.»* (Mt 15, 1-20).

For his part, Jesus, too, challenged his hearers to ask questions about obscure passages in Sacred Scripture in order to discover in them the secrets of God: «*Now while the Pharisees were gathered together, Jesus asked them a question, saying, "What do you think of the Christ? Whose son is he?" They said to him, "The son of David." He said to them, "How is it then that David, inspired by the Spirit, calls him Lord, saying, 'The Lord said to my Lord, sit at my right hand, till I put thy enemies under thy feet'? If David thus calls him Lord, how is he his son?" And no one was able to answer him a word*»

(Mt 22, 41-46), as they still did not know that the son of David was the Son of God himself.

Even though He possesses all this divine and human authority, Jesus did not wish to impugn the authority of the teachers of the time in the eyes of the people, so He restricted Himself to reprimanding in them the lack of coherence between their words and their deeds: «*The sribes and the Pharisees sit on Moses' seat; so practise and observe whatever they tell you, but not what they do; for they preach, but do not practise. (...) you are not to be called rabbi, for you have one teacher, and you are all brethren (...) Neither be called masters, for you have one master, the Christ. He who is greater among you shall be your servant; whoever exalts himself will be humbled, and whoever humbles himself will be exalted*» (Mt 23, 2-12)

In these lovely lessons of Jesus Christ which I have just transcribed, and many others that He has left to us, we see the obligation we all have to practice charity and to avoid any impurity which makes us unworthy to be with God and our neighbour. We also see how we enhance our own nobility when we respect authority and practise the virtue of humility. As our Master has said: «*whoever exalts himself will be humbled, and whoever humbles himself will be exalted*» (Mt 23, 12).

The teaching of Jesus Christ is light and life to us on our way. By following it, we are sure not to stray. Many years before Our Lord came into the world, the prophet Isaiah foretold his coming in these words: «*The people who walked in darkness have seen a great light; those who dwelt in a land of deep darkness, on them has light shined. Thou hast multiplied the nation, thou hast increased its joy; they rejoice before thee as with joy at the harvest, as men rejoice when they divide the spoil.*» (Is 9, 2-3). And Jesus himself confirmed that this prophecy had been fulfilled: «*I have come as light into the world, that whoever believes in me may not remain in darkness. If any one hears my sayings and does not keep them, I do not judge him; for I did not come to judge the world but to save the world. He who rejects me and does not receive my sayings has a judge. The word that I have spoken will be his judge on the last day. For I have not spoken on my own authority; the Father who sent me has himself given me commandment what to say and what to speak. And I know that his commandment is eternal life. What I say, therefore, I say as the Father has bidden me.*" (Jn 12, 46-50). To conclude: Jesus Christ is our Master and Teacher, and his word is the Word of God. Through it, if we follow it, we shall be saved: It marks out the way that we are to follow all the days of our life.

But Jesus, in his public life, also presented Himself as our *Doctor*, who cures our spiritual and bodily infirmities. One day, Jesus was having a meal in the house of Matthew – He had just called him to be his disciple – and the Pharisees, who were shocked to see Him eating with publicans and sinners: «*said to his disciples, "Why does your teacher eat with the tax collectors and sinners?" But when he heard it, he said, "Those who are well have no need of a physician, but those who are sick. Go and learn what this means, 'I desire mercy, and not sacrifice.' For I came not to call the righteous, but sinners."*» (Mt 9, 11-13). Jesus confirmed the certainty of this truth when He went as a guest to the house of Zacchaeus and witnessed this man's conversion: «*Today salvation has come to this house, since he also is a son of Abraham. For the Son of man came to seek and to save the lost.*» (Lk 19, 9-10).

His primary concern is always to heal the wounds inflicted on our souls by sin, and to save those suffering from such great evils. We have an example of this in the way He forgave the sinful woman who had repented. While He was at table, a woman came to Him who was known publicly as a sinner; throwing herself at his feet, she began to weep over her sins. Jesus turned to her and said: «*Your sins are forgiven. (...) Your faith has saved you; go in peace*» (Mt 7, 48.50)

However, He did not limit himself to healing souls, converting sinners and forgiving sins. He also performed physical cures. Interesting in this connection is the healing of the paralysed man in Capharnaum, because Jesus pointed to the physical cure as a proof of the power He possessed to cure spiritual ills. In fact, that is how He began: «*Be of good heart, son, your sins are forgiven*»; but He was accused of blasphemy for saying those words. Jesus defended Himself, saying: «*But that you may know that the Son of man has authority on earth to forgive sins – he then said to the paralytic – "Rise, take up your bed and go home." And he rose and went home.*» (Mt 9, 6-7).

Christ performed many other similar miracles for the benefit of people who were in despair on account of their suffering. One day, one of the leaders of the synagogue, called Jairus, came to Him and asked Him to go to his house to heal his daughter, who was at the point of death. Jesus granted his request and went with him. While they were on their way, a woman, who had been suffering from a flow of blood for twelve years, came up behind Him and touched the hem of his garment, thinking to herself that she only needed to touch Him in order to be healed. And that is what happened: «*And immediately the hemorrhage ceased; and she felt in her body that she was healed of her disease. (...) "Daughter, your faith has made you well; go in peace, and be healed of your disease.*» (Mk 5, 29, 34). While this was happening, «*there came from the ruler's house some who said, "Your daughter is dead. Why trouble the Teacher any further?" But ignoring what they had said, Jesus said to the ruler of the synagogue, "Do not fear, only believe." (...) He put them all outside, and took the child's father and mother and those who were with him, and went in where the child was. Taking her by the hand he said to her, "Talitha cumi"; which means, "Little girl, I say to you, arise." And immediately the girl got up and walked; for she was twelve years old*» (Mk 5, 35-42).

One day, Jesus was walking along and «*two blind men followed him, crying aloud, "Have mercy on us, Son of David." When he entered the house, the blind men came to him; and Jesus said to them, "Do you believe that I am able to do this?" They said to him, "Yes, Lord." Then he touched their eyes, saying, "According to your faith be it done to you." And their eyes were opened*» (Mt 9, 27-30).

Another day they brought a dumb man to Him who was possessed by the devil. Jesus drove out the devil and the dumb man spoke. When the crowd saw this, they cried out: «*Never was anything like this seen in Israel*» (Mt 9, 33). And this happened a good many times! «*And Jesus went about all the cities and villages, teaching in their synagogues and preaching the gospel of the kingdom, and healing every disease and every infirmity.*» (Mt 9, 35).

Jesus did all this out of compassion for those who were suffering, in the conviction that every opportunity was a good one for doing good. On another occasion, he went to the synagogue. There He encountered a man who had a withered hand, and the bystanders asked Jesus: «*Is it lawful to heal on the sabbath?" so that they might accuse him. He said to them, "What man of you, if he has one sheep and it falls into a pit on the sabbath, will not lay hold of it and lift it out? Of how much more value is a man than a sheep! So it is lawful to do good on the sabbath." Then he said to the man, "Stretch out your hand." And the man stretched it out, and it was restored, whole like the other.*» (Mt 12, 10-13).

When John the Baptist sent his own disciples to Jesus to ask Him whether He was himself the Messiah or whether they were to wait for another to come, Jesus replied: «*Jesus answered them, "Go and tell John what you hear and see: the blind receive their sight and the lame walk, lepers are cleansed and the deaf hear, and the dead are raised up, and the poor have good news preached to them. And blessed is he who takes no offence at me.»* (Mt 11, 4-6). This reply to the disciples of John the Baptist has the same meaning and weight as another reply that Christ made to the Jewish leaders when they asked Him the same question: *«"If you are Christ, tell us plainly." Jesus answered them, "I told you, and you do not believe. The works that I do in my Father's name, they bear witness to me; (...) If I am not doing the works of my Father, then do not believe me; but if I do them, even though you do not believe me, believe the works, that you may know and understand that the Father is in me and I am in the Father,»* (Jn 10, 24-25; 37-38).

Even before that, Jesus had touched on this subject in his preaching to the Jewish leaders: *«You sent to John, and he has borne witness to the truth. (...) But the testimony which I have is greater than that of John (the Baptist), for the works which the Father has granted me to accomplish, these very works I am doing, bear me witness that the Father has sent me. And the Father who sent me has himself borne witness to me. His voice you have never heard, his form you have never seen; and you do not have his word abiding in you, for you do not believe him whom he has sent. You search the scriptures, because you think that in them you have eternal life; and it is they that bear witness to me; yet you refuse to come to me that you may have life.»* (Jn 5, 33-40).

Thus Jesus Christ has left us his works and the sublime nature of his teaching as a proof of his divinity. And we do not wonder at it! He only asks us to use in his regard the same criterion that on another occasion He recommended to us to enable us to distinguish between true and false prophets: *«You will know them by their fruits. (...) So every sound tree bears good fruit, but the bad tree bears evil fruit. A sound tree cannot bear evil fruit, nor can a bad tree bear good fruit. (...) Thus you will know them by their fruits»* (Mt 7, 16-20).

Finally let us look at the sacred mission of *Redeemer* which was entrusted to Jesus Christ by the Father when He sent Him to earth. Various passages of Sacred Scripture present Him in this light, namely as Saviour of the world.

When St John the Baptist was administering the baptism of penance in the River Jordan, *«he saw Jesus coming toward him, and said, "Behold the Lamb of God, who takes away the sin of the world!"»* (Jn 1, 29). And He took them away. The author of the sacred text just quoted – St John the Evangelist – later wrote in his first Epistle: «*God is light and in him is no darkness(...) if we walk in the light, as he is in the light, we have fellowship with one another, and the blood of Jesus his Son cleanses us from all sin. (...) If we confess our sins, he is faithful and just, and will forgive our sins and cleanse us from unrighteousness.*» (1Jn 1, 5-9).

When holy Simeon finally had the joy of finding the Child Jesus in the Temple, he greeted in Him the salvation that all the people were waiting for, and exclaimed joyfully: «*Lord, now lettest thou thy servant depart in peace, according to thy word; for mine eyes have seen thy salvation which thou hast prepared in the presence of all peoples, a light for revelation to the Gentiles, and for glory to thy people Israel.*» (Lk 2, 29-32). Echoes of a number of prophetic oracles are to be heard in Simeon's words, including that of the prophet Isaiah: «*I will give you as a light to the nations, that my salvation may reach to the end of the earth*» (Is 49, 6).

Throughout his public ministry, Jesus Christ revealed by his words and deeds that He was a Saviour. He reached out to people in order to lead them in the ways of salvation. His comment on the parable of the good shepherd is significant: «*I came that they may have life, and have it abundantly (...) as the Father knows me and I know the Father; and I lay down my life for the sheep. (...) I give them eternal life, and they shall never perish, and no one shall snatch them out of my hand*» (Jn 10, 10; 15; 28).

It was this pastoral concern that led Jesus Christ to wait for the Samaritan woman at the well of Sichar and to ask her for a drink: «*"Give me a drink." (...) The Samaritan woman said to him, "How is it that you, a Jew, ask a drink of me, a woman of Samaria?" (...) Jesus answered her, "If you knew the gift of God, and who it is that is saying to you, 'Give me a drink,' you would have asked him, and he would have given you living water." (...) "Every one who drinks of this water will thirst again, but whoever drinks of the water that I shall give him will never thirst; the water that I shall give him will become in him a spring of water welling up to eternal life." The woman said to him, "Sir, give me this water, that I may not thirst, nor come here to draw."*» (Jn 4, 7. 9-15).

Jesus had won this soul and, with hers, those of many of the others who came to listen to Him. That was why, when the disciples urged Him to eat, He said to them:«*I have food to eat of which you do not know.(...) My food is to do the will of him who sent me, and to accomplish his work*» (Jn 4, 32.34).

To the woman taken in adultery, after her accusers had gone away and left her, Jesus «*said to her, "Woman, where are they? Has no one condemned you?" She said, "No one, Lord." And Jesus said, "Neither do I condemn you; go, and do not sin again."*» (Jn 8, 10-11). It is mercy which, when met with repentance, grants forgiveness, though on one condition – *do not sin again* – because that is how one is saved.

In the same way, when Jesus later encountered the paralytic whom He had cured by the pool of Bethzatha, He said to him: «*See, you are well! Sin no more, that nothing worse befall you.*» (Jn 5, 14). And the same is true of us today. He forgives us our sins but on condition that we are truly resolved not to sin again. A firm purpose of amendment is one of the requirements for a good confession.

In order to help us, Christ chose to remain on earth with us:«*I will not leave you desolate; I will come to you. Yet a little while, and the world will see me no more, but you will see me; because I live, you will live also. In that day you will know that I am in my Father, and you in me and I in you. He who has my commandments and keeps them, he it is who loves me; and he who loves me will be loved by my Father, and I will love him and manifest myself to him.*» (Jn 14, 18-21).

It is not a question of a mere spiritual presence within us. Jesus wished to be truly with us, under the consecrated appearances of bread and wine, in the Sacrament of the Altar. Here He remains as victim and priest on our behalf until the end of time, since He is an eternal priest: «*Thou art a priest for ever, after the order of Mel-chizedek.*» (Heb 5, 6).

This is so because «*But when Christ appeared as a high priest of the good things that have come, then through the greater and more perfect tent (not made with hands, that is, not of this creation) he entered once for all into the Holy Place, taking not the blood of goats and calves but his own blood, thus securing eternal redemption. For if the sprinkling of defiled persons with the blood of the goats and bulls and with the ashes of a heifer sanctifies for the purification of the flesh, how much more shall the blood of Christ, who through the eternal Spirit offered himself without blemish to God, purify your conscience from dead works to serve the living God. Therefore he is the mediator of a new covenant*» (Heb 9, 11-15).

Thus, Jesus Christ is the high priest who offers Himself daily on our altars, in order to offer to the Father suitable reparation for our sins. We see this in the words He used in consecrating the bread «*Take; this is my body.*» – and the wine «*This is my blood of the covenant, which is poured out for many*» (Mk 14, 24b)

In this Call of the Message we also have the apparition of Our Lady as *Our Lady of Sorrows,* with a meaning that we must not fail to recall. By means of this vision, God will have wished to show us the value of suffering, sacrifice and immolation for the sake of love. In the world of today, hardly anyone wants to hear these truths, such is the extent to which people are living in search of pleasure, of empty worldly happiness, and exaggerated comfort. But the more one flees from suffering, the more we find ourselves immersed in a sea of afflictions, disappointments and suffering.

Life brings with it the martyrdom of the Cross. There is no one in the world who does not have to suffer in some way. We have inherited the mystery of suffering as a consequence of the sin committed by the first parents of the human race: «*Because you (...) have eaten of the tree of which I commanded you, 'You shall not eat of it,' cursed is the ground because of you; in toil you shall eat of it all the days of your life*» (Gen 3, 17). The reference here is to the suffering to which all human beings are subject.

Jesus Christ came to redeem us by suffering; and his Mother shared as co-Redemptrix in the atrocious suffering of his passion, having been given to us as Mother at the foot of the Cross. In the apparition in October 1917 that we are discussing here, She presents herself to us in the image of suffering. The Church calls her the Mother of Sorrows, Our Lady of Sorrows, because in her heart she suffered the martyrdom of Christ, with Him and by his side. It is through the merits of Christ that all suffering has value and purifies us from sin. It is by our union with Christ that suffering can make us victims pleasing to the Father, and make us holy.

Mary was chosen by God to be the Mother of his Son – the Mother of Jesus Christ – and the Mother of his Mystical Body, the Church, which is her spiritual progeny. When He was dying in agony on the cross, Jesus gave her to us all as Mother, in the person of St John: «*Behold your Mother*» (Jn 19, 27). We are the children of the suffering and bitterness of the heart of Jesus Christ, and of the heart of his Mother, and ours.

It is for this reason that all suffering united with his completes our dedication and commitment to God and contributes to the salvation of our brothers and sisters who have gone astray. Jesus said: «*And I have other sheep, that are not of this fold; I must bring them also*» (Jn 10, 16). In order to collaborate with Christ in this mission, we must suffer, work, pray and love because it is by charity that we shall win back our lost brethren, as the Lord himself said: «*By this all men will know that you are my disciples, if you have love for one another.*» (Jn 13, 35).

Love is the magnet which draws souls, and it is for them that we offer to God our sacrifices, our acts of self-denial, our infirmities, our pains and aches, and our physical and moral sufferings. By means of them, we offer our entire consecration to God, and it is by means of them that our prayer is lifted up to Him before his altar. Thinking of them, we wish to be able, like Christ and with Christ, to say to the Father: «*I have guarded them, and none of them is lost but the son of perdition.*» (Jn 17, 22). This was because Judas withstood your grace, was unfaithful to your call and despised your Fatherly Love. If it is still possible, *Father, save him!*

Ave Maria!

20

The Call to a life of total consecration to God

The eighteenth Call of the Message

In my view, the apparition of *Our Lady of Mount Carmel* means total consecration to God. By showing herself clothed in a religious habit, she wished to represent all the other habits by which those who are totally consecrated to God can be distinguished from ordinary secular Christians.

Habits are the distinguishing mark of a consecration, a protection of decorum and Christian modesty, a means of defence for the consecrated person. Those who are consecrated value them in the same way as soldiers value their uniforms and graduates their coloured stripes: the habit marks them out and indicates what they are and the place they occupy, while at the same time obliging them to behave in a way that is appropriate to their status. Hence, to lay aside the habit is a retrograde step; it is to disappear into the ranks of those who have not been called or chosen for something higher; it is to strip oneself of a mark of distinction that singles a person out and raises that person up; it is to descend to a lower level, in order to live like those who have not been called to the higher one.

Those who, one day, heard the voice of God and decided to follow his call in a life of total consecration, thereby raised themselves to a higher plane that sets them apart from the rest of their brothers and sisters. This distinction must be interiorly visible in the eyes of God, and also be reflected exteriorly in the sight of others. It is a witness that we must give of the presence of Christ in us, according to the state that we embraced and the place that we occupy.

Jesus Christ knew that He was being criticised for mixing with publicans and sinners and eating with them, but this did not cause Him to conceal in any way what He was doing. He endured the criticism in order to accomplish the mission that the Father had entrusted to Him, and also to reveal who He was. We have his example, let us look at his words: «*If any man would come after me, let him deny himself and take up his cross and follow me. For whoever would saves his life will lose it; and whoever loses his life for my sake and the gospel's will save it. For what does it profit a man, to* gain the whole world and forfeit his life? For what can a man give in return for his life? For whoever is ashamed of me and of my words in this (...) generation, of him will the Son of man also be ashamed» (Mk 8, 34-38). In another place, He says: «You are the salt of the earth; but if salt has lost its taste, how shall its saltness be restored? It is no longer good for anything except to be thrown out and trodden under foot by men. You are the light of the world. (...) Let your light so shine before men, that they may see your good works and give glory to your Father who is in heaven.» (Mt 5, 13-16).

It was for this that we were called and chosen by Christ: to follow Him, turning our backs on ourselves and all earthly things, in order to bear witness to Christ and confess Him to the ends of the earth; proclaiming and teaching his doctrine by word and by example in order to be light for men and women so that they can see in us the image of Christ.

Let us reflect on these words of Jesus: «You did not choose me, but I chose you and appointed you that you should go and bear fruit and that your fruit should abide» (Jn 15, 16). We have been chosen in order to bear fruit, and our fruit remains, by our persevering fidelity to the gift that we have received from God and the promise we made when we accepted this gift.

In the Gospel, Jesus says to everyone, but in particular to consecrated souls: «Enter by the narrow gate; for the gate is wide and the way is easy, that leads to destruction, and those who enter by it are many. For the gate is narrow and the way is hard, that leads to life, and those who find it are few.» (Mt 7,13-14). Only a few, the Lord says, follow the narrow path that leads to life, while many choose the broad path that leads to perdition. If we want to follow the wide paths, the paths of an exaggerated freedom that sets aside due submission to authority in the practice of the virtue of obedience, we have gone astray because Jesus Christ has called us to follow Him, and He was «obedient unto death, even the death of the cross» as St Paul the Apostle says (Phil 2, 8).

The divine Master says to those He chose to go and preach to the people in his Name, «He who hears you hears me, and he who rejects you rejects me, and he who rejects me rejects him who sent me» (Lk 10,16). What the Lord says to us here requires the virtue of faith. All of us, but more especially consecrated souls, need to live by faith: that faith which sees God in others, in authority, and in everything that happens; that faith which assures us that authority represents God and that, by obeying, we are doing the will of God. The most outstanding example of this obedience was given to us by Jesus Christ himself when He said: «*He who sent me is with me; He has not left me alone, for I always do what is pleasing to him*» (Jn 8, 29). Every consecrated person both accepted, and promised, in imitation of the Saviour, to do always what is pleasing to our Father in heaven, or, to put it another way, to do the will of God as manifested to us by those who represent Him to us.

Renouncing our own will in order to do always the will of God is our holocaust, by which we unite ourselves with Christ's Passion for the sake of his Mystical Body, strengthening ourselves as members of that Body. We become part of it by the Sacrament of Baptism, but in order to remain in it we must be living members, both giving life and causing it to grow, remembering the words of Jesus: «*Every branch of mine that bears no fruit, he takes away*» (Jn 15,2). By renouncing our own will in order to accomplish God's, we become shoots of his stock, members of his Body and his servants: «*Whoever does the will of God is my brother, and sister and mother*» (Mk 3,35). It is by uniting our own will with God's that we become God's family.

It is faith that will lead our steps along this path of self-denial, and help us to accept the other renunciations that Jesus Christ requires of us if we are to follow Him in the choice that He has deigned to make of us: «*If any one comes to me and does not hate his own father and mother and wife and children and brothers and sisters, yes, and even his own life, he cannot be my disciple. Whoever does not bear his own cross and come after me, cannot be my disciple (...) So therefore, whoever of you does not renounce all that he has cannot be my disciple. Salt is good; but if salt has lost its taste, how shall its saltness be restored? It is fit neither for the land nor for the dunghill; men throw it away. He who has ears to hear, let him hear.*» (Lk 14, 26-27; 33-35).

These words of Jesus that I have just quoted do not mean that God requires us to hate and despise our families. This could not be the meaning because, in other places, He orders us to love them. What He requires of those who have consecrated their lives to Him, is that they should sacrifice the joys of living with their families, give up the good things of this life, the right to marry and have children, because those who are married and have children can certainly not either despise them or desert them. Otherwise, Our Lord says, «*they cannot be my disciples!*» Now, if they cannot be his disciples, how can they be his priests and teachers of his people? How can they be people entirely dedicated to his love and his service ?

One day, St Peter asked our Lord what would be the reward for those who had left everything in order to follow Him. This was Jesus' reply: «*Every one who has left houses or brothers or sisters or father or mother or children or lands, for my name's sake, will receive a hundredfold and inherit eternal life*» (Mt 19, 29). Jesus promises eternal life to those who give up everything for love of Him, including the right to marry and have children. His words show clearly the need for the virtues of poverty and chastity, and specifically for the state of celibacy.

One of the people whom the Lord had called to follow Him asked to be allowed to go first and bury his father, but Jesus replied: «*"Leave the dead to bury their own dead; but as for you, go and proclaim the kingdom of God"*» (Lk 9,60).

Another person asked only to be allowed to go home and say good-bye to his family, but Jesus advised against it: «*No one who puts his hand to the plough and looks back is fit for the kingdom of God*» (Lk 9, 62). A scribe who went to meet Jesus and was ready to follow him, saying: «*Teacher, I will follow you wherever you go.*» received this reply: «*Foxes have holes, and birds of the air have nests; but the Son of man has nowhere to lay his head*» (Mt 8,19-20).

These Gospel passages show us the demands that Jesus makes of those who are entirely dedicated to Him. They must leave everything, give up all that is material and earthly, renounce the right to marry and have children, in order to follow Christ, dedicating themselves to Him with all their hearts for the salvation of souls.

The requirement of virginity and celibacy does not mean that marriage itself is not good. On the contrary, it is an institution created by God and one which Jesus Christ raised to the level of a Sacrament. Nor does it mean that it is less pleasing to God to be married and have children, since these are the fruit of the sacrament and a blessing from God. It only means that, for those who are called and chosen for a life of total consecration to the service of God, the Lord has other requirements and other gifts, because their ultimate destiny is different.

The evangelical counsels which we embrace are the sacrifice which we offer to God, the renunciation of all things, and of ourselves, in order to follow Him with a pure heart, generously and joyfully. And once we have made our offering to God, we cannot turn back. As it says in Sacred Scripture: «*When a man vows a vow to the Lord or swears an oath to bind himself by a pledge, he shall not break his word; he shall do according to all that proceeds out of his mouth.»* (Num 30, 2-3). And in another place we read: *«When you make a vow to the Lord your God, you shall not be slack to pay it; for the Lord your God will surely require it of you, and it would be sin in you. But if you refrain from vowing, it shall be no sin in you. You shall be careful to perform what has passed your lips, for you have voluntarily vowed to the Lord your God what you have promised with your mouth»* (Deut 23, 22-24). Interpreting these orders from the Lord, Qoheleth says: *«When you vow a vow to God, do not delay paying it; for he has no pleasure in fools. Pay what you vow. It is better that you should not vow than that you should vow and not pay. Let not your mouth lead you into sin, and do not say before the messenger that it was a mistake; why should God be angry at your voice, and destroy the work of your hands?»* (Eccles 5, 4-6).

We have chosen God as our inheritance, so we cannot turn back, nor exchange Him for any earthly thing, or for ourselves, poor creatures that we are. In such an exchange we would become even poorer, and lose ourselves into the bargain. We are the children of a Father who is God; let us not leave our Father's house for the poverty-stricken hovel of sinners.

We were chosen to follow Christ, Himself a virgin and the Spouse of virgins, humble, obedient, chaste and poor.

Christ, Himself a virgin and the Spouse of virgins. Christ is a virgin; He chose a virgin for his Mother; and like a pure lily, He is to be found and takes his delight in virgins. That is how the author of the Apocalypse presents Him to us: *«Then I looked, and lo, on Mount Zion stood the Lamb, and with him a hundred and forty-four thousand who had his name and his Father's name written on their foreheads. And I heard a voice from heaven like the sound of many waters and like the sound of loud thunder; the voice I heard was like the sound of harpers playing on their harps, and they sing a new song before the throne and before the four living creatures and before the elders. No one could learn that song except the hundred and forty-four thousand who had been redeemed from the earth. It is these who have not defiled themselves with women, for they are chaste. It is these who follow the lamb wherever he goes; these have been redeemed from mankind as first fruits for God and the Lamb, and in their mouth no lie was found, for they are spotless»* (Rv 14, 1-5). Here the Lamb is Christ, and those who accompany Him everywhere are those who are virgins.

Virginity is the fruit of the pure love with which people consecrate themselves completely to Christ: they give themselves unreservedly, dedicating themselves wholeheartedly and for ever. It was to them that Christ was referring when He said: «*there are eunuchs who have made themselves eunuchs for the sake of the kingdom of heaven. He who is able to receive this, let him receive it*» (Mt 19, 12). Virginity is the gift of pure love, which is given entirely and solely to God; it is the bond of closest possible union with God; it is that language of pure love which it was not given to everyone to understand, as Jesus said: «*Not all men can receive this precept, but only those to whom it is given*» (Mt 19, 11).

Virginity is the secret of love, the echo of the divine Voice which penetrates the soul with the choice made of it by the Spouse of consecrated virgins: «*You did not choose me, but I chose you and appointed you that you should go and bear fruit and that your fruit should abide*» (Jn 15, 16). Christ has chosen us so that we may bear fruit more abundantly and that this fruit may remain; He has called us by our name and incorporated us in the retinue of virgins; He has led us to drink from the fountain of living water and fed us with the fruit from the tree of life, in accordance with the Lord's promise: «*To the thirsty I will give water without price from the fountain of the water of life. He who conquers shall have his heritage, and I will be his God and he shall be my son. (...) Blessed are those who wash their robes, that they may have the right to the tree of life and that they may enter the city by the gates. Outside are the dogs and sorcerers and fornicators and murderers and idolaters, and every one who loves and practises falsehood.*» (Rev 21, 6-7; 22, 14-15).

Jesus Christ has chosen us to follow Him, He who is Himself a virgin, humble, obedient, chaste and poor.

Humility is one of the principal virtues that we need in order to follow Christ faithfully. This is how He presents Himself to us: «*Come to me, all who labour and are heavy laden, and I will give you rest. Take my yoke upon you, and learn from me; for I am gentle and lowly in heart, and you will find rest for your souls. For my yoke is easy, and my burden is light*» (Mt 11, 28-30).

Humility of heart, the recognition of our own nothingness, of our faults and failings, of our weakness, of our inexperience and incapacity; all these things will keep us in an attitude of absolute confidence in the love and mercy of God. This is what Our Lady tells us in her lovely canticle:

«*My soul magnifies the Lord, and my spirit rejoices in God my Saviour, for he has regarded the low estate of his handmaiden (...) he has put down the mighty from their thrones and exalted those of low degree*» (Lk 1, 46-48, 52). And Jesus Christ ends the parable illustrating God's diametrically opposed reactions to the prayer of the Pharisee and that of the publican in the temple by saying: «*For every one who exalts himself will be humbled, but he who humbles himself will be exalted*» (Lk 18, 14).

And when the two disciples wanted to be given the first places in the Kingdom of Heaven, the Lord gave them the following lesson in humility: «*You know that the rulers of the Gentiles lord it over them, and their great men exercise their authority over them. It shall not be so among you; but whoever would be great among you must be your servant, and whoever would be first among you must be your slave; even as the Son of man came not to be served but to serve, and to give his life as a ransom for many*» (Mt 20, 25-28).

It is with sentiments such as these that our souls become pleasing in the eyes of God and draw down upon us the predilection of his love: «*He has filled the hungry with good things, and the rich he has sent empty away.*» (Lk 1, 53). We must sing the mercies of the Lord together with the Psalmist: «*O give thanks to the Lord, for he is good; for his steadfast love endures for ever! Let the redeemed of the Lord say so, who he has redeemed from trouble and gathered in from the lands, from the east and from the west, from the north and from the south. Some wandered in desert wastes, finding no way to a city to dwell in; hungry and thirsty, their soul fainted within them. Then they cried to the Lord in their trouble, and he delivered them from their distress; he led them by a straight way, till they reached a city to dwell in. Let them thank the Lord for his steadfast love, for his wonderful works to the sons of men! For he satisfies him who is thirsty, and the hungry he fills with good things. Some sat in darkness and in gloom, prisoners in affliction and in irons, for they had rebelled against the words of God, and spurned the counsel of the Most High. Their hearts were bowed down with hard labour; they fell down, with none to help. Then they cried to the Lord in their trouble, and he delivered them from their distress; he brought them out of darkness and gloom, and broke their bonds asunder. Let them thank the Lord for his steadfast love, for his wonderful works to the sons of men! For he shatters the doors of bronze, and cuts in two the bars of iron*» (Ps 107(6), 1-16). This psalm reveals to us how God grants his favour and help to those with contrite and humble hearts.

St Teresa of Jesus says that to be humble is to live in the truth with God, with one's own conscience, and with one's neighbour; it is to recognise sincerely what we are, and admit to it without evasion, hypocrisy or pretence, above all before God and our own conscience; not to want to deceive ourselves or our neighbour by pretending to be, or to be worth, something that we are not; not putting ourselves forward, or wanting to occupy the seats of honour, or to be honoured in the world's eyes, because all these things are false, untrue and deceitful. It was this that led the demons to perdition, and they have deceived and dragged many people after them. Pride is the denial of humility, and the most serious and subtle of all sins.

For this reason, Jesus Christ wished to leave us a lesson and example of humility almost at the end of his earthly life. While He was at table with his disciples, He got up, took a towel and a basin of water and washed their feet. Then, when He had sat down again at the table, He said to them: «*Do you know what I have done to you? You call me Teacher and Lord; and you are right for so I am. If I then, your Lord and Teacher, have washed your feet, you also ought to wash one another's feet. For I have given you an example, that you also should do as I have done to you. Truly, truly, I say to you, a servant is not greater than his master; nor is he who is sent greater than he who sent him. If you know these things, blessed are you if you do them.*» (Jn 13, 12-17). What the divine Master wants to teach us here is not so much the ceremony of washing, or not washing, one another's feet, but the charity and humility with which we must treat one another.

We were chosen to follow *Christ obedient* to his Father. Every incident in his life is for us an example of obedience.

When He was twelve years old, Jesus went with his parents to the temple in Jerusalem for the feast of Passover. When the feast was over, his parents lost him, and it was three whole days before they found Him. Afterwards, St Luke tells us, Jesus «*went down with them and came to Nazareth, and was obedient to them*» (Lk 2, 51). He obeyed those who represented for Him the authority of God, his Father. Later, He was to say: «*For I have come down from heaven, not to do my own will, but the will of him who sent me*» (Jn 6, 38). This is the kind of obedience required of consecrated souls, who have been chosen, and have acknowledged the fact of having been chosen, by pronouncing before God a vow or an oath promising to follow Him.

There is no justification at all for believing that the modern mentality provides an excuse for dispensing ourselves from the obligation that we took upon ourselves to obey. Obedience should not be looked upon as a yoke or an imposition. Religious obedience rests on a will that is free, the will of the person who pronounced the vow or the oath, and willed thereby to submit him/herself to the will of God. Such obedience is the free expression of a choice: the person chose God as guide and opted to be led by Him. Neither is obedience a diminution. Quite the contrary, it is a value which uplifts those who have not, in themselves, the generosity to achieve this.

There are, however, personal rights that the vow does not eliminate, and that we are all obliged to respect, including Superiors. The latter cannot abuse the authority that God has entrusted to them. If they were to do so, they would be responsible for the disorientation of their subjects and of their failure to make progress. They must not pile onto them more obligations than those envisaged in their rule, especially if such obligations indicate in some way a lack of trust or some form of pharisaism, by imposing on others – as Christ says in his Gospel – heavy burdens that they themselves do not carry. They should not use force in order to compel or subjugate their subjects, as if they were prisoners in gaol: this achieves nothing but only causes exasperation. St Paul perceived this danger and, after urging the children among his disciples to obey their parents, he urges the parents not to exasperate their children: «*Children, obey your parents in everything, for this pleases the Lord. Fathers, do not provoke your children, lest they become discouraged*» (Col 3, 20-21).

Jesus Christ is our model of obedience as a young labourer, working in his father's humble workshop in the obscure village of Nazareth, subject to the dictates and requirements of the customers who came to Him with their orders. With all, He behaved humbly, modestly and obligingly towards everyone. He submitted himself to the burden of toil and to the discomforts of a poor home, in order to do the will of the Father.

Hence, He is able to say: «*And he who sent me is with me; he has not left me alone, for I always do what is pleasing to him.*» (Jn 8, 29). We, too, ought to be able to say to Christ: *You are always with me because I always do what pleases you.* The primary end of our total dedication to the Lord is this: to do God's will, to please God, and to live a life of intimate union with God – a union of affection, a union of will, a union of deeds done in faith.

In Jesus Christ we also have the model for the obedience of the apostle. When the time pre-ordained by the Father came, obedient as always to his will, Jesus left everything and went off in search of souls in order to bring them the word of God and guide them in the paths of salvation.

It was with this end in view that he went to the house of Zacchaeus and that of Simon the Pharisee; that He waited by the well for the Samaritan woman and her fellow citizens, in order to give them the living water of grace, forgiveness of their sins and the light of the knowledge of the Father. With this end in view, too, He never shirked toil, or weariness, or self-sacrifice, intensifying his life of prayer and penance. To accomplish the work that the Father had given Him to do was, for Him, as important as the food He ate: «*I have food to eat of which you do not know. (...) My food is to do the will of him who sent me, and to accomplish his work*» (Jn 4, 32, 34). This is also the mission entrusted to consecrated souls: to carry out the will of God in order to accomplish the work that He has entrusted to them, in other words, their own sanctification and the salvation of souls.

Jesus Christ is also our model as victim, sacrificed in obedience to the will of the Father for the redemption of the world.

We see this obedience in the prayer which He addressed to the Father in the Garden of Olives:«*My Father, if it be possible, let this cup pass from me; nevertheless, not as I will, but as thou wilt.*» (Mt 26, 39). As in our own case, Jesus' human nature, too, abhorred the suffering, the humiliation and the death, but He put obedience to his Father's will before the repugnance of his own nature: *Not as I will, but as You will.*

The prospect of suffering caused Jesus fear and anguish, so much so that He said to his Apostles: «*My soul is very sorrowful*» (Mk 14, 34), but it did not induce Him to disobey: «*My Father, if this cannot pass unless I drink it, thy will be done*» (Mt 26, 42). If obedience were not costly, what merit should we have in obeying? It is when it demands a sacrifice of us that we prove our love for God.

The vow of chastity requires of consecrated souls purity of heart and of the affections, thoughts, words and deeds. In this, too, Jesus Christ is our model: He was chaste, pure and holy.

He loved God his Father with the pure love of a virginal heart; He loved souls and cleansed them from the stains of sin in his own blood. In the Apocalypse, St John tells us that he saw in Heaven «*a great multitude which no man could number, from every nation, from all tribes and peoples* and tongues, standing before the throne and before the Lamb, clothed in white robes, with palm branches in their hands, and crying out with a loud voice, "Salvation belongs to our God who sits upon the throne, and to the Lamb! (...) Then one of the elders addressed me, saying, "(...) These are they who have come out of the great tribulation; they have washed their robes and made them white in the blood of the Lamb. Therefore are they before the throne of God, and serve him day and night within his temple; and he who sits upon the throne will shelter them with his presence. They shall hunger no more, neither thirsty any more; the sun shall not strike them, nor any scorching heat. For the Lamb in the midst of the throne will be their shepherd, and he will guide them to springs of living water; and God will wipe away every tear from their eyes.» (Rv 7, 9-17). Although this multitude can be taken as standing for all those who have been redeemed, in a special way it represents those who have followed Christ as virgins, because it is these who are available, free from entanglements with earthly things, and ready to serve the Lord day and night in his Temple.

St John then goes on to narrate how he saw an Angel with a thurible in his hand come and stand by the altar of God: «he was given much incense to mingle with the prayers of all saints upon the golden altar (...) and the smoke of the incense rose with the prayers of the saints from the hand of the angel before God. (Rev 8, 3-4,). I don't quite know, but I believe this Angel must stand for the priest, pure and chaste, who goes up to the altar and offers to God the prayers, offerings and virtues of the people.

Purity of heart, purity of affection, and purity of intention are, as it were, the fruit of chastity and its safeguard. In one of his letters, St Paul writes: «For this is the will of God, your santification: that you abstain from immorality; that each one of you know how to control his own body in holiness and honour, not in the passion of lust like heathen who do not know God; that no man transgress, and wrong his brother in this matter, because the Lord is an avenger in all these things, as we solemnly forewarned you. For God has not called us for uncleanness, but in holiness. Therefore whoever disregards this, disregards not man but God, who gives his Holy Spirit to you.» (1 Thess 4, 3-8).

And somewhere else St Paul tells us:«Every one should remain in the state in which he was called. Were you a slave when called? Never mind. But if you can gain your freedom, avail yourself of the opportunity. For he who was called in the Lord as a slave is a freedman of the Lord. Likewise he who was free when called is a slave of Christ. You were bought with a price; do not become slaves of men. So, brethren, in whatever state each was called, there let him remain with God. (...) The unmarried man is anxious about the affairs of the Lord, how to please the Lord; but the married man is anxious about worldly affairs, how to please his wife, and his interests are divided. And the unmarried woman or girl is anxious about the affairs of the Lord, how to be holy in body and spirit; but the married woman is anxious about worldly affairs, how to please her husband. I say this for your own benefit, not to lay any restraint upon you, but to promote good order and to secure your undivided devotion to the Lord.» (1 Cor 7, 20-24; 32-35).

The primary object of our vow of chastity is this: to be free of earthly cares in order to dedicate ourselves more completely to the service of the Lord, and to love Him, and Him alone, more purely, with the purity of our hearts, our affections and our body, so that we may live more fully in intimate union with Christ.

«Do you not know – again it is the Apostle St Paul speaking to us – that your bodies are members of Christ? (...) He who is united to the Lord becomes one spirit with him. Shun immorality. (...) Do you not know that your body is a temple of the Holy Spirit within you, which you have from God? You are not your own; you were bought with a price. So glorify God in your body.» (1 Cor 3, 16-23).

By the vow of chastity we are doubly consecrated to God: He is our temple and we are the place where He dwells. St John tells us this in the Apocalypse: «And I saw no temple in the city, for its temple is the Lord God the Almighty and the Lamb. And the city has no need of sun or moon to shine upon it, for the glory of God is its light, and its lamp is the Lamb. (...) its gates shall never be shut by day – and there shall be no night there; they shall bring into it the glory and the honour of the nations. But nothing unclean shall enter it, nor any one who practises abomination or falsehood, but only those who are written in the Lamb's book of life» (Rev 21, 22-27)

What a wonderful thing this total gift of ourselves to the Lord is! By it our names are inscribed in the Lamb's Book of Life. As the Lord says: «Blessed are the pure in heart, for they shall see God» (Mt 5, 8). But already, in this life, pure souls enjoy a special intimacy and knowledge of God, who communicates and manifests Himself to them in Christ: «All things have been delivered to me by my Father, and no one knows the Son except the Father, and no one knows the Father except the Son and any one to whom the Son chooses to reveal him» (Mt 11, 26-27). And to whom should God reveal Himself if not to pure souls? They are those who have been chosen – in St Paul's words – «for the praise of his glory» (Eph 1, 14).

The vow of poverty unites us to *Christ who is poor,* deprived of the goods of this world so that He could be free to dedicate Himself completely to the work entrusted to Him by the Father. And, as we learn from the words that He addressed to the Father, He succeeded: «*I glorified thee on earth, having accomplished the work which thou gavest me to do*» (Jn 17, 4). And this is the object of our own vow of poverty: so that, freed from earthly things and the preoccupations they bring with them, we may be able, in union with Christ, to accomplish the mission which the Father has entrusted to us.

A rich young man went up to Jesus *saying, "Teacher, what good deed must I do, to have eternal life? And he said to him(...) "If you would enter life, keep the commandments" He said to him, "Which?" And Jesus said, "You shall not kill, You shall not commit adultery, You shall not steal, You shall not bear false witness, Honour your father and mother, and You shall love your neighbour as yourself." The young man said to him, "All these I have observed; what do I still lack?" Jesus said to him, "If you would be perfect, go, sell what you possess and give to the poor, and you will have treasure in heaven; and come follow me"»* (Mt 19, 16-21). Those who wish to follow Jesus Christ more closely must not be absorbed in this world's goods, as these will make them blind, impede the life of the apostolate, and prevent their full and exclusive dedication to God.

To those who give up everything in order to follow Him, the Lord gives, in exchange, in this life, the necessities of life, while inviting them to abandon themselves to divine Providence who cares for all; and in the life to come: treasure in Heaven.

This is how Jesus Christ urges us to abandon ourselves with complete confidence to our heavenly Father, who is ever mindful of us: «*Therefore I will tell you, do not be anxious about your life, what you shall eat or what you shall drink, nor about your body, what you shall put on. Is not life more than food, and the body more than clothing? Look at the birds of the air; they neither sow nor reap nor gather into barns, and yet your heavenly Father feeds them. Are you not of more value than they? And which of you by being anxious can add one cubit to his span of life? And why are you anxious about clothing?*

Consider the lilies of the field, how they grow; they neither toil nor spin; yet I tell you, even Solomon in all his glory was not arrayed like one of these. But if God so clothes the grass of the field, which today is alive and tomorrow is thrown into the oven, will he not much more clothe you, O men of little faith? Therefore do not be anxious, saying, 'What shall we eat?' or 'What shall we drink?' or 'What shall we wear?' For the Gentiles seek all these things; and your heavenly Father knows that you need them all. But seek first his kingdom and his righteousness, and all these things shall be yours as well.» (Mt 6, 25-33).

But Jesus also urges us to keep our treasures in a safe place – in Heaven:«*Do not lay up for yourselves treasures on earth, where moth and rust consume and where thieves break in and steal, but lay up for yourselves treasures in heaven, where neither moth nor rust consumes and where thieves do not break in and steal: For where your treasure is, there will your heart be also.*»
(Mt 6, 19-21).

This is the purpose of our vow of poverty: so that our hearts may rest only in God. Then God will take care of us, and anything else we may need will be given to us. I myself can bear wonderful testimony to this truth. I left home at thirteen years of age, without worrying about what I was to wear or to eat; I abandoned myself completely to divine Providence in order to follow God's will and until today, though I have never had any privileges, which I did not want, I have never lacked anything I needed.

God's generosity is manifest in the reply Jesus gave to St Peter when he asked what would be the reward for those who had left everything in order to follow Him: «*Truly I say to you (...) every one who has left houses or brothers or sisters or father or mother or children or lands, for my name's sake, will receive a hundredfold, and inherit eternal life*» (Mt 19, 27-29).

The phrase *will receive a hundredfold* shows us that what Jesus Christ requires of those who have given up the right to own material things for love of Him is not that they should be deprived of the necessities of life; otherwise He would not have promised them the hundredfold:

«*You will receive a hundredfold, now in this time*» (Mk 10, 30). What Jesus Christ asks of us, and what the vow of poverty signifies, is that we should renounce the right to possess things as if they were our own; also that we make use of everything that we need, but look upon it as if it were an alms, and use it as if it were on loan to us. In this way our heart remains free from earthly goods and can aspire to those of Heaven: «*Blessed are the poor in spirit, for theirs is the kingdom of heaven.*» (Mt 5, 3).

The mission of consecrated persons is to work and sanctify themselves in union with Christ for the Kingdom of Heaven. Thus each consecrated soul is another Christ on earth, another lamb sent by God to take away the sins of the world. The way to accomplish this mission is to give our lives: «*unless a grain of wheat falls into the earth and dies, it remains alone; but if it dies, it bears much fruit.*» (Jn 12, 24). It is by death that we attain to life, and it is by means of the life that we thus attain that we save ourselves from death. It is in this sense that Our Lord goes on to say: «*He who loves his life loses it, and he who hates his life in this world will keep it for eternal life. If any one serves me, he must follow me; and where I am, there shall my servant be also; if any one serves me, the Father will honour him.*» (Jn 12, 25-26).

This is the glory of consecrated souls, the glory that they hope for from God and that raises them up to God. In a way, they can say like, and with, Jesus: «*For this purpose I have come to this hour*» (Jn 12, 27).

It was for this reason that, there in the heavens, close to the Sun which had gone pale in the presence of the Light of God, the Message wished to give us a taste of the glory enjoyed by those who have already reached the Kingdom of God, but who, here on earth, by the example of their lives and the light of their teaching have marked out for us the way to heaven: *Jesus, Mary and Joseph!*

Ave Maria!

21

The Call to holiness

The nineteenth Call of the Message

One can discern another meaning in the apparition of Our Lady of Mount Carmel, namely the call to holiness. In it we see one who, like ourselves, lived on earth and sanctified herself, but now lives and reigns with God in Heaven, enjoying the fruit and the reward of this sanctification.

Our Lady sanctified herself as a pure and immaculate virgin by corresponding to the graces which God granted to her in that state. She sanctified herself as a faithful and devoted wife by fulfilling all the duties of her state in life. She sanctified herself as a loving mother who dedicated herself to the Son whom God entrusted to her, fondling Him in her arms, bringing Him up and educating Him, and also helping Him and following Him in the performance of his mission. With Him she travelled the narrow way of life, the rugged road to Calvary; with Him she agonised, receiving in her heart the wounds of the nails, the piercing of the lance and the insults of the hostile crowd; finally, she sanctified herself as mother, mistress and guide of the Apostles, agreeing to remain on earth for as long as God wished, in order to accomplish the mission which He had entrusted to her as co-Redemptrix with Christ of all human beings.

Thus Mary is, for each one of us, the model of the most perfect holiness to which a human being can aspire in this poor land of exile. How many times will she not have read and meditated in her heart these words of Sacred Scripture: «You shall be holy; for I the Lord your God am holy.» (Lev 19, 2). What God says to us here is for everyone and for all states in life, as we see from the context in which the phrase appears: «*And the Lord said to Moses, "Say to all the congregation of the people of Israel, You shall be holy; for I the Lord your God am holy.*» (Lev 19, 1-2).

This commandment obliges us to observe all the other commandments, because to transgress even one of them is to fall short of holiness.

Everyone is obliged to be holy, even those who have no faith. Obviously, in the case of those who have no faith, the holiness will be that dictated by their own conscience, and there will be no supernatural merit because they will not have the fundamental reason that gives value to true holiness: *to be holy because God is holy*, namely the desire to be holy in order to please God, to become like God, to do His will, to give pleasure to God and prove to Him how much we love Him.

As I was saying, those who do not have the happiness of possessing the gift of faith are also bound to become holy by a dictate of the human conscience; for the same reason, we say that even without knowing God, those who fulfil the natural law can be saved, as St Paul tells us: «*When the Gentiles who have not the law do by nature what the law requires, they are a law to themselves, even though they do not have the law. They show that what the law requires is written on their hearts, while their conscience also bears witness and their conflicting thoughts accuse or perhaps excuse them on that day, when, according to my gospel, God judges the secrets of men by Christ Jesus.*» (Rom 2, 14-16).

For us who have the happiness of possessing the gift of faith, which we received in the sacrament of Baptism, the duty to be holy obliges us to something more: to be clothed with supernatural life, to impart a supernatural character to all our actions, in other words, to be holy because God is holy. This duty obliges us to live in the shadow of the holiness of God or, to put it another way, by following the path that God has mapped out for us to be holy and to be with Him: «*For I am the Lord your God; consecrate yourselves therefore, and be holy, for I am holy*» (Lv 11,44)

God himself guides our steps along the road to holiness: «*I am God Almighty, walk before me, and be blameless.*» (Gen 17, 1). To walk in the presence of God is to realise that his gaze is upon us, and that our whole being is, as it were, in front of the mirror of the light of God. Hence, when we realise that God sees us, we will not dare to offend Him. On the contrary, there will be born in us a desire to fulfil his Law in order to please Him, to give Him pleasure, to merit his favours and graces, and to sanctify ourselves in order to become like Him. Herein lies true union with God for everyone, and it is this that makes us holy.

Consecrated souls are raised to a higher level on account of the holiness of the state of life which they have embraced. By turning their backs on the things of earth, they have placed themselves in a particular state of readiness to correspond with the working of God's grace in them. By giving themselves to God in love, they offer to Him, once and for all, a holocaust of the whole of themselves. Now, this act is of itself capable of raising them to a life of constant intimacy with God and of perfect love, provided that such consecrated souls have given themselves completely, without restriction or reservation.

By giving themselves in this way, their encounter with God becomes permanent and familiar. The soul relates with God as with a friend or a father who is always available, communicating to Him its desires, its aspirations, its ideals and its difficulties. And it is in this intimacy that God gives Himself to such souls and makes them holy. Moreover, such souls are aware of God's presence within them, experiencing God as their temple and the place where they dwell. Hence, they take refuge there every moment and day of their lives. And even when God's presence does not make itself felt, they plunge themselves into His immense Being and abandon themselves in his Fatherly arms; by faith they know that He is listening to them and is leading them by the ways that He wants them to follow. United to Christ, they offer their sacrifice to God, in accordance with the Apostle's teaching that I love so much, namely: «*Through him then let us continually offer up a sacrifice to God, that is, the fruit of lips that acknowledge his name. Do not neglect to do good and to share what you have, for such sacrifices are pleasing to God*» (Heb 13, 15-16).

Unfortunately, we have to admit that very few people attain to this degree of intimate union with God. The temptations of the devil penetrate even into the cloister and succeed in diverting some souls from the one sublime aspiration that led them to strip themselves of many things.

Then the tempter comes along and succeeds in blinding them with pathetic ambitions for places and positions of honour, to such an extent that, if they do not succeed in getting them, it seems to them the end of the world. So they have to be given the places and positions they seek, in order to reassure them. A poor kind of reassurance, this, when it is derived from the chains of pride, vanity and I don't know what else, which are the plague of monasteries and religious houses! And the devil deceives very many with such chains! The «Imitation of Christ» had already said this, and St Teresa of Jesus repeated it, but to what effect? The devil does not give up, because it is where he reaps his harvest!

That is why Jesus Christ says to us that «*Whoever would be first among you must be your slave; even as the Son of man came not to be served but to serve, and to give his life as a ransom for many*» (Mt 20, 27-28). And those who know how to overcome these temptations immerse themselves in the immense Being of God as in an ocean of grace, strength and love; they penetrate the divine secrets with heightened clarity, and understand them even though they cannot understand them fully. God reveals Himself to such souls with a certain delight, and communicates to them knowledge of a part of Himself according to the capacity of each one to attain to the essence of the divine Being.

Thus the soul identifies itself with the holiness of God to the extent to which it gives itself generously, and God takes it to himself and enriches it with his gifts. It is here that the person is ennobled with the virtue of God, as the Apostle St Paul tells us: «*But, as it is written, "What no eye has seen, nor ear heard, nor the heart of man conceived, what God has prepared for those who love him", God has revealed to us through the Spirit. For the Spirit searches everything, even the depths of God. For what person knows a man's thoughts except the spirit of man which is in him? So also no one comprehends the thoughts of God except the Spirit of God. Now we have received not the spirit of the world, but the Spirit which is from God, that we might understand the gifts bestowed on us by God*» (1 Cor 2, 9-12). And Jesus Christ says the same, but with Himself as the Revealer: «*All things have been delivered to me by my Father, and no one knows the Son except the Father, and no one knows the Father except the Son and any one to whom the Son chooses to reveal him*» (Mt 11, 26-27).

God communicates Himself and reveals Himself to whomsoever He pleases, but when He does so, such communication requires faithful correspondence on the part of the person who receives it. God's action does not destroy human nature; rather, it perfects and enhances it. It does not deprive people of their natural human, moral and physical reactions because it is through these that they are to sanctify themselves, in imitation of Christ who felt and who suffered for love of the Father. Nor does God's action make them immune to temptation, whether of pride, from the devil, the flesh or the world, because they are to sanctify themselves in the battle in which they will be victorious by the help of grace, after the example of Jesus Christ who, in spite of being the Holy of Holies, was also tempted. The harsh trials to which such souls are sometimes subjected may agitate them and even cause them to recoil, because God has not made them immune to human weakness; such trials are particularly hard to endure when they are the fruit of injustice, misunderstanding or a lack of truth. But those who cause the hurt are the ones who are responsible.

Nevertheless, it is in the midst of all these conflicts that such people – if they persevere in the fight and win through – sanctify themselves and become, for God, a true praise of his glory, as the Apostle says: «*To lead a life worthy of the Lord, fully pleasing to him, bearing fruit in every good work and increasing in the knowledge of God. May you be strengthened with all power, according to his glorious might, for all endurance and patience with joy, giving thanks to the Father, who has qualified us to share in the inheritance of the saints in light.*» (Col 1, 10-12).

Whatever favours God may grant to a soul, He will not deprive it of the natural gifts which are given to all human beings: one's own will, freedom, feelings, one's own personality, with the same rights and responsibilities as everyone else. God has given these gifts equally to everyone so that by freely using them we can sanctify ourselves and earn an eternal reward. In this way, God respects in us the gifts He has given us, and we too must respect them in others. Thus each one has a responsibility and is answerable to God for his or her own self.

To strip people of any of these gifts is to force them to live as others want them to; it is to commit an injustice and make oneself responsible for the faults or sins that a person who is forced in this way may, for this reason, commit. From the point of view of the person who has been thus humiliated, if he or she accepts the situation and endures the suffering with patience and for the love of God, then they sanctify themselves and merit a reward: «*For the eyes of the Lord are upon the righteous, and his ears are open to their prayer. But the face of the Lord is against those that do evil*» (1 Peter 3, 12).

Thus, since we have been chosen by God for holiness, let us endeavour to respond to the call with the best of ourselves, for our own personal growth and for the benefit of all. This is what St Paul urges us to do: «*As in one body we have many members, and all the members do not have the same function, so we, though many, are one body in Christ, and individually members one of another. Having gifts that differ according to the grace given to us, let us use them: if prophecy, in proportion to our faith; if service, in our serving; he who teaches, in his teaching; he who exhorts, in his exhortation; he who contributes, in liberality; he who gives aid, with zeal; he who does acts of mercy, with cheerfulness*» (Rom 12, 6-8).

Thus, by the good use that we make of the gifts that God has given us, our holiness develops in the love that we owe to God and to our neighbour; we purify ourselves and become worthy of eternal life, since love is the essence of all true holiness, as the sublime Eagle of the New Testament tells us:«*By this we know that we love the children of God, when we love God and obey his commandments. For this is the love of God, that we keep his commandments. And his commandments are not burdensome. For whatever is born of God overcomes the world; and this is the victory that overcomes the world, our faith*» (1 Jn 5, 2-4).

Can there be anyone who feels like asking: 'But why must we be saints?'

The Apostle St Paul gives us the answer in the following marvellous words: «*Blessed be the God and Father of our Lord Jesus Christ, who has blessed us in Christ with every spiritual blessing in the heavenly places, even as he chose us in him before the foundation of the world, that we should be holy and blameless before him. He destined us in love to be his sons through Jesus Christ, according to the purpose of his will, to the praise of his glorious grace which he freely bestowed on us in the Beloved. In him we have redemption through his blood, the forgiveness of our trespasses, according to the riches of his grace which he lavished upon us. For he has made known to us in all wisdom and insight the mystery of his will, according to his purpose which he set forth in Christ as a plan for the fulness of time, to unite all things in him, things in heaven and things on earth.*

In him, according to the purpose of him who accomplishes all things according to the counsel of his will, we who first hoped in Christ have been destined and appointed to live for the praise of his glory. In him you also, who have heard the word of truth, the gospel of your salvation, and have believed in him, were sealed with the promised Holy Spirit, who is the guarantee of our inheritance until we acquire possession of it, to praise of his glory.» (Eph 1, 3-14).

For this we were chosen, and for this we must become saints: to be the praise of the glory of God and to share in this same glory which we receive from Him as a grace.

Ave Maria!

22

The Call to follow the road to Heaven

The twentieth Call of the Message

As we have seen, the whole of the Message is a call to follow the road to heaven, to walk in such a way as to succeed in attaining to eternal life.

In the times in which we live, there are even those who deny the existence of Heaven, whether because they have no faith, or because they do not want to commit themselves to following the narrow path that leads to Heaven. But they are wrong. That Heaven exists is a revealed truth which cannot be denied.

There are many passages in Sacred Scripture which speak to us of Heaven. The prophet Isaiah, when pleading before God for his people, says: «*Look down from heaven and see, from the holy and glorious habitation. Where are thy zeal and thy might? The yearning of thy heart and thy compassion? (...) For thou art our Father*» (Is 63, 15-16). The same prayer is addressed to God in the Book of Deuteronomy: «*Look down from thy holy habitation, from heaven, and bless thy people*» (Deut 26, 15). And, in the New Testament, Jesus Christ taught us to pray as follows: «*Our Father who art in heaven, hallowed be thy name, thy kingdom come, thy will be done, on earth as it is in heaven*» (Mt 6, 9-10).

After narrating the baptism of Jesus in the River Jordan, St Matthew wrote: «*When Jesus was baptized, he went up immediately from the water, and behold, the heavens were opened and he saw the Spirit of God descending like a dove, and alighting on him*» (Mt 3, 16). Some time after this, John the Baptist, when replying to a question put to him by his disciples, bore witness to Jesus in the following terms: «*"No one can receive anything except what is given him from heaven. You yourselves bear me witness, that I said, I am not the Christ, but I have been sent before him. (...) He must increase, but I must decrease". He who comes from above is above all; he who is of the earth belongs to the earth, and of the earth he speaks; he who comes from heaven is above all. He bears witness to what he has seen and heard*» (Jn 3, 27-32).

When urging us to practise the love that we owe to our enemies, Jesus Christ said: «*Love your enemies and pray for those who persecute you, so that you may be sons of your Father who is in heaven*» (Mt 5, 44-45). And He concluded his proclamation of the Beatitudes by saying: *«Blessed you are when men revile you and persecute you and utter all kinds of evil against you falsely on my account. Rejoice and be glad, for your reward is great in heaven, for so men persecuted the prophets who were before you.»* (Mt 5, 11-12).

The Lord tells us that we shall be blessed if we are persecuted on his account, because the prophets before us were persecuted in a similar way. But why is it that those whom God has chosen for a special mission, and with whom He is in more direct contact, are persecuted and oppressed? It is the continuation of the mystery of the Cross which marks out for us the path to Heaven.

From the texts just cited, it is clear that the existence of Heaven is a truth that cannot be denied. Some people deny it because, they say, one does not know where it is, nor has anyone ever seen it, etc.

But many things exist which we have not yet seen, but we do not doubt that they exist because someone who really knows has told us about them. We know, for example, that there is a sea of fire at the heart of the earth; here and there, in various parts of the globe, there are volcanoes to be seen with the lava that pours forth from them, but we do not see the fire itself which produces them. Nevertheless, we know that it exists. And the one who created this fire and keeps it going is the same Lord who created the fire of Hell and will keep it going, too, for all eternity.

We also know that, out in space, there are many planets which we have not yet seen, many stars whose light has not yet reached us. No one has yet succeeded in measuring the firmament. Now, God, who created this unlimited space, can also have created a «place», a stopping place to which He has given the name of Heaven, destined to be the dwelling place of God and of his Elect for ever and ever. It is said that Heaven consists in the possession of God: there can be no doubt that God is the wellspring of all happiness, and that when we possess God we shall be eternally happy.

When describing the Ascension of Jesus Christ into Heaven, St Luke says: *«Then he led them out (his disciples) as far as Bethany, and lifting up his hands he blessed them. While he blessed them, he parted from them, and was carried up into heaven»* (Lk 24, 50-51). And St Mark describes this same event as follows: *«After he had spoken to them, was taken up into heaven, and sat down at the right hand of God»* (Mk 16, 19).

We could continue to quote many other passages from Sacred Scripture which assure us of the existence of Heaven, but we will not do so in order not to make this humble document excessively long. Let what has already been said be sufficient for those who are prepared to believe without insisting on actually seeing everything! Not that it is a bad thing to be able to see, quite the opposite, since the more we see the better we understand how much more we have yet to learn in order to know the immensity of the work created by God. While maintaining due proportions, one could apply here, in relation to the difficulty in knowing the things of earth and heaven, the phrase that Jesus Christ used when explaining to Nicodemus the need for faith in order to understand them: *«If I have told you earthly things and you do not believe, how can you believe if I tell you heavenly things?»* (Jn 3, 12).

Wishing to confirm this truth for us, the Message, too, came to recall to our minds, and to speak to us about Heaven.

When the little shepherd children asked the beautiful Lady where she was from, she replied: *«I am from heaven»*. When they heard that she was a Lady who had come from Heaven, they remembered about a friend of theirs who had died a short time before and who, people said, had gone to Heaven, so they asked about her. The Lady replied: *«She is in heaven»*.

In the prayer that the Lady taught them to say at the end of each decade of the Rosary, we ask God to *«bring all souls to heaven»*.

And when the children asked if they, too, would go to heaven, the Lady replied that they would. Hence, it is certain that heaven exists. *Heaven does exist!*

The great concern of God and of Our Lady is that people should be saved and go to heaven; and since heaven is the dwelling place prepared by God for eternal life, unless we follow the road that leads to it, we shall never get there. As far as we know, there are already two people there in soul and body: Jesus Christ and Mary most holy, his Mother and ours; and there, too, go all the souls which have the good fortune to leave this world in the state of grace, that is, without mortal sin.

On the day of the resurrection from the dead, all souls will be reunited with their bodies so that they can together share in the eternal happiness or the eternal damnation that they have deserved during the time of their pilgrimage on earth. Jesus Christ himself has told us this, He who will then be our Judge: *«For as the Father has life in himself, so he has granted the Son also to have life in himself, and has given him authority to execute judgment, because he is the Son of man. Do not marvel at this; for the hour is coming when all who are in the tombs will hear his voice and come forth, those who have done good, to the resurrection of life, and those who have done evil, to the resurrection of judgment»* (Jn 5, 26-29).

If God had created us merely in order to live out, on this earth, the few days that we spend here in the midst of toil, suffering and affliction that all of us, one way or another, have got to endure, then we could say that our life had no meaning, since it was destined to end in the dust of the earth from which we were made. But God, in his goodness, must have had greater purposes in mind, and his Love could not be content with this. We are the masterpiece of his love, since He created us to share in the immensity of his Life.

From the moment of our conception, our life continues through time and goes on to eternity, where it will abide. As long as we live on this earth, we are pilgrims on the way to heaven, if we keep to the way that God has marked out for us. This is the most important thing in our lives: that we should behave in such a way as to ensure that, when we depart from this world and at the end of time, we shall deserve to hear from the lips of Jesus Christ those consoling words: *«Come, O blessed of my Father, inherit the kingdom prepared for you from the foundation of the world»* (Mt 25, 34).

It is for this reason that the Message speaks to us of Heaven and urges us to keep to the way that will lead us there.

Ave Maria!

Part Three

THE TEN COMMANDMENTS

23

Knowledge of God

We have seen that God created us to love and serve Him here on earth, and then to see and enjoy Him forever in Heaven. The Message of Fatima reminds us that we must follow the road to Heaven. And it is observance of the Commandments that will lead us to eternal life. This is what Jesus Christ told the young man who asked Him: «*"Teacher, what good deed must I do, to have eternal life? And he said to him, "Why do you ask me about what is good? One there is who is good. If you would enter life, keep the commandments" He said to him, "Which?" And Jesus said, "You shall not kill, You shall not commit adultery, You shall not steal, You shall not bear false witness, Honour your father and mother, and You shall love your neighbour as yourself.»* (Mt 19,16-19). Therefore, the way to Heaven is this: keep the Commandments.

Since, unfortunately, the great majority of people neither know nor understand the Commandments, it will be useful to many people to recall them here, so that we may all understand what we must do in order to obtain eternal life.

It may possibly occur to someone to ask me: What have the ten Commandments got to do with the Message of Fatima? I answer that they have a great deal to do with it: they are among the chief aims of the Message. In fact, Our Lady ended the series of her apparitions in Fatima with these words: *"Do not offend the Lord our God any more, because He is already so much offended"*. And, previously, on the 13th July, she had already said: *"In October, I will tell you who I am and what I want."* Thus, what Our Lady wanted and, therefore, the main object of the Message, was to beg us not to continue to offend Our Lord because He was already so deeply offended.

There can be no doubt that what offends God most is the breaking of his law: all Sacred Scripture confirms this. All the Prophets protested against the breaking of God's law; and, in the same way, Jesus Christ condemns it also, as does the Church, which continues to speak in his name in our own day.

In order to keep God's commandments, we have to know Him. Who, then, is God?

The Book of Deuteronomy tells us how Moses, on the threshold of the Promised Land, called around him the twelve tribes of Israel in order to remind them of how God had led them from the time they left Egypt until they had arrived where they now were, at the River Jordan. This is how Moses recalls God's great gift to his people, the Decalogue: «*The Lord spoke with you face to face at the mountain, out of the midst of the fire, while I stood between the Lord and you at that time, to declare to you the word of the Lord; for you were afraid because of the fire, and you did not go up into the mountain. He said: "I am the Lord your God, who brought you out of the land of Egypt, out of the house of bondage*» (Dt 5,4-6).

God showed Himself to his people on Mount Sinai, so that they would acknowledge Him as the one true God. We were there, represented by the Israelites; to us also God makes Himself known and addresses his word.

All the Israelites saw the fire on the mountains and all understood that it was supernatural fire, since it neither burned nor consumed. In this fire, in some way, they saw God and they were terrified, as they themselves confessed, finally asking Moses to be their mediator: «*Behold, the Lord our God has shown us his glory and greatness, and we have heard his voice out of the midst of the fire; we have this day seen God speak with man and man still live. Now therefore why should we die? For this great fire will consume us; if we hear the voice of the Lord our God any more, we shall die. For who is there of all flesh, that has heard the voice of the living God speaking out in the midst of fire, as we have, and has still lived? Go near, and hear all that the Lord our God will say; and speak to us all that the Lord our God will speak to you; and we will hear and do it.*» (Dt 5, 24-27).

All this makes me think! While Moses is going peacefully up the mountain to draw near to God and talk to Him intimately, the people are terrified and are afraid they are going to die. Would that not be because, by the sin of idolatry, they have lost the strength of grace and can no longer, like Moses, see God and hear his voice? The fear which they felt certainly was not caused by the presence of God but came rather from the reproach of their own conscience, because that is what accuses us before God and condemns us. As for me, how much I would give to be absorbed in that divine flame!

In this passage from Sacred Scripture, I seem to see in Moses the figure of pure souls who are continually moving up towards God, climbing the mountain of holiness, while those who live sunk in a life of sin are descending all the time, burying themselves in a swamp of vice and moving further and further away from God. They cease to love Him, because sin extinguishes the flame of love in them; they no longer trust, because sin confuses their minds and they cannot see the mercy of God; they lose their faith, because passion blinds them and prevents them from seeing the light of God.

In Moses, I see an image of the person who corresponds to God's call. Nothing frightens him because his conscience is at peace, he believes in God, keeps his commandments and runs to meet Him. He knows that his Creator is the one true God, the Source of all that exists; therefore, he trusts in his power, his goodness, his wisdom, and his love.

God showed Himself to the Israelites in order to assure them of the reality of his existence and thus to make it possible for them to pass on the certainty of that truth. We, too, belong, spiritually, to that same people. Made one with Christ in Baptism, we became part of the People of God. We were chosen by God to become members of the mystical Body of Christ, which is his Church. And it is this Church which, all over the world, forms the People of God, as we see from the command it received from Christ: «Go into the world and preach the gospel to the whole creation. He who believes and is baptized will be saved; but he who does not believe will be condemned» (Mk 16, 15-16). Thus, it is necessary to believe in God, and be baptised, in order to be saved, to belong to the People of God and to be counted among his chosen ones.

Terrified not only by the fire which God caused on the mountain, which itself trembled, but also by the voice of thunder with which God spoke to them, the Israelites begged Moses to be their intermediary with God. When Moses returned from God's presence, he told them the laws which God had given him, and, then, said to them: «These words the Lord spoke to all your assembly at the mountain out of the midst of the fire, the cloud, and the thick darkness, with a loud voice; and he added no more. And he wrote them upon two tables of stone, and gave them to me. And when you heard the voice out of the midst of the darkness, while the mountain was burning with fire, you came near to me, all the heads of your tribes, and your elders; and you said, "(...) Go near, and hear all that the Lord our God will say; and speak to us all that the Lord our God will speak to you; and we will listen and obey. And the Lord heard your words, when you spoke to me; and the Lord said to me, 'I have heard the words of this people, which they have spoken to you;

they have rightly said all that they have spoken. Oh that they had such a mind as this always to fear me and to keep all my commandments, that it might go well with them and with their children for ever! (...) You shall be careful to do therefore as the Lord your God has commanded you; you shall not turn aside to the right hand or to the left.» (Deut 5, 22-24; 27-29;32).

It is Moses who transmits God's message to his people. Could it be that no one else is capable of speaking directly to God? It is God who chooses each one of us and endows each of us with the capacity and the necessary gifts for the accomplishment of the mission, which He entrusts to us. The fear to which God refers – *"of such a mind to fear Me"* – is the love, which should lead us not to want to offend Him, in order not to lose his friendship and his grace.

In Moses, we see represented the Head of the Church, commissioned by Jesus Christ with the task of passing on to us the laws and words of God. Therefore, we have to believe in God and in his Church, just as the Israelites believed and said to Moses: *«Go near, and hear all that the Lord our God will say; and speak to us all that the Lord our God will speak to you; and we will listen and obey».* (Deut. 5, 27). This should be our response too: to listen to the Church, and believe what it says – certain that what it tells us is the word of God – and obey. *"We will listen and obey"*

Just as God said to Moses: *«Arise, go on your journey at the head of the people, that they may go in and possess the land, which I swore to their fathers to give them.»* (Deut. 10, 11) so also He says to his Church: *«Go therefore and make disciples of all nations, baptizing them in the name of the Father, and of the Son and of the Holy Spirit,»* (Mt 28,19). Thus, the Church is the Messenger of God to direct his People in the ways which He himself has traced out for them by means of the laws and the doctrine which He has confided to it. And just as the Israelites believed and followed the directions of Moses because he was the messenger of God, so we must follow the guidance of the Church because she is, for us, the messenger of God.

And let us not waver or move away from the Church when we see imperfections in some of her members, because, individually, we are all weak and sinful. But the Church does not cease to be holy for all that: holy in her laws and in the doctrine entrusted to her by God, holy in her Head, Jesus Christ, her divine Founder and Saviour, holy in the divine Spirit which animates and helps her, and in the life of grace generated and nourished by the Sacraments.

In Moses, God found imperfections also; and, as a punishment, He did not grant him the grace of entering the Promised Land with his people. But, in spite of that, he was still the man chosen by God as leader of his people.

Moses doubted when he struck the rock in the desert, as God had commanded, so that water would gush from it. Because of this, the Lord said to him, and to Aaron: «*Because you did not believe in me, to sanctify me in the eyes of the people of Israel, therefore you shall not bring this assembly into the land which I have given them*» (Num 20,12). This passage of Sacred Scripture shows us how God wants us to believe not only in his existence from all eternity, but also in the efficacy of his word. Moses carried out the command that God had given him; he struck the rock as God had ordered him to do, but with a certain lack of faith and confidence. He was afraid that God would not work the promised miracle.

As a punishment, he was not to enter the Promised Land, but only glimpsed it from afar, as the sacred text tells us: «*And Moses went up from the plains of Moab to mount Nebo, to the top of Pisgah, which is opposite Jericho. And the Lord showed him all the land, Gilead as far as Dan, all Naphtali, all the land of Ephraim and Manas-seh, all the land of Judah as far as the western sea, the Negeb, and the Plain, that is, the valley of Jericho and the city of palm trees, as far as Zoar. And the Lord said to him, "This is the land of which I swore to Abraham, to Isaac, and to Jacob, 'I will give it to your descendants'. I have let you see it with your eyes, but you shall not go over there. So Moses the servant of the Lord died there in the land of Moab, according to the word of the Lord, and he buried him in the valley in the land of Moab opposite Beth-peor*» (Dt 34, 1-6).

All this shows how firm our conviction should be and the extent of our faith in God; we have to believe in the immense power of His operative word, in the eternal wisdom of his Being, which is the very source of life, in his laws which trace out the way we should go, in his creative and redemptive work, in what his Word, his Son Jesus, says and in the truths which He taught us, in his Church which is the treasure-house of the truths entrusted to Her by the Eternal Word, in his mercy, in his forgiveness and in his love.

The beginning of the whole spiritual life is belief in God. This faith opens up to us the marvels of infinite Being, leads us to find God in his works, to live the life of God present within us. We ourselves are poor and have nothing; but in God we possess everything and lack for nothing.

The person who believes in God is happy, because he knows he has a Father from whom all things come, yet is above all human paternity. He loves his Father, rests in his arms and lives for this Father who is goodness, mercy, forgiveness and love! One thing only He asks: «*Fidelity in the observance of His laws*» God gave this advice to his people through Moses: «*The Lord said to me (...) 'Go and say to them, "Return to your tents." But you, stand here by me, and I will tell you all the commandments and the statutes and the ordinances which you shall teach them, that they may do them in the land which I give them to possess'. You shall be careful to do therefore as the Lord your God has commanded you; you shall not turn aside to the right hand or to the left. You shall walk in all the way which the Lord your God has commanded you, that it may go well with you*» (Deut 5, 28, 30-33).

The fact that God is invisible does not justify the incredulity of those who do not want to believe in his existence. God created, for the good of humanity, many invisible forces, whose existence nobody doubts. Who, for instance, has seen the wind? We hear it, we feel it when it blows upon us, and we see its effects when it shakes the trees and tosses the seas. The same is true of oxygen, hydrogen, electricity, etc. There are other invisible elements, which are used for the benefit of humanity. Well then! Before all this existed, God, who created it and formed it from nothing, was already present. And it was to these invisible forces that God gave most power: electric energy, different sounds, etc.

God manifests Himself also in the preservation of created beings. We see that the achievements of men are realised by using materials created by God; and, with time and use, these wear out, deteriorate and disappear. How different is the destiny of the works which originate solely from the hand of God! Consider the sun: it has always the same strength, the same degree of heat, the same brilliance, follows always the same course laid out for it by God! The same is true of the moon, the stars, the planets, the earth, the seas and all that exists and was created by God! It all must remain the same because that is what God wishes, since that depends on his omnipotent will. And they are here, before our eyes, indisputable witnesses to the power, the wisdom, the will and the eternal existence of God.

We have no difficulty in believing that such and such famous men lived, because history mentions them. But it also speaks of the existence of God, his deeds, and his works. Why, then, do we not believe? Is sacred history less worthy of belief than profane history? Are the sacred writers less truthful than profane ones? Now, the sacred writers tell us: *In the beginning God created the heavens and the earth.*» (Gen 1, 1)

«*In the beginning was the Word, and the Word was with God, and the Word was God. He was in the beginning with God; all things were made through him, and without him was not anything made that was made*» (Jn 1, 1-3)

«*Worthy art thou, our Lord and God, to receive glory and honour and power, for thou didst create all things, and by thy will they existed and were created*» (Rev 4, 11).

Ave Maria!

24

You shall adore the true God and Him alone

«You shall have no other gods before me. You shall not make for yourself a graven image, or any likeness of anything that is in heaven above, or that is on earth beneath, or that is in the water under the earth; you shall not bow down to them or serve them; for I the Lord your God am a jealous God» (Deut 5, 7-9)

Already, in the second Call of the Message, we spoke of the adoration which we give to God. We will now look at the reasons why God commands us to adore Him only. Does God need our adoration? Certainly not! God is infinitely happy in Himself. He does not need anyone or anything; He already has in Himself all that is good, and all that exists belongs to Him, since He created it. He can freely dispose of everything without any possible opposition. Why, then, does He require us to adore Him only?

The reason for giving us such a command is that He is the one living and true God, eternal and worthy of being adored; He is the only God capable of accepting our adoration and rewarding it.

This commandment is an order inspired by love. God has commanded us to adore Him only, so that we may not turn to adoring false gods – gods which in reality are nothing, of no value, and can do nothing for us.

I call it also the precept of love, since our adoration should be the result of our love of God, and of our gratitude, because He loved us first: He loved us with an everlasting love and it was because of that love that He created us, surrounded us with so many benefits in the order of nature and in the order of grace, and destined us for eternal life where we will share in all his gifts.

The observance of this commandment brings us close to God; through it we will find mercy, forgiveness and grace.

Sacred Scripture tells us that, when Moses went up to Mount Sinai to receive from God the laws that were to govern his people, they, who meanwhile had remained at the foot of the mountain, made a golden calf and began to adore it. Seeing this, God complained to Moses, saying: *«Go down; for your people, whom you brought up out of the land of Egypt, have corrupted* themselves; they have turned aside quickly out of the way which I commanded them; they have made for themselves a molten calf, and have worshipped it and sacrificed to it, and said, 'These are your gods, O Israel, who brought you up out of the land of Egypt!'" (...) And Moses turned, and went down from the mountain with the two tables of the testimony in his hands, tables that were written on both sides; on the one side and on the other were they written. And the tables were the work of God, and the writing was the writing of God graven upon the tables (...) And as soon as he came near the camp and saw the calf and the dancing, Moses' anger burned hot, and he threw the tables out of his hands and broke them at the foot of the mountain. And he took the calf which they had made, and burnt it with fire, and ground it to powder, and scattered it upon the water, and made the people of Israel drink it» (Ex 32, 7-8.19-20)

«On the morrow Moses said to the people, "You have sinned a great sin. And now I will go up to the Lord; perhaps I can make atonement for your sin." So Moses returned to the Lord and said, "Alas, this people have sinned a great sin (...) But now if thou wilt forgive their sin – and if not, blot me, I pray thee, out of thy book which thou hast written." But the Lord said to Moses, "Whoever has sinned against me, him will I blot out of my book. But now go, lead the people to the place of which I have spoken to you» (Ex 32, 30-34)

«Moses said to the Lord, "See, thou sayest to me, 'Bring up this people'; but thou hast not let me know whom thou wilt send with me (...) The Lord said, "My presence will go with you, and I will give you rest." Moses said, "If thy presence will not go with me, do not carry us up from here. (...) I pray thee, show me thy glory." And he said, "I will make all my goodness pass before you, and will proclaim before you my name 'The Lord' and I will be gracious to whom I will be gracious, and will show mercy on whom I will show mercy."» (Ex 33, 12-16;18-19).

«And the Lord descended in the cloud and stood with him there, and proclaimed the name of the Lord. (...) And Moses made haste to bow his head toward the earth, and worshipped. And he said, "If now I have found favour in thy sight, O Lord, let the Lord, I pray thee, go in the midst of us, although it is a stiff-necked people; and pardon our iniquity and our sin, and take us for thy inheritance".» (Ex 34, 5;8-9)

These events show us how Moses, with the love he had for God and his neighbour, with his humble prayer and adoration, obtained pardon for the people, reconciling them with God from whom they had turned away by the sin of idolatry.

By divine choice, we are the successors of this people of God, as Jesus Christ shows us in the parable of the Good Shepherd: «*I am the good shepherd. The good shepherd lays down his life for the sheep (...) And I have other sheep, that are not of this fold; I must bring them also, and they will heed my voice. So there shall be one flock, one shepherd.*» (Jn 10, 11.16)

I have no doubt that these sheep which the divine Saviour came to gather and lead to his sheepfold are all the people who have heard his voice and followed Him. Therefore, I believe we must consider as addressed to us, the words spoken by Moses to the Israelites: «*Behold, to the Lord your God belong heaven of heavens, the earth with all that is in it; yet the Lord set his heart in love upon your fathers and chose their descendants after them, you above all peoples, as at this day. Circumcise therefore the foreskin of your heart, and be no longer stubborn. For the Lord your God is God of gods and Lord of lords, the great, the mighty, and the terrible God, who is not partial and takes no bribe. (...) You shall fear the Lord your God; you shall serve him and cleave to him*» (Dt 10, 14-17;20).

As Moses tells us here, we hold fast to God, Him only we adore, Him only we serve and love, because our adoration is the result of a love which believes, hopes, trusts and loves, giving itself in complete surrender to the loved One, who is God.

"*Lord, I believe, I adore, I hope and I love You*".

Ave-Maria!

25

You shall not take the name of the Lord, your God, in vain.

«*You shall not take the name of the Lord your God in vain: for the Lord will not hold him guiltless who takes his name in vain.*» (Deut 5, 11).

This commandment obliges us to live in the truth with God, with our neighbour and with ourselves. God abhors lies, because God is truth. In the Gospel of St. John we read: «*And the Word became flesh and dwelt among us, full of grace and truth; we have beheld his glory, glory as of the only Son from the Father.*» (Jn 1,14). And in another place in the same Gospel, Jesus Christ says of Himself: «*I am the way, and the truth, and the life; no one comes to the Father, but by me.*» (Jn 14, 6). If, as Jesus says, we cannot go to the Father except by Him, and He is the Truth, this shows that we cannot go to God except by the way of truth.

We cannot deceive God, because He sees right into everything, just like the crystalline water which flows out of the clearest spring. God always has before Him our works, our intentions, and our desires.

We speak the truth to God when we are faithful to our promises, our vows, and our oaths. In Sacred Scripture we read: «*When you make a vow to the Lord your God, you shall not be slack to pay it; for the Lord your God will surely require it of you, and it would be sin in you. But if you refrain from vowing, it shall be no sin in you. You shall be careful to perform what has passed your lips, for you have voluntarily vowed to the Lord your God what you have promised with your mouth.*» (Deut 23, 21-23) .

However, when we do not keep our promises, we lie to God. Our vows, our oaths and our promises have invoked God in vain. Besides, as the sacred text says, nobody obliged us to promise; we made this offering to God of our own free will. Hence, once it is made, we are obliged to keep it.

In the same way, we cannot deceive our neighbour, and still less call on God to witness our false, deceitful and guileful statements. God takes as done to Himself the good or evil done to our neighbour. Jesus Christ teaches us this in the Gospel: «*Truly I say to you, as you did it to one of the least of these my brethren, you did it to me*» (Mt 25,40). And God takes it into account in order to punish or reward. That is what we see in the scene of the Last Judgement: «*When the Son of man comes in his glory, and all the angels with him, then he will sit on his glorious throne. Before him will be gathered all the nations, and he will separate them one from another as a shepherd separates the sheep from the goats, and he will place the sheep at his right hand, but the goats at the left. Then the King will say to those at his right hand, 'Come, O blessed of my Father, inherit the kingdom prepared for you from the foundation of the world; for I was hungry and you gave me food, I was thirsty and you gave me drink, I was a stranger and you welcomed me, I was naked and you clothed me, I was sick and you came to me.' Then the righteous will answer him, 'Lord, when did we see thee hungry and feed thee, or thirsty and give thee drink? And when did we see thee a stranger and welcome thee, or naked and clothe thee? And when did we see thee sick or in prison and visit thee? And the King will answer them, 'Truly I say to you, as you did it to one of the least of my brethren, you did it to me.' Then he will say to those at his left hand. 'Depart from me, you cursed, into the eternal fire prepared for the devil and his angels; for I was hungry and you gave me no food, I was thirsty and you gave me no drink, I was a stranger and you did not welcome me, naked and you did not clothe me, sick and in prison and you did not visit me.' Then they also will answer, 'Lord, when did we see thee hungry or thirsty or a stranger or naked or sick or in prison, and did not minister to thee?' Then he will answer them, 'Truly, I say to you, as you did it not to one of the least of these, you did it not to me.' And they will go away into eternal punishment, but the righteous into eternal life.*» (Mt 25, 31-46).

Here, God reveals Himself as a father who considers as done to himself whatever good or evil is done to his children. If God speaks to us like this about the good which we have neglected to do to others, what will He say to us about the evil we have caused them? What will He say to us if, through craft, trickery or cunning, we have deceived our neighbour? And we do this whenever we take advantage of someone's ingenuousness or the confidence that he or she had in us, and then we excuse ourselves, saying: "If they hadn't been so stupid, if they hadn't let themselves be deceived!" But, what will God's answer be to all lies of this kind, of which, unfortunately, the world is full?

Any deceit, any hypocrisy, any pretence is a lie. Its gravity is measured by the degree of harm done to the glory of God or the good of others. We see, in the Gospel, how God condemns this sin. «*Woe to you, scribes and Pharisees, hypocrites! for you tithe mint and dill and cummin, and have ne-*

glected the weightier matters of the law, justice and mercy and faith; these you ought to have done, without neglecting the others.(...) Fill up, then, the measure of your fathers. You serpents, you brood of vipers, how are you to escape being sentenced to hell?» (Mt 23: 23, 32-33).

Jesus rebuked the doctors of the law, saying:«Woe to you lawyers also! for you load men with burdens hard to bear, and you yourselves do not touch the burdens with one of your fingers» (Lk 11,46). And He was to conclude this discourse with the following recommendation to his disciples: «Beware of the leaven of the Pharisees, which is hypocrisy. Nothing is covered up that will not be revealed, or hidden that will not be known. (...) Do not fear those who kill the body, and after that have no more that they can do. But I will warn you whom to fear: fear him who, after he has killed, has power to cast into hell; yes, I tell you, fear him!» (Lk 12, 1-5).

This language on the part of Jesus Christ may strike us as harsh, but its severity is directed against such behaviour on our part towards others. For his part, God is simply the Father defending His children and the Judge who, to an equal degree, rewards good and punishes evil.

If we look at the world, considering how people lived in the time of Jesus and, unfortunately, how they live today, the picture we see is frightening! And yet, it is reality, in so far as it refers to the word of God and what it tells us about human life. Taking advantage of other people's ignorance, their weakness, their need, their confidence, all this is lying, a sin against justice, against the law of charity and against the truth. Thinking about these abuses the Lord says: «Beware of false prophets, who come to you in sheep's clothing but inwardly are ravenous wolves. (...) Every tree that does not bear good fruit is cut down and thrown into the fire» (Mt 7,15.19).

Often we lie to ourselves, and thus deceive ourselves. Carried away by blind passion, we promise ourselves happiness where it is not to be found.

God created us free, able to think, desire and decide. We are beings who think and know, as far as the power of understanding in our own intelligence allows us. It is in virtue of our own power of thought and our own intelligence that we are responsible for everything we do of our own free will.

We deceive ourselves when we exchange good for evil, following what is attractive to our evil inclinations, without thinking of the grave consequences which ensue. Jesus Christ, speaking to the Jews, said: «Truly, truly, I say to you, every one who commits sin is a slave to sin. (...) You are of your *father the devil, and your will is to do your father's desires. He was a murderer from the beginning, and has nothing to do with the truth, because there is no truth in him. When he lies he speaks according to his own nature, for he is a liar and the father of lies»* (Jn 8, 34.44). The devil, prompted by pride, caused his own downfall and that of those he dragged after him; he deceived himself and deceived those who followed him. Wanting to raise himself above God, he fell into the depths of the abyss; wanting to climb higher, he sank even lower!

The same thing happens to us, if we let ourselves be carried away by the temptations of the devil, the world and the flesh. This is how the sacred text describes one of the temptations prepared by the devil for Jesus Christ: *«Then the devil took him to the holy city, and set him on the primacy of the temple, and said to him, "If you are the Son of God, thrown yourself down; for it is written, 'He will give his angels charge of you,' and 'On their hands they will bear you up, lest you strike your foot against a stone". Jesus said to him, "Again it is written, 'You shall not tempt the Lord your God.'»* (Mt 4, 5-7). It is the temptation to pride, which often seduces us, and we do not know how to resist it as Christ did. Throw yourself down, you will come to no harm! The Angels will come and bear you up on their hands; you will not be injured by the stones on which you fall. And you will be a spectacle to the world which will stand and admire you.

The temptation to pride is a lie! Throw yourself over the precipice of vice, no harm will come to you! Go down! Why do we not rather set ourselves to climb upwards instead of descending? Mount, climb higher! Be pure, chaste, just, be faithful to God and to your neighbour, be restrained in your conduct. Go higher and God will embrace you in his fatherly arms. Why does temptation not urge us to go upwards instead of going down? Because to go up is truth, and to go down is falsehood; and, like the devil, vice, passion and the world are false, they cannot give us true advice. Thus, very often, we allow ourselves to be deceived, and it is only when we find ourselves lost that we realise the fact.

In order to overcome the temptations which surround us, we have to struggle against falsehood because that is what all temptations are. In the Book of Revelation, St. John describes the struggle between the good Angels who remained faithful to God and the bad Angels who rebelled: *«Now war arose in heaven, Michael and his angels fighting against the dragon; and the dragon and his angels fought, but they were defeated and there was no longer any place for them in heaven. And the great dragon was thrown down, that ancient serpent, who is called the Devil and Satan, the deceiver of the whole world – he was thrown down to the earth, and his angels were thrown down with him»* (Rev 12, 7-9). See what Sacred Scripture calls the devil: the deceiver of the whole world. Temptation is always seductive, whether it comes from ourselves, from the world or from the devil; it is always deceitful: it promises us what it cannot give.

True happiness is found only in God: the further we draw away from God, the more we sink down, and the more unhappy we become; the nearer we draw towards God, the happier we are and the greater we become as persons, because only in God are truth, justice, true love and greatness to be found. Therefore, God forbids us to take his name in vain.

Ave Maria!

26

Remember to keep holy the sabbath day

«Six days you shall labour, and do all your work; but the seventh day is a sabbath to the Lord your God; in it you shall not do any work, you, or your son, or your daughter, your manservants, or your maidservant, or your cattle, or the sojourner who is whithin your gates; for in six days the Lord made heaven and earth, the sea, and all that is in them, and rested the seventh day» (Ex 20, 9-11).

The sacred text tells us that God prescribed rest on the seventh day of the week so that it would be a holy day, consecrated to the Lord in memory of, and in thanksgiving for, the week of creation. We know that, in the Old Testament, the day of the week reserved for rest and consecrated to the Lord was Saturday. The Church, authorised by God – *«I will give you the keys of the kingdom of heaven, and whatever you bind on earth shall be bound in heaven, and whatever your loose on earth shall be loosed in heaven.»* (Mt 16, 19) – substituted Sunday for Saturday, in order to commemorate, along with the work of creation, the work of redemption brought about by Christ, our Saviour, who rose from the dead on a Sunday.

Now that we understand this much, let us fix our attention on the words which God uses when laying down this commandment: *«Six days you may labour (...) But the seventh day is the Sabbath of the Lord, your God»* (Ex 20, 9). Thus, Sunday is not only a day of physical rest, with abstention from servile work, but it is also, and above all, a day to be «consecrated to the Lord», a day of prayer in which we encounter God, to thank Him for all his benefits to us, to sing his praises, to remember his infinite gifts in which He has made us sharers, and to ask his help in all our needs.

In order to fulfil all these duties to God, the Church has commanded us to hear an entire Mass on Sundays and Holy Days. And we must not limit ourselves to simply being present at Mass; we must take part in it. Indeed, it is not only the priest who celebrates Mass: he presides, and consecrates, in the name of Christ, but all the faithful gathered around the altar, live and celebrate the one Sacrifice of Christ. Hence, we must be prepared, so that, giving the responses, praying with the priest, we may, with the priest, draw near to the altar to receive Holy Communion, the Body of Jesus Christ.

I say that it is important to be prepared, because, in order to receive the Body of Christ, it is necessary that our conscience does not accuse us of grave sin. If we are in a state of grave sin, we must first receive absolution in the Sacrament of Penance, or Confession, before receiving Holy Communion.

The celebration of the Eucharist is not a mere ceremony at which we are present; it is a real event in which we meet the living God, in the person of his Son, the renewal of whose passion, death and resurrection we celebrate, and we receive his Body and Blood, as He Himself has told us: «*This is my body which is given for you. Do this in remembrance of me*» (Lk 22, 19) and «*I am with you always, to the close of the age*» (Mt 28, 20).

In reference to the consecrated bread and wine, the Lord says to us,: "*This is My Body*". Hence, if the Lord says that "*this is*", then it is, and does not cease to be, because the word of God effects what it signifies. By virtue of this word, under the species of the consecrated bread and wine, the Body and Blood of Jesus Christ are present, for as long as the species remain. By virtue of the word of God, the phenomenon of transubstantiation has taken place. Here our faith must be firm, because it is nourished and enlightened by the word of God, which, for us, is life and light. We are not walking in darkness, we know where we are going, we follow the road which God has marked out for us, we follow Him who said: «*I am the way, the truth and the life*» (Jn 14,6). We follow Jesus Christ, the Word of God, the Word of the Father.

In this way, if our observance of Sunday is limited to merely abstaining from work, we cannot say, with an easy conscience, that we are keeping God's commandment since we have respected the part of it that refers to rest, but failed to observe the part that bids us consecrate the day to the Lord. God did not make us just material beings, there is also a part of us which is spiritual, which makes us like God: we can think, know, choose freely and decide; we are the result of God's thought, created by his Will. Therefore, our physical and corporal rest has to be accompanied, and sanctified, by the spiritual element in us.

Still less will this commandment be observed by those who use this day only for distractions, pastimes and amusements, especially such as are sinful. In that case, the day, which should be consecrated to the Lord, becomes a day of sin which offends God and corrupts souls. In this respect, Sacred Scripture tells us «*Everyone who profanes it shall be put to death; whoever does any work on it, that soul shall be cut off from among his people. Six days shall work be done, but the seventh day is a sabbath of solemn rest, holy to the Lord*» (Ex 31, 14-15) .

As we see, the text insists on this day of rest being consecrated to the Lord. And this consecration demands that at least part of the day should be spent in an encounter with God: an encounter where we communicate directly and consciously with the Lord, by means of prayer, individually and with others, assisting at Mass, hearing the word of God which, by the ministry of priests, is addressed to us in the general assembly of the faithful. It was to them that the Lord confided the mission of preaching his word to us and guiding us in the way of salvation.

If we should happen to see some priests who seem to have lost their way and have gone astray, let us not be surprised! They, too, are human, subject to frailty like ourselves. In the course of time, we meet many who have lost their way and been unfaithful to God and to the mission entrusted to them by the Lord. This is a fact about which God Himself complains and which He deplores thus: «*And now, O priests, this command is for you. If you will not listen, if you will not lay it to heart to give glory to my name, says the Lord of hosts, then I will send the curse upon you and I will curse your blessings; indeed I have already cursed them, because you do not lay it to heart. Behold, I will rebuke your offspring, and spread dung upon your faces, the dung of your offerings, and I will put you out of my presence. So shall you know that I have sent this command to you, that my covenant with Levi may hold, says the Lord of the hosts. My covenant with him was a covenant of life and peace, and I gave them to him, that he might fear; and he feared me, he stood in awe of my name. True instruction was in his mouth, and no wrong was found on his lips. He walked with me in peace and uprightness, and he turned many from iniquity. For the lips of a priest should guard knowledge, and men should seek instruction from his mouth, for he is the messenger of the Lord of hosts*» (Ml 2, 1-7).

God shows us here the figure of a priest who was unfaithful, and that of another who was faithful to the Lord and the mission entrusted to him. The fact that some priests fall away, must not mean that our respect, our esteem and our veneration for those who persevere should be any less: rather, the weakness of some should heighten the merit of the rest. Therefore, we should always listen with faith to the priest, because he is a light for our path, a guide for our life and a source of strength for our weakness.

Christ is the true and eternal Priest of the New Covenant, and all of us, who remain united to Him, share in his priesthood; each of us in the sphere where we have been placed by God. All of us, united in the same faith, the same hope and the same charity; together constitute the People of God, described by Sacred Scripture as a *priestly* people. St. Peter, in his first Letter, says to us: «*But you are a chosen race, a royal priesthood, a holy nation, God's own people, that you may declare the wonderful deeds of him who called you out of darkness into the marvellous light. Once you were no people but now you are God's people; once you had not received mercy but now you have received mercy.*» (1 Peter 3, 9-10). «*And like living stones be yourselves built into a spiritual house, to be a holy priesthood, to offer spiritual sacrifices acceptable to God through Jesus Christ*» (1 P 2, 5). It was in Baptism that we received this priestly dignity, in virtue of which we can *offer spiritual sacrifices*: all the good works of a Christian, making known the wonders of God, all the prayers of supplication and thanksgiving offered by ourselves and our neighbours, the witness of a holy life, self-sacrifice and the gift of ourselves in the service of others.

We must realise that we have been made sharers in the priesthood of Christ in order to co-operate in his work of Redemption. The realisation of this will help us to observe worthily the precept concerning Sunday as a day consecrated to the Lord: the day must be used also for our own evangelisation, by the study of the laws and truths of God, so that, in our daily lives, we may know how they apply in each case, how to live them ourselves and transmit them to those around us, above all to those entrusted by Heaven to our responsibility.

If, on the contrary, we spend our Sunday solely in physical rest and distractions, can we say that we are fulfilling our priestly mission in respect of those whom the Lord has confided to our care? Will we not have failed to give the good example which we should give to those who see us? We must not forget that the apostolate of good example is superior to that of the word, unless this latter is translated coherently into action in our practical life. The Portuguese have a saying, which is very true: *"Words move us, but example induces us"*. In other words, our lives must be in harmony with our words.

All of us, to a greater or lesser extent, in whatever situation we are placed, have a responsibility for the good of others, and the salvation of their souls. By our attitude towards them, by our words, our actions, and the prayers we should say for them, either in private or in public, with them and for them, we have to help one another to keep on the right road; the road of faith in Christ, the road of hope and love which unites us all in Christ, Head and Leader of his People, the Church. If we do not do this, how in fact do we consecrate our Sunday to the Lord?

In his Gospel, St John tells us that, when many of those who had followed Christ heard Him proclaiming the mystery of the Eucharist, they refused to believe, were scandalised and left the Lord. Then Jesus, seeing this, said to them: «*Do you take offence at this? Then what if you were to see the Son of man ascending where he was before? It is the spirit that gives life, the flesh is of no avail; the words that I have spoken to you are spirit and life. But there are some of you that do not believe.*" For Jesus knew from the first who those were that did not believe, and who it was that should betray him. And he said, "This is why I told you that no one can come to me unless it is granted him by the Father." After this many of his disciples drew back and no longer went about with him. Jesus said to the twelve, "Will you also go away?" Simon Peter answered him, "Lord, to whom shall we go? You have the words of eternal life; and we have believed, and have come to know, that you are the Holy One of God." Jesus answered them, "Did I not choose you, the twelve, and one of you is a devil?" He spoke of Judas the son of Simon Iscariot, for he, one of the twelve, was to betray him.*» (Jn 6, 61-71).

This Gospel passage shows us how, from the very beginning, in God's Church there were those who did not believe, were unfaithful or deserted altogether. They left God to succumb to temptations to pride, avarice, sins of the flesh, the devil and the world. They take no notice of what the Lord said; "*It is the spirit that gives life, while the flesh is of no avail*". Of what use is the flesh when the spirit leaves it? Let us go into a cemetery and look at the graves: they will give us the answer!

But this answer is still incomplete. A day will come when these bodies, by then reduced to ashes, must rise to eternal life and, united once more to the souls which animated them in life, will go to share in the same destiny ordained for the souls after death, merited by each one according to his or her works. This is why Jesus Christ tells us that the flesh is of no use because it is the spirit which gives life. And the words that He spoke are indeed *"spirit and life"*, at any rate for those who believe and follow them. St. Peter answered: *"To whom shall we go, Lord, You have the words of eternal life?"*

Like the Apostle, we must believe in Christ and remain united to Him, in the person of the Successor of St. Peter, the Pope and Bishop of Rome, and say, with him: *"We have come to believe and are convinced that You are the Holy One of God, the Christ, the Son of the living God, who came into the world to save us; and that You only have the words of eternal life".* (Jn 6:69). And when we see that others are falling away, we should stand all the more firmly in our faith, united to Christ, in the person of his representative, the Pope, the one true Head of the one true Church of God, founded by Jesus Christ. He is still present and will be with us until the end of time: «*I am with you always, to the close of the age*» (Mt 28, 20).

This is the door of salvation which God has opened for us, and the way by which we will go to Him: Christ and his Church. We are members of Christ's Church, we are part of the Assembly of Christ and we live united to Christ, so that we may be saved by Christ. And Sunday is the day appointed by God for all the members of the Mystical Body of Christ who form His Church to gather together in assembly.

Ave Maria!

27

Honour your father and your mother

«*Honour your father and your mother, as the Lord your God commanded you*» (Deut 5:16)

In his letter to the Ephesians, St Paul reminds his disciples of this commandment, given by God for all human beings: «*Children, obey your parents in the Lord, for this is right. "Honour your father and mother" (this is the first commandment with a promise), "that it may be well with you and that you may live long on earth."*» (Eph 6, 1-3). We must observe this law, which requires us to honour our father and mother, not only in order to be happy on earth, but above all to avoid eternal punishment, since to fail to observe this commandment is to sin against justice and charity, and thus to fall into grave sin, which can result in eternal damnation. «*Whoever curses his father or his mother shall be put to death.*» (Ex 21, 17).

The severity with which God enjoins on us the observance of this commandment shows us the gravity of any infringement of it. In a liturgical celebration of the Law of God – for which Moses convoked the whole people of God who took part in it by declaring their individual acceptance of each statement of the Levites – the maledictions which the latter had to proclaim against those who transgressed the divine laws, included the following: «*'Cursed be he who dishonours his father and his mother'. And all the people shall say, 'Amen.'*» (Deut 27, 16). And the Book of Sirach reminds us of this commandment, stressing the debt of gratitude we owe to our parents: «*With all your heart honour your father, and do not forget the birth pangs of your mother. Remember that through your parents your were born; and what can you give back to them that equals their gift to you?*» (Sir 7, 27-28).

And Jesus Christ, confirming this commandment and emphasising how very pleasing faithful observance of it is to God, who has no patience with any of the many pretexts we invent for evading it, censures the Pharisees in these terms: «*'Honour your father and your mother,' and, 'He who speaks evil of father or mother, let him surely die.' But you say, 'If any one tells his father or his mother, 'What you would have gained from me is given to God, he need not honour his father.' So, for the sake of your tradition, you have made void the word of God. You hypocites! Well did Isaiah prophesy of you,* when he said: 'This people honours me with their lips, but their heart is far from me; in vain do they worship me, teaching as doctrines the precepts of men.'» (Mt 15, 8-9).

Here is this commandment of God, as spelt out in a memorable page by the author of the Book of Sirach: «Listen to me your father, O children; and act accordingly, that you may be kept in safety.

For the Lord honoured the father above the children, and he confirmed the right of the mother over her sons.

Whoever honours his father atones for his sins, and whoever glorifies his mother is like one who lays up treasure.

Whoever honours his father will be gladdened by his own children, and when he prays he will be heard.

Whoever glorifies his father will have long life, and whoever obeys the Lord will refresh his mother; he will serve his parents as his masters.

Honour your father by word and deed, that a blessing from him may come upon you. For a father's blessing strengthens the houses of children, but a mother's curse uproots their foundations.

Do not glorify yourself by dishonouring your father, for your father's dishonour is no glory to you.

For a man's glory comes from honouring his father, and it is a disgrace for children not to respect their mother.

O son, help your father in his old age, and do not grieve him as long as he lives; even if he is lacking in understanding, show forbearance; in all your strength do not despise him.

For kindness to a father will not be forgotten, and against your sins it will be credited to you; in the day of your affliction it will be remembered in your favour; as frost in fair weather, your sins will melt away.

Whoever forsakes his father is like a blasphemer, and whoever angers his mother is cursed by the Lord.» (Sir 3,1-16).

All these sayings are the voice of God, which tell us how we should behave towards our parents.

But the observance of this commandment goes further than this, and extends to all God-given authority. Thus, St. Paul, having said that children should obey and respect their parents, exhorts subjects to obey their superiors:

«Children, obey your parents in everything, for this pleases the Lord. (...) Slaves, obey in everything those who are your earthly masters, not with eye *service, as men-pleasers, but in singleness of heart, fearing the Lord. Whatever your task, work heartily, as serving the Lord and not men, knowing that from the Lord you will receive the inheritance as your reward; you are serving the Lord Christ.* (Col 3, 20-24). These words are a call to faith inviting us to serve our superiors, seeing God in them and hoping that He will reward us with his inheritance.

So, we must look upon our superiors as parents, loving them, serving them, honouring them as sent by God to us so that, as servants of God – because their mission to us is a service – they may help us, guide our steps and lead us on the right road through life.

And let us remember that we are all of us sent by God, each of us in our own particular place: children are sent by God to their parents, to be brought up, educated and started off on the road of life; teachers are sent by God to instruct their pupils; pupils are sent by God to their teachers to be taught the arts, the natural and supernatural sciences. In this way, everything is service, whether in the case of parents, teachers, children, pupils or employees. It is all service in the Lord's name.

Contractors and employers serve their employees, giving them work, paying their salaries, providing them with a steady and honourable livelihood. In this way, we are all servants of God, serving Him in the person of our neighbours.

This doctrine is confirmed by the words of Jesus Christ: «*Truly, truly, I say to you, he who receives any one whom I send receives me; and he who receives me receives him who sent me.*» (Jn 13, 20). And, speaking to his disciples after the mother of the sons of Zebedee had asked Him to allow them to occupy the seats of honour in the kingdom of Heaven, the Lord said to them: «*You know that the rulers of the Gentiles lord it over them, and their great men exercise authority over them. It shall not be so among you; but whoever would be great among you must be your servant, and whoever would be first among you should be your slave; even as the Son of man came not to be served but to serve, and to give his life as a ransom for many.*» (Mt 20, 25-28).

Moreover, since we are Christians, followers of Christ, we must all become servants of our brothers and sisters; we must serve them with love, with respect for the personality and dignity of our neighbour, because the dignity of each one does not come from the place he or she occupies but rather from each person's right to that respect. In one case, it is a father's right, in another a son's; in one it is the right of a teacher, in another that of a pupil.

It is true that some people are in charge and give orders, and others have to carry them out; but we are all of us beings created by God, in his image and likeness, destined for eternal life when we shall share in the life of God. Therefore, God created us intelligent beings who can think and know, capable of discovering God. He made us living beings, able to discern good and evil and decide for one or the other and, on the basis of this choice, merit either eternal reward or eternal punishment.

We have all come from the mind of God. And, thanks solely to the divine goodness, our intelligence is capable of reaching this creative thought, in the measure in which God wills to transmit it. Hence, we must use this intelligence to know God, the marvels of his creative work which are the object of human science, and the divine mysteries which He has revealed to us. Above all, by availing of all this knowledge which God has conveyed to us in so many ways and, last of all, by means of his own Son, we must seek to love Him and serve Him in the person of our brothers and sisters, who, like us and with us, are children of the same Father in Heaven.

It was under this aspect of service that Jesus Christ founded his Church: to bring the founts of salvation to the whole human race! All the members of the Church must consider themselves as servants of God, working in the interest of this saving plan, like Christ who came «*to serve, and to give his life as a ransom for many*» (Mt 20.28); for the benefit of the members of his Mystical Body, He set up the holy Hierarchy, to whom He entrusted the mission which He had received from his Father: «*As the Father has sent me, even so I send you.*» (Jn 20, 21)

This is why the Pope, the true and universal representative of Christ, Leader and visible Head of His Church, signs himself: "*Servant of the Servants of God*".

In this way, the commandment which orders us *to honour our father and mother* embraces all authority, which, as in the case of our parents, represents God for us and was established by Him.

Thus, the Church was instituted by Christ, to serve God and the People of God. We should, therefore, respect it, love it and follow everything that it teaches. Just as, in the Old Testament, God sent his prophets to instruct and guide the Chosen People in the way of his commandments, so also Jesus Christ has given us the Church to continue by means of it, the work of our redemption. Hence, we must love this Church of which we are members, serve it and respect it as the spiritual Mother given us by God for the glory of his name and Mother also of the Mystical Body of Jesus Christ, his Son and our Saviour.

Ave Maria!

28

You shall not kill

«*You shall not kill*» (Deut 5 : 17)

With this commandment, God forbids any attempt against human life. To decide when a life is to end is a right which God has reserved for Himself alone. Therefore, it is not lawful for us to destroy human life, even if it is only in embryo.

This prohibition against murder, which God has laid on humanity, is placed before us in various parts of Sacred Scripture: The story of Cain and Abel, sons of Adam and Eve, is a clear example:

«*Abel was a keeper of sheep, and Cain a tiller of the ground. In the due course of time Cain brought to the Lord an offering of the fruit of the ground, and Abel brought of the firstlings of his flock and of their fat portions. And the Lord had regard for Abel and his offerings, but for Cain and his offering he had no regard. So Cain was very angry, and his countenance fell. The Lord said to Cain, "Why are you angry, and why has your countenance fallen? If you do well, will you not be accepted? And if you do not do well, sin is couching at the door; its desire is for you, but you must master it."*

Cain said to Abel his brother, "Let us go out to the field." And when they were in the field, Cain rose up against his brother Abel, and killed him.

Then the Lord said to Cain, "Where is Abel your brother?" He said, "I do not know; am I my brother's keeper?" And the Lord said, "What have you done? The voice of your brother's blood is crying to me from the ground. (...) you shall be a fugitive and a wanderer on the earth." Cain said to the Lord, "My punishment is greater than I can bear. Behold, thou hast driven me this day away from the ground; and from thy face I shall be hidden; and I shall be a fugitive and a wanderer on the earth, and whoever finds me will slay me."

Then the Lord said to him, "Not so! If any one slays Cain, vengeance shall be taken on him sevenfold." And the Lord put a mark on Cain, lest any who came upon him should kill him. Then Cain went away from the presence of the Lord, and dwelt in the land of Nod, east of Eden.» (Gen 4, 2-16).

This passage in Sacred Scripture gives us some marvellous teaching about this commandment of God: "*You shall not kill*". The first thought that occurs to me is this: in spite of the fact that Cain was his brother's assassin, the Lord did not allow anyone to kill Cain himself. The right to send death to anyone when He so wills it is one that God reserves to Himself. God acts in this way so as to allow time for repentance and penance.

If, instead of becoming embittered because of his punishment and fearing to be killed himself, Cain had acknowledged his sin and humbly asked the Lord's forgiveness, he would certainly have been pardoned. But, instead of this act of humility and confidence in the goodness of God, he flew into a passion.

Possibly, Cain was afraid that somebody, knowing what he had done to his brother, would want to avenge Abel's death by doing the same to him. But God also forbids murder as a form of revenge, so He took steps to ensure that the crime was not repeated and further sin committed. With this commandment, God forbids the sin of vengeance, because this is an act of rebellion, provoked by excessive pride. We cannot, therefore, take revenge on our neighbour, nor should we punish offenders in a spirit of vengeance.

In cases where those in authority find themselves obliged to punish crime in order to maintain order, the punishment must always be accompanied by a spirit of charity with regard both to the common good and towards the guilty person, so that he may acknowledge his crime, repent of it and be ready to amend his life.

Normally, we do not take into account certain kinds of slow death inflicted on people and, yet, these, too, are weighed in God's balance. The injustice which one or other of our neighbours is often made to suffer; the calumny by which they are robbed of their good name, their personal dignity and the respect which is their due; the abuse by which they are deprived of their rights; and many other things of this kind, on account of which our neighbour suffers a kind of martyrdom and which bring about a slow death.

When Jesus Christ was arrested in the Garden of Gethsemane, St. Peter, wanting to defend his Master, took a sword and attacked one of the soldiers, cutting off his ear. But the Lord healed the wound and said to Peter: «*Put your sword back into its place; for all who take the sword will perish by the sword.*» (Mt 26, 52). This means that every crime has a punishment and is forbidden and rejected by God. Not even in defence of Himself did the Lord allow St. Peter to use a sword. That does not mean that, in case of attack, we cannot defend ourselves, but it does mean that we cannot attack our neighbour unjustly and can do so only if forced by the need of self-defence.

Returning to the case of Cain and Abel, we find there an admonition combined with an order given to Cain by God, one which we cannot pass over without serious reflection:« *Why are you angry, and why has your countenance fallen? If you do well, will you not be accepted? And if you do not do well, sin is couching at the door; its desire is for you, but you must overcorme it.*» (Gen 4, 6-7). We should all identify which temptation it is that assails us most frequently, and tries to drag us on to the wrong path; in other words, which is the sin that, as God said to Cain, has most appeal for us. We must overcome it, as God asked: "You must overcome it". In fact, every sin brings with it a sentence of eternal death because it is a transgression of God's Law: «*But the tree of knowledge of good and evil you shall not eat, for in the day that you eat of it you shall die.*» (Gen 2,17). We could read this phrase as follows: if you transgress my commands, you will incur the penalty of death, or of eternal damnation. Every sin falls within the scope of this sentence, because all sin is a transgression of God's law, bringing with it eternal death and, very often, temporal death also; consequently, it is never lawful for us to sacrifice either our neighbour's life, or our own. This commandment is absolute: "*You shall not kill*".

Jesus Christ, in the Sermon on the Mount, confirms this divine commandment, saying: «*You have heard that it was said to the men of old, 'You shall not kill; and whoever kills shall be liable to judgment.' But I say to you that every one who is angry with his brother shall be liable to judgment; whoever insults his brother shall be liable to the council, and whoever says, 'You fool!' shall be liable to the hell of fire.*» Mt 5 : 21-22).

The Lord said: "*He will be liable to judgement*". In fact, anyone who commits this crime can still be saved, if he is willing to repent, ask pardon and undertake some penance, making reparation as far as possible for the harm caused to his neighbours.

Ave-Maria!

29

You shall not commit adultery

«*You shall not commit adultery*» (Deut 5:18)

In these days when society seems to want to make a law of this sin, Sacred Scripture continues to repeat the commandment of God: "*You shall not commit adultery*". It is the word of God, and the word of God does not change, nor does his Law: «*It is easier for heaven and earth to pass away, than for one dot of the law to become void*» (Lk 16, 17).

This commandment obliges us all, each one according to his or her state of life, to preserve chastity. Those who feel they are called to the state of matrimony are obliged to preserve chastity until the time comes to contract a definite union blessed by God in the sacrament of Matrimony; they must treat each other with respect as in the case of a tree whose fruit is still green and which must mature so that its fruit may be gathered at the proper time.

Once they have received the sacrament of Matrimony, the union between the couple is definitive and cannot be shared with others: it is indissoluble while the partners live. It was thus that God instituted the marriage union, and nobody has the right to modify or transgress what God has ordained. We know about this institution from Sacred Scripture when it describes the creation of the human race: «*So God created man in his own image, in the image of God he created him; male and female he created them. And God blessed them, and God said to them, "Be fruitful and multiply, and fill the earth and subdue it.*» (Gen 1, 27-28).

Let us look for a moment at the way in which God established the marriage bond. He created man and woman, next He blessed them and only after blessing them did He allow them a definitive union, expressed thus by its fruits, that is, the growth of the human race. This blessing of God, which must precede the union of the spouses, has today, for those who are baptised, a concrete form: the sacrament of Matrimony. Only after the couple have received this Sacrament can the union be considered lawful and sanctioned.

God instituted this union, formed of two people only, and not to be shared by any other person while the couple are alive. This is the order given by the Lord from the beginning: «*Therefore a man leaves his father and his mother and cleaves to his wife, and they become one flesh.*» (Gen 2, 24). "*The two become one flesh*": the two and no more!

These two, blessed by God and now one body, remind us of the tree of life planted by the Creator in the earthly paradise so that, when cultivated, it might yield fruit in due time. If we look for fruit on a tree outside its proper time, we will not find it. And, if we pluck the fruit before it is ripe, it will be green, tasteless and harmful to our health if we eat it; if, on the other hand, we pluck the fruit when it is ripe, in the season appointed by God, then the fruit is delicious, a source of life and happiness. New flowers will blossom on the tree, new spring-times will smile in our homes and new lives will intone songs to their Creator.

This is the principal reason why God instituted the marriage bond, and all who choose this way of life must assume this obligation. By means of this union, God has willed to associate humanity with his creative work; He has given it, we may say, a position of honour; but, in this position, along with the honour, there are laws imposed by God which must be observed faithfully. Each family, like a tree, has a single trunk, and from that trunk grow many branches, that is, children: growing from the tree, they will cover it with fruit.

It is necessary; then, that this tree, which is the family, should give God all the fruit He wants from it. It is not lawful to destroy buds which are the germs of new life, because this means destroying and refusing to use the fruit of the tree and rendering it barren, thus incurring the same condemnation which Jesus Christ uttered in the case of the barren fig-tree. One day, early in the morning, Jesus was on his way to the city of Jerusalem and; «*"May no fruit ever come from you again!" And the fig tree withered at once.*» (Mt 21,19).

Now, who would want a fig tree covered with fresh, green foliage, but never yielding fruit in his field? Its wood is of no use for building; it is taking up space on the land to no purpose. It is fit only to be cut down and thrown into the fire, because it has not fulfilled the mission entrusted to it by God, which is to yield fruit in due time. God has laid down the appropriate time for everything; a time for sowing, a time for planting, a time for weeding, a time for harvesting; and the whole of creation which has been given us to contemplate, follows the laws which God has prescribed for it; all creation except human beings!

One day, the Pharisees wanted to know Jesus' opinion about all this and «asked, *"Is it lawful for a man to divorce his wife?"* He answered them, *"What did Moses command you?"* They said, *"Moses allowed a man to write a certificate of divorce, and to put her away."* But Jesus said to them, *"For your hardness of heart he wrote you this commandment. But from the beginning of creation, 'God made them male and female'. 'For this reason a man shall leave his father and mother and be joined to his wife, and the two shall become one. So they are no longer two but one. What therefore God has joined together, let not man put asunder."»* (Mk10, 2-9). We have here a confirmation of the law imposed by God from the beginning: the two are one flesh; they are the trunk of the tree of life which cannot be divided. And if, on account of the hardness of the human heart, the two are forced to separate, each of the two is nonetheless required to preserve the virtue of chastity because, as Jesus says: «*Every one who divorces his wife and marries another commits adultery, and he who marries a woman divorced from her husband commits adultery.*» (Lk 16,18).

This law of God is very clear, and it is not lawful for anyone to give it an interpretation which distorts it. Only the Church can interpret the Law of God, and, hence, we have to follow the teaching of the Supreme Head of the Church, who is the Pope, Bishop of Rome. And if anyone happens to proclaim to us a doctrine which is different or contrary to this, we must not believe him or follow the doctrine, because only to the Roman Catholic Apostolic Church has Christ promised, and granted, the help of the Holy Spirit; therefore, it is the Church, in the person of its Supreme Head and Vicar of Christ on earth, which has the light and grace necessary to define, teach and govern spiritually the People of God.

There is no shortage today of people who interpret this law of God in a sense contrary to the teachings of the Head of the Church, but these false doctrines were, at all times, condemned by God. Already in the Old Testament, God complained and accused his people of profaning the sanctuary of the family, saying to them, by the voice of the prophet Malachi, that this was the only reason that their offerings were not acceptable to Heaven: «*You cover the Lord's altar with tears, with weeping and groaning because he no longer regards the offering or accepts it with favour at your hand. You ask, "Why does he not?" Because the Lord was witness to the covenant between you and the wife of your youth, to whom you have been faithless, though she is your companion and wife by covenant. Has not the one God made and sustained for us the spirit of life? And what does he desire? Godly offspring. So take heed to yourselves, and let none be faithless to the wife of his youth. For I hate divorce, says the Lord the God of Israel, and covering one's garment with violence, says the Lord of hosts. So take heed to yourselves and do not be faithless.»* (Mal 2, 13-16).

All these divine words show us the seriousness of sins against the commandment, which forbids adultery. The answer, which Jesus Christ gave to the Pharisees when they asked Him about divorce, is worth our consideration. *"It was because of the hardness of your hearts that Moses allowed a writ of divorce"*. Hence, this hardness of heart is something that should not exist, because, apart from anything else, it is contrary to justice, since it violates the promise that the spouses made to love each other forever. Let them not forget what the Lord went on to say: *"What God has joined together, no human being must separate"* and then, *"Whoever divorces his wife and marries another commits adultery against her"*. Hence, all acts against this commandment are grave in the sight of God.

It is therefore alarming to see, in today's world, the disorder which prevails in this respect, and the ease with which people plunge into immorality. To remedy the situation, there is only one solution: that people should repent, reform their lives and do penance. For those who do not want to take this road Jesus Christ says: *«unless you repent you will likewise perish»* (Lk 13,5), or else like the eighteen victims who perished when the tower of Siloe fell on them.

That the solution lies in repentance and a change of life-style is confirmed in the case of the adulterous woman, whom Jesus succeeded in saving from death by stoning, as St. John describes. He tells us that when Jesus was teaching in the Temple, the Scribes and Pharisees came to Him bringing a woman who had been caught in adultery. Presenting her to the Lord, they asked Him whether He thought she should be stoned, as the Law of Moses commanded. At first, Jesus did not answer: so they persisted: *«he stood up and said to them, "Let him who is without sin among you be the first to throw a stone at her. (...) But when they heard it, they went away, one by one, (...) and Jesus was left alone with the woman standing before him. Jesus looked up and said to her, "Woman, where are they? Has no one condemned you?" She said, "No one, Lord." And Jesus said, "Neither do I condemn you; go, and do not sin again."»* (Jn 8, 7-11).

We see here, in Jesus Christ, what the mercy of God to a repentant sinner is like. Most certainly He saw repentance in that woman's heart and He pardoned her, promising not to condemn her if she did not sin again: *"Neither do I condemn you; go, and do not sin again."*». The interpreters of this Gospel passage may say that these words of Jesus referred to the death sentence laid down in the Mosaic Law for such cases. That may be so, but I think that, when the Lord ordered the woman not to sin any more, He was stating the condition for not being condemned to eternal death. For every sin we commit puts us in danger of eternal damnation, since we do not know whether God will give us the time or the grace to repent and do penance. *"Go in peace and sin no more!"* is the road marked out by God for all those who, having sinned, want to repent and change their lives in order to be saved.

With reference to what we have been talking about, consider these words of St. Paul: «*To the married I give charge, not I but the Lord, that the wife should not separate from her husband (but if she does, let her remain single or else be reconciled to her husband) – and that the husband should not divorce his wife.*» (1 Cor 7,10-11). Here again we have a clear affirmation of the indissolubility of marriage; it is not lawful for anyone to separate what God has joined together. And if, because of the hardness of the human heart, a separation becomes necessary, then each partner must observe chastity, that is, must keep under control their passions, their unruly inclinations and vices, because God did not create us to satisfy the desires of the flesh, but to save our souls and with them our bodies, for the day of resurrection.

Thus, we must avoid falling into the slavery of sin, because, as the Lord says: «*every one who commits sin is a slave to sin*» (Jn 8, 34). This will drag us down to Hell. The Apostle St. Paul warns us against this danger, saying: «*immorality and all impurity or covetousness must not even be named among you (...) Be sure of this, that no immoral or impure man, or one who is covetous (that is an idolater), has any inheritance in the kingdom of Christ and of God. Let no one deceive you with empty words, for it is because of these things that the wrath of God comes upon the sons of disobedience. Therefore do not associate with them*» (Eph 5, 3,5-7).

The Apostle urges us not to have anything to do with immoral people, so that they will not lead us into evil ways. The Portuguese have a proverb, which is certainly true: *Walk with good people and you will be like them, walk with evil people and you will be worse than they are.* Therefore, we must keep away from bad companions, so that they will not lead us into discreditable ways: however, let us continue to love these brothers and sisters of ours and treat them with discretion, seeking to help them with our prayers, win them with our words and our good example so that they may walk on a better path, the path of purity, truth, justice and love. We must do so in imitation of Jesus Christ, who loved sinners while detesting sin, and gave his life for our salvation: «*For God sent the Son into the world, not to condemn the world, but that the world might be saved through him*» (Jn 3, 17).

Ave Maria!

30

You shall not steal

"You shall not steal" (Ex 20, 15)

God forbids us to steal, because stealing is an act of injustice; it is unjust to take possession of something which does not belong to us. Such an act is contrary to God's justice; hence, He tells us: *"You shall not covet your neighbour's house... Nor anything else that belongs to him"* (Ex 20, 17).

"You shall not covet your neighbour's house" With this commandment God forbids us to covet what belongs to our neighbour; and, if we do not covet, we will not steal either, because it is covetousness which leads to theft.

If we do not have all that we need – and if we are able-bodied – we must work seriously and honourably to earn it. In fact, anyone who, despite good health and appropriate age, does not work, fails to observe the law of work imposed by God on the whole human race: «*The Lord God took the man and put him in the garden of Eden to till it and keep it.*» (Gen 2, 15).

In the beginning, when God gave this command to man, work was a form of entertainment and recreation: but, after man sinned by disobeying the order which God had given him not to eat the fruit of the forbidden tree, the command to work was felt as a penance and a punishment for the sin committed. «*And Lord commanded the man, saying, "You may freely eat of every tree of the garden; but of the tree of the knowledge of good and evil you shall not eat, for in the day that you eat of it you shall die.(...) So when the woman saw that the tree was good for food, and that it was a delight to the eyes, and that the tree was to be desired to make one wise, she took of its fruit and ate; and she also gave some to her husband, and he ate. (...) And to Adam he said, "Because you have listened to the voice of your wife, and have eaten of the tree of which I commanded you, 'You shall not eat of it', cursed is the ground because of you; in toil you shall eat of it all days of your life; thorns and thistles it shall bring forth to you; and you shall eat the plants of the field. In the sweat of your face you shall eat bread till you return to the ground, for out of it you were taken; you are dust, and to dust you shall return.*» (Gn 2,16; 3,6.17-19).

Thus, according to this sacred text, because of the sin of the first human beings, we are all subject to the law of work and to temporal death: "*By the sweat of your face shall you get bread to eat, until you return to the ground from which you were taken; for you are dust and to dust you shall return*" (Gen 3, 10). I say that we were subjected to temporal death, since we were ransomed from eternal death by the Redemption wrought by Jesus Christ. Now, in order to be saved, it only remains for us to co-operate with the grace which He has won for us.

The only exceptions to the law of work are children, because they have not yet the necessary physical strength, helpless invalids, and those who, because of their age and the work they have done in the past, have exhausted their strength. To provide what is necessary for these is the task of all those who are bound in justice to do so, especially those who are now enjoying what was gained by the effort and sacrifice of those who can no longer work; this is the charity of all who understand and love their neighbour. In this way, all will be able to live, seriously and honourably, as brothers and sisters, children of the same Heavenly Father, without transgressing his commandment: "*You shall not steal*".

There are so many and such different ways of stealing that it is impossible for me to enumerate them all here, but I will mention a few. Thus, in business, it is stealing to charge more than a just price for any goods, perhaps taking advantage of need, or of our neighbour's ignorance. On the part of those who work and receive payment for it, it is stealing not to give the proper amount of time to our work and not to work with the diligence and perfection required if things are to be done properly. And, on the part of those who are served by these workers, it is stealing not to pay them their due, and in good time.

To steal is to deprive others of their legitimate rights, either by oppressing them in such a way that they cannot use something to which they are entitled, or depriving them of their freedom as the free beings that they are, since God created them thus, or in any other way whatsoever.

It is also stealing to deceive our neighbour, by selling goods as of high quality when in reality they are damaged or worthless, selling animals which appear to be healthy and perfect but are really sickly or defective.

God has forbidden all these forms of stealing, saying to us: «*You shall not steal, nor deal falsely, nor lie to another.*» (Lv 19, 11). And St. Paul recommends the observance of this commandment in the following words: «*give no opportunity to the devil. Let the thief no longer steal, but rather let him labour, doing honest work with his hands, so that he may be able to give to those in need.*» (Eph 4, 27-28). And he says in another place: «*Now we command you, brethren, in the name of our Lord Jesus Christ, that you keep away from any brother who is living in idleness and not in accord with the tradition that you received from us (...) For even when we were with you, we gave you this command: If any one will not work, let him not eat. For we hear that some of you are living in idleness, mere busy-bodies, not doing any work. Now such persons we command and exhort in the Lord Jesus Christ to do their work in quietness and to earn their own living.*» (2 Thess 3, 6. 10-12). The Apostle bids us not to associate with those whose bad habits are known to us, those who break God's laws, because they will lead us into evil ways and ruin us. And he exhorts us, if we ourselves have got into bad habits, to amend our ways, beginning once more to work honestly, in order to earn our living and help our neighbour in need.

Another type of theft is when we rob someone of their good name. Slandering our neighbour, depriving him or her of the esteem and confidence of others is one of the most serious kinds of theft we can commit, because we steal what we all value above all else, our good name, our honour, the confidence and appreciation of others, thereby placing the person in a difficult situation, both in his or her private life as well as in his or her public and social affairs.

Condemning all this, God declares to the sinner:

«*What right have you to recite my statutes, or take my covenant on your lips? For you hate discipline, and you cast my words behind you. If you see a thief, you are a friend of his; and you keep company with adulterers. You give your mouth free rein for evil, and your tongue frames deceit. You sit and speak against your brother; you slander your own mother's son. These things you have done and I have been silent; you thought that I was one like yourself. But now I rebuke you, and lay charge before you.*» (Ps 50 (49),16-21). And the psalmist concludes: «*Mark this, then, you who forget God, lest I rend, and there be none to deliver!*» (Ps 50(49), 22).

Let us accept this divine reminder because what is involved is our eternal salvation. Let us make sure that our life with God is all that it should be by our faithful and constant observance of his law and his word which is his Word incarnate, Jesus Christ our Saviour: *«He who hears my word and believes him who sent me, has eternal life; he does not come into judgment, but has passed from death to life.»* (Jn 5, 24).

Ave Maria!

31

You shall not bear false witness against your neighbour

«You shall not bear false witness against your neighbour» (Deut. 5, 20)"

With this commandment, God forbids all kinds of calumny and lies, which damage our neighbour. The Lord speaks thus: *«You shall not utter a false report. You shall not join hands with a wicked man, to be a malicious witness. You shall not follow a multitude to do evil; nor shall you bear witness in a suit, turning aside after a multitude, so as to pervert justice; nor shall you be partial to a poor man in his suit. (...) You shall not pervert the justice due to your poor in his suit. Keep far from a false charge, and do not slay the innocent and righteous, for I will not acquit the wicked. And you shall take no bribe, for a bribe blinds the officials, and subverts the cause of those who are in the right.»* (Ex 23, 1-8).

This commandment of God also forbids all unjust criticism, backbiting and slander of our neighbour: that great defect of putting the worst interpretation on our neighbour's actions, attributing to them an evil intention, which they never had. Condemning this conduct, St. James says: *«Do not speak evil against one another, brethren. He that speaks evil against a brother or judges his brother, speaks evil against the law and judges the law. But if you judge the law, you are not a doer of the law but a judge. There is one lawgiver and judge, he who is able to save and destroy. But who are you that you judge your neighbour?»* (Jm 4, 11-12).

All backbiting, censure, and unjust and detracting criticism are contrary to this commandment because they are founded on falsehood and calumny. In the Book of Proverbs, it is written: *«A false witness will not go unpunished, and he who utters lies will perish»* (Prov 19, 9).

If we apply this to our own case, we understand the meaning of this commandment very well, since we would like to see it observed with regard to ourselves. Why, then, do we not understand it in the same way in our neighbour's case? Surely it is because we live carelessly or else in ignorance of the truth?

In St. John's Gospel, there is a passage, which has always impressed me greatly, the one which refers to Jesus' trial before Pilate. At a given moment, the accusation is made that Jesus had wanted to be king, the true sense of which the Lord sought to make clear. «*Pilate said to him, "So you are a king?" Jesus answered, "You say that I am a king. For this I was born, and for this I have come into the world, to bear witness to the truth. Every one who is of the truth hears my voice." Pilate said to him, "What is truth?" After he had said this, he went out to the Jews again, and told them, "I find no crime in him.*» (Jn 18, 37-38).

This Gospel text shows us what life in the world is like. Pilate was a man who occupied a very high place in the society of his day, wielding great power, including that of judge of the Supreme Court, and, yet, he does not know what truth is! Neither did he want to know, because he did not wait for Jesus' answer. He was not interested in learning; he simply went out and spoke to the Jews. So many people in the world live like this: they are not interested in the truth, and yet we will never arrive in Heaven unless we follow the way of truth.

Thus, Pilate, having listened to calumny, condemned an innocent man to death. And he was aware of this, since he himself admitted that the victim was innocent; moreover, to stifle the voice of his conscience, he staged the hypocritical ceremony of washing his hands, declaring before all the people that he himself was innocent of the blood of that just Man. «*Pilate (...) took water and washed his hands before the crowd saying, "I am innocent of this righteous man's blood"*» (Mt 27, 24)." «*Then he handed him over to them to be crucified.*» (Jn 19, 16).

If it were possible to unroll the whole web of human history, how many examples would we not find of people condemned to death or to punishments just as cruel as death, victims of calumny, of lies, of unjust judgements, of hatred, envy and vengeance? And, yet, the Law of God has been given to us and is still valid, repeating always: "*You shall not kill. You shall not bear false witness against your neighbour. You shall not repeat a false report. Do not join the wicked in putting your hand, as an unjust witness, upon anyone. You shall keep away from anything dishonest*".

Even if people do not want to heed this voice of God, its echo must vibrate in the human conscience for as long as the race exists and afterwards, in eternity, in the despair of those who, because they did not follow it, are lost forever.

To transgress this commandment is a very grave matter: for, in doing so, we offend God in the person of our neighbour. It is a sin against the precepts of the justice and charity with which Jesus Christ bids us treat our neighbour: «*This is my commandment, that you love one another as I have loved you*» (Jn 15, 12) and the Lord loved us to the point of giving his life for us. In another place, He recommends the same thing, saying: «*So whatever you wish that men would do to you, do so to them; for this is the law and the prophets.*» (Mt 7, 12).

Ave Maria!

32

You shall not covet your neighbour's wife

«*You shall not covet your neighbour's wife nor shall you desire his house(...),or anything that is your neighbour's.*» (Deut 5,18).

There is so much disregard of this commandment in the world today that I ask myself if it is even worthwhile talking about it? The answer is in the affirmative; because, even if the whole world is drowning in the abyss, the word of God remains, repeating: "*You shall not covet your neighbour's wife*".

The sin against this commandment is so serious that, in the Old Testament, it was punished by death. «*If a man commits adultery with the wife of his neighbour, both the adulterer and the adulteress shall be put to death.*» (Lv 20, 10). And, in another place: «*If a man is found lying with the wife of another man, both of them shall die, the man who lay with the woman, and the woman*» (Deut 22, 22).

In the Sermon on the Mount, when Jesus Christ was talking to the multitude which had gathered around Him, He said: «*You have heard that it was said, 'You shall not commit adultery'. But I say to you that every one who looks at a woman lustfully has already commited adultery with her in his heart.*» (Mt 5, 27-28) . We see from this that God forbids not only the act in itself but also the covetousness and the desire involved, since these lead afterwards to the consummation of the act. And the divine Master concludes his affirmation with this very harsh advice «*If your right eye causes you to sin, pluck it out and throw it away; it is better that you lose one of your members than that your whole body be thrown into hell.*» (Mt 5, 29). In this extreme example, Jesus wants to emphasise the gravity of this sin and how it incurs the punishment of eternal damnation.

The sin against this commandment involves the violation of two others, namely, the one which orders the observance of chastity, and the one which forbids theft. In fact, to take possession of someone who belongs to, or has been entrusted to, another is stealing. Such an act is thus contrary to both justice and charity. Hence, God includes in this commandment a list of things which we may not covet: «*Neither shall you covet your neighbour's wife; and you shall not desire your neighbour's house (...) or anything that is your neighbour's»* (Dt 5, 21).

The law of civil divorce, which various nations permit, is opposed to the law of God which lays down that the marriage bond is indissoluble: *«What therefore God has joined together, let no man put asunder.»* (Mt 19, 6). St. Paul, wishing to discuss the limits proper to this law, proposed the concrete case of the union of man and woman, which only the death of one of them can sever. *«Thus a married woman is bound by law to her husband as long as he lives; but if her husband dies she is discharged from the law concerning the husband. Accordingly, she will be called an adulteress if she lives with another man while her husband is alive. But if her husband dies she is free from that law, and if she marries another man she is not an adulteress»* (Rm 7, 2-3).

The same Apostle does not conceal from us the terrible fate awaiting those who transgress this law. *«Be sure of this, that no immoral or impure man, or one who is covetous (that is an idolater), has any inheritance in the kingdom of Christ and of God. Let no one deceive you with empty words, for it is because of these things that the wrath of God comes upon the sons of disobedience. Therefore do not associate with them»* (Eph 5, 5-7). And this is what he wrote to the Corinthians: *«I wrote to you in my letter not to associate with immoral men; not at all meaning the immoral of this world, or the greedy and the robbers, or idolaters, since then you would need to go out of the world. But rather I wrote to you not to associate with any one who bears the name of brother if he is guilty of immorality or greed, or is an idolater, reviler, drunkard, or robber – not even to eat with such a one.»* (1 Cor 5, 9-11).

St. Paul also reminds us that God has called us all to sanctity *«For this is the will of God, your sanctification: that you abstain from immorality; that each one of you know how to control his own body in holiness and honour, not in the passion of lust like heathen who do not know God; that no man transgress, and wrong his brother in this matter, because the Lord is an avenger in all these things, as we solemnly forewarned you. For God has not called us for uncleanness, but in holiness. Therefore whoever disregards this, disregards not man but God, who gives his Holy Spirit to you.»* (1 Thess 4, 3-8).

Concerning St. Paul's remark, *"The Lord always avenges all these things";* here is a page from the prophet Jeremiah, where God resolves to exterminate his unfaithful people. *«How can I pardon you? Your children have forsaken me, and have sworn by those who are no gods. When I fed them to the* full, they committed adultery and trooped to the houses of harlots. They were well-fed lusty stallions, each neighing for his neighbour's wife. Shall I not punish them for these things? says the Lord; and shall I not avenge myself on a nation such as this? Go up through her vine-rows and destroy, but make not a full end; strip away her branches, for they are not the Lord's.» (Jer 5, 7-10).

The story of King David tells that he sinned against this commandment; and as one sin usually leads to many others, he also violated the commandment which forbids us to appropriate to ourselves the right of our neighbours, the precept which commands everyone to observe chastity according to his state of life; the commandment which forbids us to make an attempt on our neighbour's life, etc. God dealt mercifully with him, sending him the prophet Nathan to make him acknowledge his sins, and let him know the chastisements with which God had intended to punish him. After hearing the prophet's words, David repented and did penance. Therefore, God ordered the prophet to say to him: «*The Lord also has put away your sin; you shall not die. Nevertheless, because by this deed you have utterly scorned the Lord, the child that is born to you shall die*» (2 Sam 12, 13-14).

In the New Testament, St. John the Baptist, too, had to rebuke King Herod for having taken his brother Philip's wife, in these words: «*It is not lawful for you to have your brother's wife.*» (Mk 6, 18). But in John's case, zeal for God's law brought him the palm of martyrdom: he was imprisoned and, at the request of the adulterous woman, beheaded.

How happy I should be if God were to give me, too, the grace of giving my life in defence of his Law and if, by so giving it, men, in imitation of David, acknowledged their sins, asked God's pardon, amended their lives and did penance, so that thus they might be saved and gain eternal life!

We are deluded if we think, or say, that these divine laws were given solely for the Israelites because they were the people chosen by God to be saved. In fact, Jesus Christ, in the Gospel, told us that He did not come to abolish the Law but to complete and perfect it. And He commanded his apostles to go and teach it to the whole world, so that all people might be saved: «*Go into all the world and preach the gospel to the whole creation. He who believes and is baptized will be saved; but he who does not believe will be condemned.*» (Mk 16, 15-16).

This command that Jesus Christ gave to his Apostles proves that all of us belong to the People of God. We were chosen, or rather, created in order to be saved, on condition that we believe, are baptised, and fulfil the Law of God. Yes, we must fulfil the Law of God, as Jesus tells us: «*Think not that I have come to abolish the law and the prophets; I have come not to abolish them but to fulfil them. For truly I say to you, till heaven and earth pass away, not an iota, not a dot, will pass from the law until all is accomplished.*» (Mt 5, 17-18. And it will endure until the last day when the same Word of God will pronounce the sentence of condemnation on the transgressor: «*If any one hears my sayings and does not keep them, I do not judge him; for I did not come to judge the world but to save the world. (...) the word that I have spoken will be his judge on the last day.*» (Jn 12, 47-48).

Thus we see that we will be saved by observing the Law of God, whereas by violating it we will be condemned. It is certain that God is a kind Father, always ready to receive the repentant sinner but only when He sees sorrow for the sin and a firm purpose of amendment in the sinner's heart. It was for the benefit of souls like this that the Lord said: «*Those who are well have no need of a physician, but those who are sick. Go and learn what this means, 'I desire mercy, and not sacrifice.' For I came not to call the righteous, but sinners.*» (Mt 9, 12-13). Yes, because the just follow the Lord's ways; it is the sinners who have gone astray that must be called back and led into the ways of truth, of purity, of justice and of God's love.

Ave Maria!

33

The Commandments are summed up in charity

We have gone through the commandments of God's Law, one by one, to discover how we should observe them. We have seen that by observing them we shall be saved, and by violating them we shall be condemned.

And we cannot say: *That is my own business!* as some do who are indifferent, cynical, defeatists or individualists:

But is it their own business? What if all Heaven was moved in order to save you? How can you assert that this business of saving your soul concerns you only? The Son of the Eternal Father died on the cross instead of you and in your place; are you now going to hand yourself over to hell which He has already conquered? Stop this nonsense of defying eternal death. Your Heavenly Father does not want you to be lost; how can you forget Him, despise Him, destroy his image within you? Does a Father's grief, your Father's grief, leave you utterly indifferent? If that is so, are you sure that you are still in the realm of the living, have you not, rather, gone down alive into the realm of the dead?

God's suffering because of the sins of men is very great! In the apparition of October 1917, Our Lady ended her series of spoken messages, saying: *"Do not offend the Lord our God any more, because He is already so much offended."* And we offend God when we transgress his Law, the Commandments.

But why does God feel so deeply offended when we sin against his commandments? God Himself, properly speaking, is not affected by it. He continues to be what He is: eternally happy, great, powerful, immense, source of life and of all good. But God is *love*, and by sin we diminish love: not the love of God for us, but our love for Him. The moment we transgress one of his laws, we cease to love God; we create a void in our love. How can a son say he loves his father, if, in the father's own house, he disobeys and despises his orders, his instructions, his favours and his caresses. He must be – and he is – a rebellious son, not a son who loves his father.

All true love demands giving, renunciation, self-sacrifice, self-surrender. This was how God loved us from the beginning. He created us in his image, making us sharers in his life, in his gifts such as intelligence, power of reflection, wisdom, free will, freedom, and destined us for eternal life. All this sharing in his gifts which He has granted us, in the order of nature as well as of grace, is, on God's part, a self-sacrifice, a self-surrender, a self-revelation and a descent, out of love, so as to raise us up, to honour us, to perfect us and to associate us with Himself.

All sin on our part is a breach of love. When God saw us in our fallen state, He was inflamed with great love and compassion for us; and He gave Himself for our redemption in the person of his Son, Jesus Christ, whom the Father sent into the world to save us. Unfathomable abyss of divine love, which St. John described thus: «*And the Word became flesh and dwelt among us, full of grace and truth; we have beheld his glory, glory as of the only Son from the Father (...) For the law was given through Moses; grace and truth came through Jesus Christ.*» (Jn 1, 14-17). And Jesus declares that He came down from Heaven because that was his Father's will, and that He came to save us and give us eternal life, which we had lost through sin: «*All that the Father gives me will come to me; and him who comes to me I will not cast out. For I have come down from heaven, not to do my own will, but the will of him who sent me; and this is the will of him who sent me, that I should lose nothing of all that he has given me, but raise it up at the last day. For this is the will of my Father, that every one who sees the Son and believes in him should have eternal life; and I will raise him up at the last day*» (Jn 6, 37-40).

The extent to which the Father loves us may be seen in the gift He makes to us of his own Son: «*For God so loved the world that he gave his only Son, that whoever believes in him should not perish but have eternal life. For God sent the Son into the world, not to condemn the world, but that the world might be saved through him. He who believes in him is not condemned; he who does not believe is condemned already, because he has not believed in the name of the only Son of God. And this is the judgment, that the light has come into the world, and men loved darkness rather than light, because their deeds were evil. For every one who does evil hates the light, and does not come to the light, lest his deeds should be exposed. But he who does what is true comes to the light, that it may be clearly seen that his deeds have been wrought in God*» (Jn 3, 16-21).

Thus, Jesus Christ is the manifestation of the Father's love; this love was sent into the world to be poured into the hearts of men, and enkindle in them the fire of that charity which burns and consumes Him for the good of His children, so as to unite them in the same perfection of supernatural life, of faith and of love of Him who created and saved them. God is love, St. John tells us: «*He who does not love does not know God; for God is love. In this the love of God was made manifest among us, that God sent his only Son into the world, so that we might live through him. In this love, not that we loved God but that he loved us and sent his Son to be the expiation for our sins.*» (1 Jn 4, 8-10) .

As we see, God gives Himself to us through love, and this love, when it is kindled in a heart, softens everything, sweetens everything, because it extinguishes the fire of unruly passions and smoothes the ways of holiness, which consist in the observance of the divine Law, through love. It is then that the person's love for God becomes more fervent, and the union between them is made closer by strong and unbreakable bonds, until this love becomes the person's very life. And, led by this love, such a person gives him/herself completely to God and to others, for the love of God. What one then desires is to communicate to others this treasure of grace and happiness which we ourselves now possess within us, to make the way smooth for them and help them to continue on it, so that they may enjoy the same good fortune which has made us happy: *love.*

It is the new commandment which Christ came to give the world, and which, until then, was unknown or badly interpreted: «*A new commandment I give to you, that you love one another; even as I have loved you, that you also love one another.*» (Jn 13,34). Christ loved us and surrendered Himself unto death for us. Thus Christ is for us the model of pure, chaste love, sacrificed for God and others; He is the model for our self-surrender, our consecration and our fidelity to God and to our neighbour. These words make me think not only of religious, but of everyone, because, by Baptism, we are all consecrated and dedicated to a religious life of love of God and our neighbour.

Already in the Old Testament, God had given this law: «*You shall not take vengeance or bear any grudge against the sons of your own people, but you shall love your neighbour as yourself: I am the Lord. You shall keep my statutes*» (Lv 19,18-19). Yes, God ordered us to love our neighbour; He asked us to love Himself:«*Hear, O Israel: The Lord our God is one Lord; and you shall love the Lord your God with all your heart, and with all your soul, and with all your might. And these words which I command you this day shall be upon your heart; and you shall teach them diligently to your children, and shall talk of them when you sit in your house, and when you walk by the way, and when you lie down, and when you rise. And you shall bind them as a sign upon your hand, and they shall be as frontlets between your eyes. And you shall write them on the doorposts of your house and on your gates.»* (Dt 6, 4-9)

Although this commandment was so explicit in the Old Law, it was misinterpreted and distorted, as Jesus showed the Scribes and Pharisees in the case of the commandment to honour our father and mother. *«You hypocrites! Well did Isaiah prophecy of you, when he said: 'This people honours me with their lips, but their heart is far from me; in vain do they worship me, teaching as doctrines the precepts of men.'»* (Mt 15, 7-9). A further proof of the confusion and difficulty with which people surrounded the Law of God can be seen in the question which an expert in the Law, with some others, put to Jesus: *«"Teacher, which is the great commandment in the law?" And he said to him, "You shall love the Lord your God with all your heart, and with all your soul, and with all your mind. This is the great and first commandment. And a second is like it, You shall love your neighbour as yourself. On these two commandments depend all the law and the prophets."»* (Mt 22, 36-40).

As Jesus teaches us, the whole Law is summed up in the love of God and of our neighbour for love of Him; in other words, we love others because they are children of God like ourselves and, therefore, our brother or sister, with free will like ours, with the same rights as we have, and destined for eternal life. Accordingly, it is this love which leads us to observe each and all of the commandments, because all of them, in one way or another, refer to God and our neighbour. Their observance always redounds to the glory of God, our own good and that of our neighbour. On the other hand, their transgression affects God's external glory – that is, in his creation, not in Himself – does harm to our own good and the good of our neighbour, considered both as an individual and as a member of society.

The reason is this: we are members of the Mystical Body of Christ which is his Church. What happens in it is similar to what occurs in any living body: if one member is ailing, the whole body suffers; and, when one member is lost, the whole body feels the deprivation. Now, to transgress the commandments is a breach of love. Whenever we break a Commandment in a serious matter, the bond of charity, which binds us to God and our neighbour, is broken. We cannot say we love when we offend!

In fact, with our transgression, we lesson the application of the redemptive work of Jesus Christ to ourselves and, consequently, its fruit; we offend our neighbour by our bad example, either by leading them into evil ways or by harming them in their rights, their health, their life, their possessions, their good name, honour, reputation, personal dignity, etc.

But we also damage ourselves, depriving ourselves of the grace of God, putting ourselves in danger of eternal damnation, throwing away our personal dignity, our good name, honour, material, moral and spiritual goods and, in many cases, even the possibility of exercising our freedom, since, as the Lord says: *the sinner becomes the slave of sin.* We sacrifice our health and, very often, our temporal and eternal life. Sad consequences of our transgressing the Law of God!

And it is not difficult to see how any and every violation of the different Commandments ends by offending against the law of charity, which is the love of God, Whom we ceased to love when we transgressed his Law; love of our neighbour, which is damaged directly or indirectly; love of ourselves because we diminish and defraud ourselves by depriving ourselves of good things which are irretrievable either in time or in eternity. Perhaps without realising it, we disgrace ourselves completely.

The Commandments are summed up in love. They are all the expression of that living fire of love, which is God. *God is charity, God is love!* It was through love that God gave us these precepts; like a good father who gives his children precise instructions so that they may walk in the right paths and be happy.

The Commandments are our best guardians; the best defence of human life. If everyone kept these divine precepts today, there would be no assailants, thieves, adulterers, idolaters, no enemies of any kind. We would all love one another like brothers and sisters, helping one another in joy, peace and happiness, like children in their father's house. Yes, because the world is just that: the house of our God and Father who created us all, so as to live united under his Fatherly eye, enjoying the same goods and the same loving relations, following the same road marked out by the same laws, living the same ideal which leads to the possession of the same kingdom, where life never ends, joy has no limits, and love is eternal; eternal because love is God, the love and life of God which are poured out on his children.

But how can we say that we possess charity if we do not love God and our neighbour; if we cannot manage to make the sacrifices necessary in order to fulfil each and all of the Commandments? We have no charity if we cannot deny ourselves sufficiently in order to be pure, chaste, humble, faithful to God and to our neighbour; if we cannot sacrifice ourselves for the benefit of our neighbours who are poor and need our help, our assistance in their difficulty, our alms and our comfort; if we cannot deny ourselves enough so as to give to our needy neighbour what we do not preferring to waste it on what is useless and unnecessary.

Think of all the money wasted on sinful amusements, in the indulgence of vices, on alcoholic drink, in cafés, in gambling – houses and places of licentious conduct, in luxuries and exaggerated vanities, on smoking, etc.! If we are foolish and selfish enough to waste completely what we could, and should, give to our brothers and sisters who are in need, cold and hungry, where, then, is our charity, our love of God and of our neighbour?

Where is our charity, if we cannot forgive from our heart, or pay back good for evil? If we allow ourselves to be carried away by the spirit of vengeance, by envy, jealousy, prejudice malevolence, hatred, etc.?

Sacred Scripture tells us: «*You shall not go up and down as a slanderer among your people, and you shall not stand forth against the life of your neighbour: I am the Lord. You shall not hate your brother in your heart (...) You shall not take vengeance or bear any grudge against the sons of your own people, but you shall love your neighbour as yourself: I am the Lord. You shall keep my statutes.*» (Lv 19, 16-19).

And Jesus Christ taught us to ask the Father to forgive us our sins as we forgive those who have offended us, and He tells us why: «*For if you forgive men their trespasses, your heavenly Father also will forgive you; but if you do not forgive men their trespasses, neither will your Father forgive your trespasses.*» (Mt 6,14-15).

In his Gospel, referring to the question put to Jesus by a scribe: "*Which is the first of all the commandments?*" St. Mark describes the joy which filled that scribe at the answer he received and to which he replied: «"*You are right, Teacher; you have truly said that he is one, and there is no other but he; and to love him with all the heart, and with all the understanding, and with all the strength, and to love one's neighbour as oneself, is much more than all whole burnt offerings and sacrifices*"» (Mk 12, 32-33). In these words, we have a marvellous explanation of the first and greatest of all the Commandments, that is to say, love – love of God and of our neighbour. But we must keep in mind that we will not be fulfilling it completely as long as we transgress any one of the various commandments given by God, all of which are included in these two, to the extent that a violation of any one of them involves a sin against the commandment of charity. The commandments are a kind of more detailed explanation given to us by God of the manner in which we should observe the commandment of love.

And, to end this little reflection on the Ten Commandments of God – as an integral part of his Message, sent to us through his Mother and ours, calling our attention to the path traced out by Him for all who wish to be saved – I leave you here what Jesus Christ recommended to his Apostles, and to us also, during the last hours of his earthly life: «*As the Father has loved me, so have I loved you; abide in my love. If you keep my commandments, you will abide in my love, just as I have kept my Father's commandments and abide in his love. These things I have spoken to you, that my joy may be in you, and that your joy may be full. This is my commandment, that you love each one another as I have loved you. Greater love has no man than this, that a man lay down his life for his friends. You are my friends if you do what I command you. (...) This I command you, to love one another*» (Jn 15, 9-14.17).

But Jesus takes the perfection of love of God and of our neighbour even further. It is easy to love our friends; but we also have to love our enemies, paying back with good the evil they have done to us. It is here that our charity touches the sphere of heroism! The Lord gave his life for his friends and also for his enemies «*Father, forgive them; for they know not what they do*» (Lk 23,34). He asked pardon for his enemies and wanted to save them, leaving an example to confirm what He had once said:«*Love your enemies, do good to those who hate you, bless those who curse you, pray for those who abuse you. (...) your reward will be great, and you will be sons of the Most High; for he is kind to the ungrateful and selfish. Be merciful, even as your Father is merciful*» (Lk 6, 27. 35-36).

Ave Maria!

Part Four

THE ROSARY.

34

A remarkable and powerful prayer

We have seen already how God, knowing the great need we have to pray, but also that everyone cannot be asked to pray in the same way because the possibilities and situations in each one's life are so different, called for the daily recitation of the Rosary, thus condescending to the simple level which is common to all of us. During the very first apparition, on 13th May, 1917, Our Lady asked: *"Pray the Rosary every day"*; and this request was to be repeated by her every month until October.

So, calling to mind the insistence with which God, by means of the Fatima Message, recommends the prayer of the Rosary, and also all that the Church's Magisterium has said about it over the years, we can conclude that the Rosary is a form of vocal prayer which, in general, suits all of us, for which we should have the highest regard, and which we should make the greatest effort never to abandon.

Unfortunately, in these confused times, there are those who venture to criticize the Rosary, saying, for example, that it is not a liturgical prayer. Some time ago, I heard about an article of this nature and was greatly saddened by it. Someone asked the author of it how he had dared to write and publish such nonsense, to which he replied: *I was forced to do it!* Did he not know, then, that there is no authority in the world which can force us to go against our own conscience ? It is the mystery of human weakness, which, in many cases, in order to please creatures, perhaps for earthly reasons, does not mind incurring God's anger and the penalties with which He punishes sin. Contrary to what this person, and others of the same mind, have written, I assure you that the Rosary is a biblical prayer and that it is part of the sacred Liturgy.

We begin the Rosary with the words: *"Deus in adjutorium meum intende, Domine ad adjuvandum me festina"* or, in English: *"O God, come to our aid, Lord, make haste to help us"*. This is the prayer we say at the beginning of the different parts of the Liturgy of the Hours.

Then we pray: *Gloria Patri, et Filio, et Spiritui Sancto. Sicut erat in principio, et nunc et semper, et in saecula saculorum, Amen"*. Or, in English, *"Glory be to the Father, and to the Son, and to the Holy Spirit. As it was in the beginning, is now and ever shall be, world without end. Amen"*. This prayer of praise, which we recite at the end of each decade of the Rosary, is the same as that with which we end the psalms in the Liturgy of the Hours, and it is also used at Mass, whether in the Gospel Acclamation on the Solemnity of the Blessed Trinity, or in the longer form of the hymn: "Glory to God in the highest", begun by the Angels in Bethlehem.

The Our Father, which we recite at the beginning of each decade, was taught to us by Jesus Christ when his disciples asked Him to teach them to pray: «*Pray then like this: "Our Father who art in heaven, hallowed be thy name, thy kingdom come, thy will be done, on earth as it is in heaven. Give us this day our daily bread; and forgive us our debts, as we also have forgiven our debtors; and lead us not into temptation, but deliver us from evil."*» (Mt 6, 9-13). This prayer, which we say in all the decades of the Rosary, is a biblical prayer and is part of the Liturgy; it is recited daily in the Mass and in the Liturgy of the Hours.

The next prayer is the Hail Mary, which we repeat ten times, thus forming a decade of our Rosary. It, too, is a biblical prayer. It begins with the words which the Angel Gabriel addressed to Mary when he was sent by God to announce to her the Incarnation of the Word: «*The angel Gabriel was sent from God (...) to a virgin (...) and the virgin's name was Mary. And he came to her and said, "Hail, full of grace, the Lord is with you!"*» (Lk 1,26-28). I think that when He was sending the Angel, God must have suggested to him the words with which he was to salute Mary, announcing to her, on the part of God, the mystery of the incarnation of the Word.

And St. Elizabeth, moved by the Holy Spirit, said: «*Blessed are you among women, and blessed is the fruit of your womb!*» (Lk 1, 42).

Thus, the Hail Mary was formed under God's inspiration: "*Hail Mary, full of grace, the Lord is with you; blessed are you among women, and blessed is the fruit of your womb, Jesus*".

We must regard this salutation as having been addressed to the Virgin Mary by God Himself, on the natural level insofar as the words of the heavenly messenger are concerned, and supernaturally in the case of the words which were spoken by St. Elizabeth under the inspiration of the Holy Spirit: «*And when Elizabeth heard the greeting of Mary, the babe leaped in her womb; and Elizabeth was filled with the Holy Spirit and she exclaimed with a loud cry, "Blessed are you among women, and blessed is the fruit of your womb!"*» (Lk1, 41-42). If St. Elizabeth was moved by the Holy Spirit when she uttered these words, as Sacred Scripture tells us; then this praise comes from the Holy Spirit.

But it is more praise of God than of Mary: You are blessed because the fruit of your womb is blessed; and it is in this fruit, and by this fruit, that the blessing of God has come to you and that you are blessed among all women. And this was how the Virgin Mary understood it when she sang: *«My soul magnifies the Lord, and my spirit rejoices in God my Saviour, for he has regarded the low estate of his handmaiden. For behold, henceforth all generations will call me blessed; for he who is mighty has done great things for me, and holy is his name. And his mercy is on those who fear him from generation to generation»* (Lk 1, 46-50). As we see, all praise of Mary rises up to God; He looked with mercy on his lowly handmaid.

So the Ave Maria is indeed a biblical prayer. But it is also part of the Liturgy, being recited on various feasts of the year, both in the Mass and in the Liturgy of the Hours.

Later on, the Church, guided by the Holy Spirit Who enlightens and helps it, rounded off the formula of the Ave Maria with the humble supplication: *"Holy Mary, Mother of God, pray for us sinners, now and at the hour of our death. Amen".*

This prayer, in which we ask Mary to intercede for us with the Lord, does not contradict in any way the truth taught by St. Paul: *«There is one mediator between God and men, the man Christ Jesus»* (1 Tm 2, 5). There is only one Mediator endowed with the divine nature and possessing natural access to God, namely: Jesus Christ. Nevertheless, *«an intermediary implies more than one; but God is one.»* (Gal 3, 20) which means that there is a second party to be served and represented by the Mediator, namely humanity.

And *"Jesus Christ, Man"* is our Mediator by nature – the human nature which He assumed in the womb of the Virgin Mary. But Christ did not become man to be the one and only survivor of humanity, but to be *«the first born among many brethren»* (Rom 8, 29) whom He saved, restoring to them the access to the presence of God and intimacy with Him which they had enjoyed in the earthly paradise. In fact He did more: He bound us to Himself as members of his Mystical Body which is the Church, the saving presence of Jesus until the end of time and to the ends of the earth, sharing, by grace and calling, the Saviour's threefold mission – that of prophet, priest and king.

There is, thus, only one divine Mediator: Jesus Christ; but as suppliant intercessors we have Mary, the Saints, and each one of us, if we so wish. St. Paul himself, in various passages in his letters, asks people to pray both for him and for one another. «*To that end keep alert with all perseverance, making supplication for all the saints, and also for me, that utterance may be given in opening my mouth boldly to proclaim the mystery of the gospel, for which I am an ambassador in chains; that I may declare it boldly, as I ought to speak*» (Eph 6,18-20).

So, if the Apostle tells us to pray for one another, we have much more reason to ask Mary to pray for us, because her prayer will be much more pleasing to the Lord in view of her dignity as Mother of God and her closer union with Christ, true God and true Man, by reason of her mission of co-Redemptrix with Christ as well as of her great sanctity.

Returning, now, to the biblical and liturgical dimension of the Rosary, let us consider the prayer which the Message taught us to pray at the end of each decade. A similar request occurs in the Mass, since the rubrics order us to begin the Holy Sacrifice by confessing our sins, and the prayer taught us by Our Lady leads us to ask pardon for these same sins: "*Oh my Jesus, forgive us, save us from the fire of hell. Lead all souls to heaven, especially those who are most in need.* (Apparition of 13th July, 1917).

"*Those who are most in need*". I think this refers to those in greatest danger of damnation. With this prayer, we ask God to apply to us the fruit of the Holy Sacrifice of the Mass, that is, the salvation of souls, together with forgiveness for our own sins.

Thus, I believe that, after the liturgical prayer of the Holy Sacrifice of the Mass, the prayer of the holy Rosary, because of its origin and the sublime nature of the prayers which compose it and also on account of the mysteries of our redemption which we recall and contemplate in each decade, is the most pleasing prayer we can offer to God, and the one most beneficial to our own souls. If this were not so, Our Lady would not have recommended it to us with such insistence.

The saying of the Rosary is the form of prayer which has been most recommended by all the Popes who have served the Church in recent centuries, beginning with Gregory XIII who, in the Bull "Monete Apostolos", calls it "*the Psalter of the Most Holy Virgin which we pray in order to placate God's anger and implore her intercession*". (1st April, 1573).

Sixtus V also, in the Bull "Dum ineffabilis" of 30th January, 1586, calls the Rosary the *"Psalter of the glorious and ever Virgin Mary, Mother of God, instituted by the inspiration of the Holy Spirit"*.

Before these two Popes, St. Pius V had also governed the Church. He attributed the victory obtained by the Christians against the Turks at Lepanto on 7th October, 1571 to the praying of the Rosary. In thanksgiving, he ordered the Feast of Our Lady of Victories to be celebrated annually on that day, a feast which one of his successors changed to that of Our Lady of the Rosary.

About three hundred years after that war, Pope Pius IX was serving the Church. On his death bed, he said to those around him: *"The Rosary is a compendium of the Gospel, and gives to those who pray it those rivers of peace of which the Scriptures speak; it is the most beautiful devotion, the most abundant in grace, and the most pleasing to the Heart of Mary. My sons, let this be the testimony by which you remember me on earth"*. (February, 1878). It is marvellous to see how this great Pope linked the prayer of the Rosary to the Immaculate Heart of Mary. But was he not the Pope of Mary Immaculate, the one who proclaimed the dogma of the Immaculate Conception of Mary by the Bull "Ineffabilis Deus" in 1854?

Leo XIII, in the Encyclical "Fidentem piumque", of 20th September, 1896, said: «*In the devotion of the Rosary, Christ occupies the first place; (......) by means of the vocal prayers of which it is formed, we can express and profess our faith in God, our most provident Father, in eternal life, in the forgiveness of sins, and also in the mysteries of the Most Holy Trinity, the Incarnate Word, the divine Maternity, and others. Certainly, nobody is ignorant of the great value and merit of faith. Faith, in fact, is nothing else than the chosen seed which, in the present, produces the flowers of all the virtues which render us pleasing to God and yield fruits which will last for eternity: since "To know You is indeed the perfect virtue and to know Your power is the root of immortality"* (cf. Wisdom, 15 : 3)».

This affirmation of Pope Leo XIII is admirable. He is telling us that the Most Holy Trinity and the saving work of Christ are at the centre of this great prayer, the Rosary, making it a profession of faith in these central mysteries of Catholic doctrine. The faith which we profess, and exercise, in this prayer, is of great spiritual value. Hence, the same Pope, using the words of the Apostle St. Paul, says: «*For man believes with his heart and so is justified, and he confesses with his lips and is saved*» (Rom 10, 10). "*Therefore, the Rosary provides us with the opportunity for this external profession of faith*".

In his Encyclical «*Ingravescentibus malis*» of 29th September 1937, Pope Pius XI says: "*The Holy Rosary is not only a weapon to put to flight the enemies of God and of Religion but, above all, it fosters and nourishes the Gospel virtues. And, in the first place, it reanimates the Catholic faith by contemplation of the divine mysteries and improves our understanding of the truths revealed by God.*" And he granted a plenary indulgence for the recitation of the Rosary in the presence of the Blessed Sacrament.

On 16th October, 1940, His Holiness Pius XII said, "*The Rosary is, as its name signifies, a necklace of roses; not those roses with which the ungodly adorn themselves insolently, according to the words of Scripture – "Let us crown ourselves with roses before they wither!" (Wisdom 2 : 8) – but roses whose freshness is ceaselessly renewed in the hands of those devoted to Mary*".

Pope John XXIII in his Apostolic Letter on the Rosary, dated 29th September, 1961, says: "*Moreover, this is a characteristic of the liturgical prayer of the Missal and the Breviary: each one of its parts is introduced by "Oremus", which supposes plurality and a crowd, those who are praying, those who are hoping to be heard, and those who are being prayed for. It is the crowd which prays, united in supplication, for the whole human family, religious and civil. The Rosary of Mary is raised to the dignity of a great prayer, public and universal, for the ordinary and extraordinary needs of Holy Church, of nations and of the whole world.*"

Here the Holy Father recognises, in the prayer of the Rosary, that dimension of plurality and universality characteristic of the liturgical prayer of the Mass and the Liturgy of the Hours. "*Moreover, this is a characteristic of the liturgical prayer of the Missal and the Breviary*". And he says that the Rosary is the supplication of the multitude praying for the ordinary and extraordinary needs of Holy Church, of nations and of the world. "*It is the crowd which prays, united in supplication for the whole human family, religious and civil*".

His Holiness Paul VI, after the last voting session of the Council Fathers on 21st November, 1964, promulgated the dogmatic constitution "*Lumen Gentium*" on the Church In it we read: "*The sacred synod teaches this Catholic doctrine (the devotion offered by the Church to the Blessed Virgin) advisedly, and at the same time admonishes all the sons of the Church that the cult, especially the liturgical cult, of the Blessed Virgin, be generously* fostered, and that the practices and exercises of devotion towards her, recommended by the teaching authority of the Church in the course of centuries, be highly esteemed, and that those decrees, which were given in the early days regarding the cult of images of Christ, the Blessed Virgin and the saints, be religiously observed". (*Lumen Gentium*, 67).

Reading this document of the Second Vatican Council, I believe that no well-disposed person could deny that the prayer of the Rosary is one of the *principal practices and exercises of Marian piety* which, just then, were in the mind and the thoughts of the Council Fathers, just as it cannot be denied that this prayer is one of the practices and exercises of piety which have been most recommended and approved by the Church's Magisterium.

Then, on 2nd February, 1974, Pope Paul VI published the Apostolic Exhortation "*Marialis cultus*", in which he dedicated paragraphs 42 to 55 to the prayer of the Rosary, confessing: "*We, too, from the first General Audience of our Pontificate on 13th July 1963 onwards, have shown our great esteem for the pious practice of the Rosary*" (n° 42).

He also declares that he has followed very attentively the numerous meetings and researches which took place on the subject of this Marian devotion: «*As a result of modern reflection, the relationships between the liturgy and the Rosary have been more clearly understood. (...) Not many years ago, some people began to express a desire to see the Rosary included in the rites of the liturgy, while others, anxious to avoid a repetition of former pastoral mistakes, unjustifiably disregarded the Rosary. Today the problem can easily be solved in the light of the principles of the Constitution 'Sacrosanctum Concilium'. Liturgical celebrations and the pious practice of the Rosary must neither be set in opposition to one another nor considered as being identical.*

The more an expression of prayer preserves its own true nature and individual characteristics, the more fruitful it becomes. Once the pre-eminent value of liturgical rites has been reaffirmed, it will not be difficult to appreciate the fact that the Rosary is a practice of piety which easily harmonises with the liturgy. In fact, like the liturgy, it is communal in nature, draws its inspiration from Sacred Scripture and is oriented towards the mystery of Christ. The commemoration in the liturgy and the contemplative remembrance proper to the Rosary, although existing on essentially different planes of reality, have as their object the same salvific events wrought by Christ. The former presents anew, under the veil of signs and operative in a hidden way, the great mysteries of our redemption. The latter, by means of devout contemplation, recalls these same mysteries to the mind of the person praying, and stimulates the will to draw from them the norms of living.

Once this substantial difference has been established, it is not difficult to understand that the Rosary is an exercise of piety that draws its motivating force from the liturgy and leads naturally back to it, if practised in conformity with its original inspiration. It does not however become part of the liturgy. In fact meditation on the mysteries of the Rosary, by familiarising the hearts and minds of the faithful with the mysteries of Christ, can be an excellent preparation for the celebration of those same mysteries in the liturgical action, and can also become a continuing echo thereof. However, it is a mistake (...) to recite the Rosary during the celebration of the liturgy.» (n° 48)

His Holiness John Paul II expressed his intimate feelings, and his way of living the prayer of the Rosary, in these words of 29th October, 1978: "A prayer marvellous in its simplicity and in its depth! In this prayer, we repeat over and over again the words which the Virgin Mary heard from the Archangel and from her cousin Elizabeth. The whole Church joins in these words. (...) At the same time our heart can include in these decades of the Rosary all the events which go to make up the life of the individual, the family, the nation, the Church, and the whole of humanity. Incidents which affect us personally or our neighbour and, in a special way, those who are closest to us, whom we keep in our heart. Thus the simple prayer of the Rosary marks the rhythm of human life. (...) A prayer which is so simple and so rich! I cordially exhort all to pray it".

To conclude this list of recommendations of, and appreciation for, the holy Rosary, I leave you one last quotation from a prominent figure in the Church. In the homily which the Archbishop of Colombo (Sri Lanka), His Eminence Cardinal Cooray, gave in Fatima on 12th August, 1967, he spoke of the religious life being lived at that time in the Sri Lankan Shrine in honour of Our Lady of Fatima: "Our ideal is to make the devotion in our Shrine a continual repetition of the Message of Fatima, that is, penance and prayer. For this purpose, two institutions were founded. On one side is the Convent of the Poor Clares whose life is made up of penance and prayer. On the other side there is the Convent of a Diocesan Congregation of native Sisters called Sisters of the Rosary: daily fast and abstinence together with hard manual work are part of their life of penance. Their special prayer is the Rosary, which is recited day and night except during Mass and the Liturgy of the Hours. The Sisters take it in turns, two by two, with arms outstretched, to recite the meditated *Rosary before the Blessed Sacrament. Their ideal is the authentic personification of the Message of Fatima, that is, penance and prayer, especially the Rosary"*.

There are those who say that the Rosary is an antiquated and monotonous prayer, because of the constant repetition of the prayers which compose it. But I put the question: Is there anything at all which lives except through the continual repetition of the same actions?

God created everything that exists in such a way that it is kept alive by the continual repetition of the same actions. Thus, in order to preserve our life, we breathe in and breathe out always in the same way; our heart beats all the time according to the same rhythm. The stars, the sun, the moon, the planets, the earth follow always the same course, which God has laid down for them. Day follows night, year after year, always in the same way. Likewise the sun gives us light and warmth. In so many plants the leaves appear in the Spring, then they are clothed with flowers, next they yield fruit and, in autumn or winter, they lose their leaves.

Thus, everything follows the law which God has laid down for it, and yet it never occurs to anyone to say that it is monotonous; hence, nobody says so; the fact is that we need all this in order to live! Well then! In the spiritual life we experience the same need to repeat continually the same prayers, the same acts of faith, hope and charity, in order to live, since our life is a continued participation in the life of God.

As we have already seen, when the disciples asked Jesus Christ to teach them to pray, He taught them the beautiful formula of the Our Father, saying: "*When you pray say: Father...*" (Lk 11, 4). The Lord ordered us to pray thus, and did not say that, after a certain number of years, we were to look for a new formula of prayer, since that one had become old-fashioned and monotonous.

When lovers are together, they spend hours and hours repeating the same thing: "I love you!" What is missing in the people who think the Rosary monotonous is Love; and everything that is not done for love is worthless. Hence, the Catechism tells us that the Ten Commandments of God can be summed up in one: to love God above all things and our neighbour as ourselves.

Those who say the Rosary daily are like children who, every day, manage to find a few moments just to be with their father, to keep him company, to show him their gratitude, to do some service for him, to receive his advice and his blessing. It is an exchange of love, the love of the father for the child and the child for the father; it is a mutual giving.

Ave Maria!

35

Contemplation of the Joyful Mysteries

Having seen that the prayer of the Rosary is the one which God has recommended most for all of us in general, both by means of the Church's Magisterium and through the Message which He sent to us by Our Lady, we will now look at the mysteries of our Redemption which this prayer leads us to recall and contemplate in each decade.

For the majority of Christians who live in the corrupt atmosphere of the world, it is almost pointless to talk about mental prayer. Hence, what is most suitable for them is vocal prayer, in common or in private: the liturgical prayer of the Holy Mass and the recitation of the Rosary.

In the Rosary, we find all the riches of God's truths, or rather, the revelation of God to men. From the mystery of the Most Holy Trinity which God revealed to us in the Annunciation of the Archangel Gabriel to Mary, to the mystery of the Word made man, his life, passion, death, resurrection and ascension into heaven, where He is seated at the right hand of the Father, and is also present in his Church, in the Sacraments, in the tabernacle where He remains in the consecrated hosts, and in our brothers and sisters who form, with us, his Mystical Body, of which we are all living and functioning members.

This is the faith, which we imbibe in prayer, and it is prayer which sustains and increases our faith. As we pray the mysteries of the Rosary, we receive the light of truth and the strength of grace in order to accept willingly, and co-operate in, the redemptive work of Christ.

First Joyful Mystery: The Annunciation.

In the first decade, we recall the annunciation of the Angel Gabriel to Mary: «*The angel Gabriel was sent from God to a city of Galilee named Nazareth, to a virgin (...) and the virgin's name was Mary. And he came to her and said, "Hail, full of grace, the Lord is with you!" But she was greatly troubled at the saying, and considered in her mind what sort of greeting this might be. And the angel said to her, "Do not be afraid, Mary, for you have found favour with*

God. And behold, you will conceive in your womb and bear a son, and you shall call his name Jesus. He will be great, and will be called the Son of the Most High; and the Lord God will give to him the throne of his father David, and he will reign over the house of Jacob for ever; and of his kingdom there will be no end." And Mary said to the angel, "How can this be, since I have no husband?" And the angel said to her, "The Holy Spirit will come upon you, and the power of the Most High will overshadow you; therefore the child to be born will be called holy, the Son of God"» (Lk 1, 26-35.

In this passage, God reveals to us how the incarnation of the Word took place; He speaks to us of the mystery of the Most Holy Trinity, that is one God in three distinct Persons: *"The Holy Spirit will come upon you, and the power of the Most High will overshadow you; therefore the child to be born will be called holy, the Son of God"*.

God also reveals to us the virginity and immaculate purity of Mary: God did not choose just any woman to be the Mother of His Son who, of course, could not assume a nature stained by sin. Therefore, He made Mary immaculate from the first instant of her life, the moment of her conception; and she remained always a virgin, because the Son of God could not be confused with any other, according to his human nature, which would happen if another child were born of the same Mother.

The Angel told Mary that she was full of grace: *Hail, full of grace, the Lord is with you!* If Mary had not been full of grace and all holy, the Angel could not have said to her that she was full of grace, because she would have some stain of sin in her. *"The Lord is with you,"* – said the Angel – because Mary belongs totally to God and exists totally for God. To think that Jesus shared his Mother with us! He gave us Mary to be our Mother in the spiritual order of grace. What a great gift God has given us!

And the Angel continued: *"Mary, do not be afraid: you have won God's favour"*. Yes, she had caught God's attention because she was a virgin, pure and spotless, and, therefore, was chosen to be the first human temple inhabited by the Most Holy Trinity. Through the merits of the Word made flesh, from whom we receive pardon and grace, we also, if we are fortunate enough to possess the gift of faith and to live a good life, are living temples of the adorable Trinity, which dwells in us according to the sacred texts: «*If you love me, you will keep my commandments. And I will pray the Father, and he will give you another Counsellor, to be with you for ever, even the Spirit of truth, whom the world cannot receive, because it neither sees him nor knows* him; you know him, for he dwells with you, and will be in you.» (Jn 14, 15-17). And St. Paul draws our attention to the same truth: «*Do you not know that you are God's temple and that God's Spirit dwells in you? If any one destroys God's temple, God will destroy him. For God's temple is holy, and that temple you are. Let no one deceive himself.*» (1 Co 3, 16-18).

Jesus Christ and the Apostle tell us here that we are living temples of God and that we must keep our temple pure, because we are God's dwelling-place, and also in order that God's life may grow in us and may give us immortality.

Ave Maria!

Second Joyful Mystery: The visit of Our Lady to St. Elizabeth.

In the second decade, we recall Our Lady's visit to her cousin, St. Elizabeth. In the first mystery, we left the Angel talking to Mary and adding afterwards: «*And behold, your kinswoman Elizabeth in her old age has also conceived a son; and this is the sixth month with her who was called barren. For with God nothing will be impossible. And Mary said, "Behold, I am the handmaid of the Lord; let it be to me according to your word," And the angel departed from her.*»

«*In those days Mary arose and went in haste into the hill country, to a city of Judah, and she entered the house of Zechariah and greeted Elizabeth. And when Elizabeth heard the greeting of Mary, the babe leaped in her womb; and Elizabeth was filled with the Holy Spirit and she exclaimed with a loud cry, "Blessed are you among women, and blessed is the fruit of your womb! And why is this granted me, that the mother of my Lord should come to me? (...) And blessed is she who believed that there would be a fulfilment of what was spoken to her from the Lord"*» (Lk 1, 36-45).

This meeting of Our Lady and her cousin St. Elizabeth shows us Mary's great faith and deep humility. This is obvious at once in her answer to the Angel, when he announced that she had been chosen to be the Mother of God. She does not feel herself exalted, or raised to a higher level. She believes the Angel's words; she recognises her lowliness before God and offers herself to serve Him as a slave: *"Behold, I am the handmaid of the Lord; let it be to me according to your word,"*.

And, thinking always of God's mercy, Mary answers her cousin: «*My soul magnifies the Lord, and my spirit rejoices in God my Saviour, for he has regarded the low estate of his handmaiden.*» (Lk 1, 46-48).

The Virgin Mary and St. Elizabeth intone here the most beautiful canticle of praise to God. Their lips are moved by the Holy Spirit. But, after all, was not Mary the living temple of the adorable Trinity!

Ave Maria!

Third Joyful Mystery: The Birth of Jesus Christ.

In the third decade of the Rosary, we recall the birth of Jesus Christ, God made man. He is the masterpiece of love! God who comes down from heaven to earth, to save his poor creatures.

«*I am the living bread which came down from heaven*» (Jn 6, 51) – He would say later, in the synagogue at Capernaum. Yes, He came from heaven; He became man, assuming the humble condition of a creature! He who is God, co-eternal with the Father, equal to the Father in power, wisdom and love! He is born as man, but He is eternal like God! A mystery which the Apostle St. John describes thus: «*In the beginning was the Word, and the Word was with God, and the Word was God. (...) And the Word became flesh and dwelt among us, full of grace and truth; we have beheld his glory, glory as of the only Son from the Father*» (Jn 1,1.14).

He came into the world as a man and manifested Himself as Light. Light, which shines in the darkness: present among us, today as then, but now his humanity is veiled. He is present in his word and in his works, in the Eucharist and in the Sacraments, in the Church and in the person of each of our brothers and sisters. He says: «*I am the light of the world; he who follows me will not walk in darkness, but will have the light of life*» (Jn 8,12). Those who follow Christ will find in Him light and life.

This is how the birth of Jesus Christ took place: «*In those days a decree went out from Caesar Augustus that all the world should be enrolled. This was the first enrollment, when Quirinius was governor of Syria. And all went to be enrolled, each to his own city. And Joseph also went up from Galilee, from the city of Nazareth, to Judea, to the city of David, which is called Bethlehem, because he was of the house and lineage of David, to be enrolled with Mary, his betrothed, who was with child. And while they were there, the time came for* her to be delivered. And she gave birth to her first-born son and wrapped him in swaddling cloths, and laid him in a manger, because there was no place for them in the inn.

And in the region there were shepherds out in the field, keeping watch over their flock by night. And an angel of the Lord appeared to them, and the glory of the Lord shone around them, and they were filled with fear. And the angel said to them, "Be not afraid; for behold, I bring you good news of a great joy which will come to all people; for to you is born this day in the city of David, a Saviour, who is Christ the Lord. And this will be a sign for you; you will find a babe wrapped in swaddling cloths and lying in a manger." And suddenly there was with the angel a multitude of the heavenly host praising God and saying, "Glory to God in the highest, and on earth peace among men with whom he is pleased!"

When the angels went away from them into heaven, the shepherds said to one another, "Let us go over to Bethlehem and see this thing that has happened, which the Lord has made known to us." And they went with haste, and found Mary and Joseph, and the babe lying in a manger. And when they saw it they made known the saying which had been told them concerning this child; and all who heard it wondered at what the shepherds told them. But Mary kept all these things, pondering them in her heart. And the shepherds returned, glorifying and praising God for all they had heard and seen, as it had been told them» (Lk 2, 1-20).

As St. Luke says here, the shepherds came and heard what was said to them, they believed and praised God. In the same way, we, too, must renew our faith in the revelation which God gives us here; we must believe and say, "My God, I believe, I adore, I hope and I love You! I ask pardon of You for those who do not believe, do not adore, do not hope and do not love You". And, like Our Lady, we must keep all these truths in our hearts, with faith, hope and love.

Ave Maria!

Fourth Joyful Mystery: The Presentation of Jesus in the Temple.

In the fourth decade of the Rosary, we call to mind the presentation of Jesus in the temple. St. Luke describes this event in the life of Christ in the following terms: «And at the end of eight days, when he was circumcised, he was called Jesus, the name given by the angel before he was conceived in the womb.

And when the time came for their purification according to the law of Moses, they brought him up to Jerusalem to present him to the Lord (as it is written in the law of the Lord), "Every male that opens the womb shall be called holy to the Lord"» (Lk 2,21-23).

Circumcision, prescribed by God in the Old Law, was replaced by Baptism, of which it was a figure, and which Jesus Christ was to institute later as a Sacrament, to wipe out the stain of original sin in us, to make us members of his Mystical Body and sharers in the graces of his redemptive work.

The example of fidelity in the observance of God's Law which Our Lady gives us here should move us to follow the same road of fidelity to God and his Church.

Fulfilling this commandment to present her first-born in the Temple to be offered to the Lord, Mary is, at the same time, carrying out the mission entrusted to her by God, that of co-Redemptrix of the human race. Mary knows the Sacred Scriptures and, through them, she knows that her Son is destined to be a victim of expiation for the sins of men and a sacrifice of praise offered to God.

Reflect on what Isaiah prophesied about this:

«Who has believed what we have heard? And to whom has the arm of the Lord been revealed? For he grew up before him like a young plant, and like a root out of dry ground; he had no form or comeliness that we should look at him, and no beauty that we should desire him. He was despised and rejected by men; a man of sorrows, and acquainted with grief; and as one from whom men hide their faces he was despised, and we esteemed him not. Surely he has borne our griefs and carried our sorrows; yet we esteemed him stricken, smitten by God and afflicted. But he was wounded for our transgressions, he was bruised for our iniquities; upon him was the chastisement that made us whole, and with his stripes we are healed. All like sheep have gone astray; we have turned every one to his own way; and the Lord has laid on him the iniquity of us all. He was oppressed, and he was afflicted, yet he opened not his mouth; like a lamb that is led to the slaughter, and like a sheep that before its shearer is dumb, so he opened not his mouth. By oppression and judgment he was taken away; and as for his generation, who considered that he was cut off out of the land of the living, stricken for the trangression of my people? And they made his grave with *the wicked and with a rich man in his death, athough he had done no violence, and there was no deceit in his mouth. Yet it was the will of the Lord to bruise him; he has put him to grief; when he makes himself an offering for sin»* (Is 53,1-10).

Mary knows that this prophecy is to be fulfilled in the person of her Son; she knows that He has been sent by God to carry out the work of our redemption. And far from wanting to save Him from such pain and suffering, she takes Him in her pure arms, brings Him to the temple with her virginal hands and places Him on the altar so that the priest may offer Him to the eternal Father as an expiatory victim and a sacrifice of praise.

Here, Mary does not simply offer her Son, she offers herself with Christ, because Jesus had received his body and blood from her; thus she offers herself in and with Christ to God, co-Redemptrix, with Christ, of humanity.

In this mystery of the presentation of Jesus, the pure hands of Mary are the first paten on which God placed the first host; and, from this paten, the priest on duty in the temple of Jerusalem took it, to place it on the altar and offer it to the Father as something which is owed to Him and an offering with which He is well pleased. Here we have a figure; later will come the real Mass, when the sacrifice of expiation will be consummated on Calvary; Jesus, by His own hands, will offer Himself to the Father for men, under the consecrated species of bread and wine, saying to the priests of the New Covenant: «*Do this in remembrance of me*» (Lk 22,19), that is, offer My sacrifice to the Father so that it will be renewed on the altar for the salvation of the world. Because «*This is my body which is given for you. (...) This cup which is poured out for you is the new covenant in my blood*» (Lk 22, 19.20).

Ave Maria!

Fifth Joyful Mystery: The prayer of Jesus in the temple of Jerusalem.

In the fifth decade of the Rosary, we recall the journey of Jesus Christ to the temple in Jerusalem, to take part in the communal prayer of the people of God. St. Luke describes this event in Our Lord's life thus: «*Now his parents went to Jerusalem every year at the feast of the Passover. And when he was twelve years old, they went up according to custom; and when the feast was ended, as they were returning, the boy Jesus stayed behind in Jerusalem. His parents did not know it, but supposing him to be in the company they went a day's journey, and they sought him among their kinsfolk and acquaintances; and when they did not find him, they returned to Jerusalem, seeking him. After three days they found him in the temple, sitting among the teachers, listening to them and asking them questions; (...) and his mother said to him, "Son, why have you treated us so? Behold, your father and I have been looking for you anxiously." And he said to them, "How is it that you sought me? Did you not know that I must be in my Father's house?»* (Lk 2,41-49).

The Holy Family here gives us a great example of Christian life. Neither distance nor lack of transport deters them from journeying to the temple in Jerusalem to join their prayer to that offered to God by his people. The Jerusalem temple reminds us of the places of worship which, today, for us, are our Churches where we too should go, all together, to offer to God our prayer and praise.

In the answer He gave his mother, Jesus Christ tells us that the temple is the house of God: *"Did you not know that I must be in My Father's house?"* For us, the Churches are our Father's house and so we must enter them with faith, with respect and with love.

We go to our Father's house, so that, there, united around the same table, we can be fed by the same bread: the bread of the Eucharist, the bread of the word of God. Like Jesus Christ, we must listen there to the word of God, which is spoken to us by his ministers, as it was formerly imparted to the people of God by the doctors of the law.

Today, we are the successors of that people; we who, happily, have received Baptism and, with it, the gift of faith, members, now, of the Mystical Body of Christ, which is the Church.

Ave Maria!

36

Contemplation of the Sorrowful Mysteries of the Rosary

Having looked at the events in the life of Jesus, which are recalled in the first part of the Rosary, we now pass on to the second part, the five Sorrowful Mysteries.

First Sorrowful Mystery: The prayer of Jesus in the Garden of Olives.

In this mystery of the Rosary, we recall the prayer of Jesus Christ in the Garden of Olives.

The Gospels tell us that the Lord spoke several times during his public life of the way He was to die and thus accomplish the work of our redemption. When the time came, after He had celebrated the last Supper with his disciples, during which He instituted the Eucharist to perpetuate his real presence among us, and to prepare Himself for his imminent Passion and Death, He went with them to a place called Gethsemane and there He said to them: « *"Sit here, while I go yonder to pray." And taking with him Peter and the two sons of Zebedee, he began to be sorrowful and troubled. Then he said to them, "My soul is very sorrowful, even to death; remain here and watch with me." And going a little farther he fell on his face and prayed, "My father, if it be possible, let this cup pass from me; nevertheless, not as I will, but as thou wilt." And he came to the disciples and found them sleeping; and he said to Peter, "So, could you not watch with me one hour?" Watch and pray that you may not enter into temptation (...)" Again, for the second time, he went away and prayed, "My Father, if this cannot pass unless I drink it, thy will be done."* (Mt 26, 36-42).

Here as in the other events of his life, Jesus Christ is for us a model, which we must follow and seek to imitate. Although He was God and had, therefore, all grace and strength, He was also truly human; and He chose to prepare Himself, by prayer, to submit his human will to that of his Father, who needed Him as an expiatory victim for the sins of humanity. To his human nature, suffering, humiliation and death were repugnant, as it is for all of us, because they are the punishment for sin; sin which He did not commit, but for which He chose to make satisfaction on our behalf. And so, He spent a long time in prayer, repeating: «*Father, if thou art willing remove this cup from me; nevertheless not my will, but thine, be done.*" (...) *And being in an agony he prayed more earnestly; and his sweat became like great drops of blood falling down upon the ground*» (Lk 22, 42.44).

When suffering and anguish oppress us, let us remember Jesus Christ in the Garden of Olives and, like Him, let us say to God: «*Father, if thou art willing remove this cup from me; nevertheless not my will, but thine, be done.*» Even if our distress is great, let us reflect that the anguish of Jesus was greater, because his face was covered with "*great drops of blood, which fell to the ground*".

Oh! If I only could have been there beside the Lord at that moment, to wipe his face with a soft towel and then to keep such a relic of the Blood of my God! But what I could not do then, I want to do today, because, every day, from his wounded face, from his pierced hands and feet, from his open heart, flows the blood of our Redemption, present in the consecrated bread and wine on the altar of sacrifice; and I have the happiness of being nourished on that Body and that Blood.

Ave Maria!

Second Sorrowful Mystery: Jesus is taken prisoner.

In this second sorrowful mystery of the Rosary, we recall the arrest of Jesus Christ. The Gospel tells us that, instigated by the devil and by the love of money, Judas, one of the Twelve whom the Lord had chosen to be with Him, undertook, in return for thirty wretched coins, to deliver the Master into the hands of his enemies who wanted to get hold of Him in order to put Him to death.

Judas, knowing that Jesus used to go to the Garden of Olives to pray, left the supper room before the other disciples and went to the chief priest to tell them that the opportune moment to seize the Master had come. Then, accompanied by the escort which the high priest had prepared for the occasion, the traitor went to find the Lord in Gethsemane.

In the meantime "*Jesus, knowing all that was going to happen*", arose from his prayer and went to meet his enemies. When He came near them, Judas advanced to salute the Master with the treacherous kiss. It was the sign he had given the soldiers so that they would recognise Him. "*The one*

I kiss, he is the man. Arrest him, and see he is well guarded when you lead him away!"

Then Jesus *«said to them: "Whom do you seek?" They answered him, "Jesus of Nazareth." Jesus said to them, "I am he." (...) When he said to them, "I am he." they drew back and fell to the ground. Again he asked them, "Whom do you seek?" And they said, "Jesus of Nazareth." Jesus answered, "I told you that I am he; so if you seek me, let these men go." This was to fulfil the word which he had spoken, "Of those whom thou gavest me I lost not one."(...) So the band of soldiers and their captain and the officers of the Jews seized Jesus and bound him. First they led him to Annas; for he was the father-in-law of Caiaphas, who was high priest that year»* (Jn 18, 4-13). Then *«Annas then sent him bound to Caiaphas the high priest»* (Jn, 18, 24).

The sacred text says that Jesus *'knew all that was going to happen to Him'* – He had already spoken of it several times! He could have taken advantage of that long period of prayer to hide Himself, but He did not. He allowed Himself to be given up to martyrdom and to death, since that was the Father's will.

He had assumed our human nature in order to be able, in this way, to bring about our Redemption by allowing Himself to be immolated on the cross, thus offering to the Father a worthy reparation for our sins. Those pure animals which were sacrificed in the Old Law, as expiatory victims for the sins of the people of God, were merely figures of Christ, the only victim of infinite merit, capable of offering adequate reparation and thus of making satisfaction for our iniquities.

Ave Maria!

Third Sorrowful Mystery: Jesus is scourged and crowned with thorns.

In this mystery, we recall Christ scourged and crowned with thorns. After He had given Himself into the hands of his enemies to be a victim immolated for our sins, He was condemned by the Sanhedrin, presided over by the high priest, Caiaphas, and brought to the Praetorium of the Roman Governor, Pontius Pilate. He was insulted, mocked, acclaimed king in jest, scourged and then crowned with thorns. The Gospel says that Pilate, having recognised that Jesus was innocent, gave Him over to be scourged: *«Then Pilate took Jesus and scourged him. And the soldiers plaited a crown of thorns and put it on his head, and arrayed him in a purple robe; they came up to him, saying, "Hail, King of the Jews!" and struck him with their hands»* (Jn 19, 1-3).

Before ordering Him to be scourged. Pilate asked Jesus if He was a king. «*Jesus answered, "My kingship is not of this world (...) I am a king. For this I was born, and for this I have come into the world, to bear witness to the truth. Every one who is of the truth hears my voice."* (Jn 18, 36-37). It was this answer which gave the soldiers a pretext for making fun of Him as king.

The soldiers left Him in a pitiable state. Pilate, seeing Him like this and still wanting to save Him, brought Him out once more to the people, declaring that Jesus was innocent: «*"Behold I am bringing him out to you, that you may know that I find no crime in him."* (...) *They cried out, "Away with him, away with him, crucify him!" Pilate said to them, "Shall I crucify your King?" The chief priests answered, "We have no king but Caesar." Then he handed him over to them to be crucified.*» (Jn 1 9, 4. 15-16).

If, some day, God allows us to be victims of the injustice of men, let us look at Jesus and follow Him in faith.

Ave Maria !

Fourth Sorrowful Mystery: Jesus carries his cross to Calvary.

In this fourth sorrowful mystery, we think of Jesus Christ with his cross on the way to Calvary.

After Pilate had delivered Jesus to be crucified, the soldiers obliged Him to walk the road to Calvary amid the insults and taunts of the people who had been stirred up against Him, carrying on his shoulders the cross to which He was to be nailed. St. John describes all this as follows: «*So they took Jesus, and he went out, bearing his own cross, to the place called the place of a skull, which is called in Hebrew Golgotha. There they crucified him*» (Jn 19, 17-18).

Following the example of Jesus Christ, who for us bore the cross of suffering, let us tread in his footsteps, carrying our daily cross with faith, hope and love.

Ave Maria!

Fifth Sorrowful Mystery: Jesus dies on the cross.

In this last sorrowful mystery of the Rosary, we recall the death of Jesus Christ, nailed to the cross. When He arrived at the summit of Mount Calvary, led by the soldiery who ill-treated Him, He was nailed to the cross where, for several hours, He suffered and agonised until He died. It was three o'clock in the afternoon.

St. John describes the end of the Lord's earthly life in these words: «Standing by the cross of Jesus were his mother,(...). *When Jesus saw his mother, and the disciple whom he loved standing near, he said to his mother, "Woman, behold, your son!" Then he said to the disciple, "Behold, your mother!" And from that hour the disciple took her to his own home. After this Jesus, knowing that all was now finished, said (to fulfil the scripture), "I thirst." A bowl full of vinegar stood there; so they put a sponge full of the vinegar on hyssop and held it to his mouth. When Jesus received the vinegar, he said, "It is finished"; and he bowed his head and gave up his spirit.*» (Jn 19,25-30).

The death of Jesus Christ is our life, because He died to give us eternal life. Some time earlier, He had said: «*I lay down my life, that I may take it again. No one takes it from me, but I lay it down, and I have power to take it again; this charge I have received from my Father.*» (Jn 10, 17-18)".

In His passion and death, what the prophet Isaiah had said about Him was fulfilled to the letter: «*He was oppressed, and he was afflicted, yet he opened not his mouth; like a lamb that is led to the slaughter, and like a sheep that before its shearer is dumb, so he opened not his mouth. By oppression and judgment he was taken away; and as for his generation, who considered that he was cut off the land of the living, stricken for the transgression of my people (...) because he poured out his soul to death, and was numbered with the transgressors; yet he bore the sin of many, and made intercession for the transgressors.*» (Is 53, 7-8. 12).

Therefore, on the cross, Jesus Christ asked the Father to pardon his enemies: «*"Father, forgive them; for they know not what they do."*» (Lk 23, 34).

Ave Maria!

37

Contemplation of the Glorious Mysteries.

We have looked at the events in the life of Jesus which we recall in the first two parts of the Rosary: now we will look at those in the third part, the glorious Mysteries.

First Glorious Mystery: the Resurrection of Jesus.

In this first glorious mystery of the Rosary, we recall the Resurrection of Jesus Christ. At the end of the previous decade, we reflected on these words of Jesus:«*I lay down my life, that I may take it again. No one takes it from me, but I lay it down, and I have power to take it again; this charge I have received from my Father.*»* (Jn 10,17-18). This reference to his Father's commandment and to his own power to lay down his life and take it up again, forms part of the various predictions which Jesus made to his disciples during his public life, when He warned them that He would die, as the prophets had foretold, but that He would rise from the dead on the third day. Jesus made the first of these predictions immediately after having heard from the lips of Peter the confession of faith whereby Peter recognised Jesus as "*the Christ, Son of the living God*". The Evangelist says: «*From that time Jesus began to show his disciples that he must go to Jerusalem and suffer many things from the elders and chief priests and scribes, and be killed, and on the third day be raised*» (Mt 16, 21)

In the Upper Room, He had celebrated with the Apostles the Passover of the Old Covenant and afterwards instituted the sacred rite which was to perpetuate the New Covenant. And, «*when they had sung a hymn, they went out to the Mount of Olives. And Jesus said to them, "You will all fall away; for it is written, 'I will strike the shepherd, and the sheep will be scattered.' But after I am raised up, I will go before you to Galilee."*» (Mk 14, 26-28).

The truth of the Lord's Resurrection rests on historical signs and events which are absolutely authentic. First, the fact that it was clearly predicted by Jesus Himself, a fact which prompted the Jews themselves to place a guard at the tomb where his body lay. When the Resurrection took place, the empty tomb attested the fact and, in particular, the many witnesses who saw Him after He had risen from the dead. They ate at table with Him, they touched the wounds on his hands and his side, they lived with Him for forty days, during which the Risen Jesus instructed them and gave them the powers necessary for the Church. The Apostles and many disciples were so sure of this that they gave their lives in defence of the truth they proclaimed.

The first announcement that the Resurrection had taken place was made to women who, unable to anoint the Lord's body properly the evening before, came early on Sunday morning to pay Him this last homage. The announcement was made to them by the Angel who rolled back the stone from the sepulchre. St. Matthew tells us this fact as follows: «*Now after the sabbath, toward the dawn of the first day of the week, Mary Magdalene and the other Mary went to see the sepulchre. And behold, there was a great earthquake; for an angel of the Lord descended from heaven and came and rolled back the stone, and sat upon it. His appearance was like lightning, and his raiment white as snow. And for fear of him the guards trembled and became like dead men. But the angel said to the women, "Do not be afraid; for I know that you seek Jesus who was crucified. He is not here; for he has risen, as he said. Come, see the place where he lay. Then go quickly and tell his disciples that he has risen from the dead, and behold, he is going before you to Galilee; there you will see him. Lo, I have told you." So they departed quickly from the tomb with fear and great joy, and ran to tell his disciples. And behold, Jesus met them and said, "Hail!" And they came up and took hold of his feet and worshipped him. Then Jesus said to them, "Do not be afraid; go and tell my brethren to go to Galilee, and there they will see me"*» (Mt 28, 1-10).

In St. Mark's Gospel we have an account of the same fact: «*And when the sabbath was past, Mary Magdalene, and Mary the mother of James, and Salome, bought spices, so that they might go and anoint him. And very early on the first day of the week they went to the tomb when the sun had risen. (...) And entering the tomb, they saw a young man sitting on the right side, dressed in a white robe; and they were amazed. And he said to them, "Do not be amazed; you seek Jesus of Nazareth, who was crucified. He has risen, he is not here; see the place where they laid him. But go, tell his disciples and Peter that he is going before you to Galilee; there you will see him, as he told you."*» (Mk 16,1-7).

We also have the same announcement of the Resurrection to the women, from the pen of St. Luke, with some details of his own: «*The women who had come with him from Galilee followed, and saw the tomb, and how his body was laid; then they returned, and prepared spices and ointments. (...) On the first day of the week, at early dawn, they went to the tomb, taking the spices which they had prepared. And they found the stone rolled away from the tomb, but when they went in they did not find the body. While they were perplexed about this, behold, two men stood by them in dazzling apparel (...) the men said to them, "Why do you seek the living among the dead? He is not here, but has risen. Remember how he told you, while he was still in Galilee, that the Son of man must be delivered into the hands of sinful men, and be crucified, and on the third day rise." And they remembered his words, and returning from the tomb they told all this to the eleven and to all the rest. Now it was Mary Magdalene and Joanna and Mary the mother of James and the other women with them who told this to the apostles; but these words seemed to them an idle tale, and they did not believe them. But Peter rose and ran to the tomb; stooping and looking in, he saw the linen cloths by themselves; and he went home wondering at what had happened.»* (Lk 23, 55-56. 24,1-2).

When we compare these three Gospel accounts, we see the different details proper to each one. There is nothing strange in that! The same thing happens when a number of people witness the same event. The account which they give of it afterwards, contains the details which most struck each one; and even when the same person relates the same fact on different occasions, he or she does so with different details, because our memory does not register everything at the same time, sometimes recalling some details, sometimes others. And the Gospels originated in the accounts narrated by the actual witnesses when founding, or visiting, the earliest Christian communities. After these witnesses had departed, the accounts were preserved in the memory of each community, whence the Evangelist collected and put them together, naturally with whatever details they contained. And this is a further proof of the truth of the Resurrection: it was not something carefully worked out to be told in a mathematical fashion, always with the same words, the same full stops and commas, but rather as an event which had been witnessed.

St. John describes the appearance of Jesus to the Apostles, who were gathered together in the Upper Room with the doors firmly closed. The Lord «*Jesus came and stood among them and said to them, "Peace be with you." When he had said this, he showed them his hands and his side. Then the disciples were glad when they saw the Lord. Jesus said to them again, "Peace be with you. As the Father has sent me, even so I send you." And when he had said this, he breathed on them, and said to them, "Receive the Holy Spirit. If you forgive the sins of any, they are forgiven; if you retain the sins of any, they are retained."* (Jn 20, 19-23).

However, Thomas, the apostle, was absent on that occasion, and later he stubbornly refused to believe what the other Apostles told him. Eight days afterwards, Jesus came back to visit them, *«Jesus came and stood among them, and said, "Peace be with you." Then he said to Thomas, "Put your finger here, and see my hands; and put out your hand, and place it in my side; do not be faithless, but believing." Thomas answered him, "My Lord and my God!"* (Jn 20, 26-28).

Some days later, in the very early morning, the disciples, who had spent the night fishing without having caught anything, saw Jesus who, from the shore, asked them: *« "Children, have you any fish?" They answered him, "No." He said to them, "Cast the net on the right side of the boat, and you will find some." So they cast it, and now they were not able to haul it in, for the quantity of fish. (...) When they got out on land, they saw a charcoal fire there, with fish lying on it, and bread. Jesus said to them, "Bring some of the fish that you have just caught." (...) "Come and have breakfast." (...) Jesus came and took the bread and gave it to them, and so with the fish»* (Jn 21, 5-13).

But let us return to the day of the Resurrection and look at the story of the two disciples of Emmaus who, disheartened and saddened by the events of the passion and death of the Master, decided to go back home. They were on their way when a traveller – Jesus Himself though they did not recognise Him – overtook them and began to talk to them, asking them what had happened in Jerusalem and how they themselves had been affected by it. *«And he said to them, "What things?" And they said to him, "Concerning Jesus of Nazareth, who was a prophet mighty in deed and word before God and all people, and how our chief priests and rulers delivered him up to be condemned to death, and crucified him. (...) And he said to them, "(...) Was it not necessary that the Christ should suffer these things and enter into his glory?" And beginning with Moses and all the prophets, he interpreted to them in all the scriptures the things concerning himself. So they drew near to the village to which they were going. He appeared to be going further, but they constrained him, saying, "Stay with us, for it is toward evening and the day is now far spent." So he went in to stay with them. When he was at table with them, he took bread and blessed, and broke it, and gave it to them. And their eyes were opened and they recognized him»* (Lk 24, 19-31).

With these facts and many others that are related in the Scriptures, the resurrection of Jesus is emphatically authenticated. It is not a matter of a figment of the imagination, still less of a collective suggestion, because the incidents took place with different people, on various occasions, and were quite dissimilar.

In these appearances, Jesus Christ presents Himself as He is: true God and true man. The disciples touch Him and can thus verify that He is the same Jesus who was crucified, since He makes them see and touch the scars of the wounds in his hands caused by the nails, and the wounds in his side where the lance pierced it. The Lord thus invites them to convince themselves of his reality, seeing for themselves that He has flesh and blood and that He still has the marks of his martyrdom. Thus, He says to Thomas, in the presence of the other disciples: « *Put your finger here, and see my hands; and put out your hand, and place it in my side; do not be faithless, but believing.* » *Thomas answered him, "My Lord and my God!"* (Jn 20,27-28).

On the shore by the Sea of Tiberias, Jesus shows Himself to the disciples as a companion who goes to meet them and offers His help, pointing out where they will find the best catch. In the meantime, on the shore, He prepares a meal for them: fish cooked on a charcoal fire and bread, which He himself serves, distributing it to them, like a father who prepares and serves food to his children.

To the disciples of Emmaus, Jesus shows Himself as an ordinary traveller on the same road as themselves, He takes part in their conversation, enlightens them about the destiny of the Messiah, patiently points out and opens up for them the prophecies concerning Him in the Scriptures. He accepts the invitation to spend the night, and shares their meal. At table, He uses gestures which reveal his identity, since the two disciples had often seen the Master doing just this: He took bread, gave thanks, broke it and gave it to them. It was this gesture that made them realise that their companion on the road had been the Lord Himself.

So, Jesus Christ rose from the dead, and his resurrection is the reason for ours: « *He who believes has eternal life (...) and I will raise him up at the last day.* » (Jn 6, 47. 54).

Ave Maria!

Second Glorious Mystery: The Ascension of Jesus into Heaven.

In this mystery, we recall the Ascension of Jesus Christ into Heaven. After his Resurrection, Jesus Christ stayed with his apostles and disciples for forty days, during which He lived and talked with them familiarly and told them about his approaching departure to Heaven. The Lord also appeared to Mary Magdalen, one of the women who went to the tomb on the morning of the Resurrection. When she threw herself at his feet as if to detain Him, Jesus said to her: « *"Do not hold me, for I have not yet ascended to the Father; but go to my brethren and say to them, I am ascending to my Father and to your Father, to my God and your God."*» (Jn 20, 17).

The Ascension of Jesus into Heaven is described by St. Mark in these words: «*After he had spoken to them, he was taken up into heaven, and sat down at the right hand of God*» (Mk 16, 19).

In the Gospel of St. Luke, the Ascension of Jesus is described as follows: « *Then he led them out as far as Bethany, and lifting up his hands he blessed them. While he blessed them, he parted from them, and was carried up into heaven. And they worshipped him, and returned to Jerusalem with great joy*» (Lk 24, 50-52).

It is also St Luke who, in the Acts of the Apostles, in a sense, fills out the details of the story: «And while staying with them he charged them not to depart from Jerusalem, but to wait for the promise of the Father, which, he said, *"you heard from me"*, (...)*You shall receive power when the Holy Spirit has come upon you; and you shall be my witnesses in Jerusalem and in all Judea and Samaria and to the end of the earth." And when he had said this, as they were looking on, he was lifted up, and a cloud took him out of their sight. And while they were gazing into heaven as he went, behold, two men stood by them in white robes, and said, "Men of Galilee, why do you stand looking into heaven? This Jesus, who was taken up from you into heaven, will come in the same way as you saw him go into heaven."*» (Ac 1, 4-11).

St. Peter, speaking to the crowd after the coming of the Holy Spirit, said: «*Men of Judea and all who dwell in Jerusalem, let this be known to you, and give ear to my words. (...) the patriarch David both died and was buried, and his tomb is with us to this day. Being therefore a prophet, and knowing that God had sworn with an oath to him that he would set one of his descendants upon his throne, he foresaw and spoke of the resurrection of the Christ, that he was not abandoned to Hades, nor did his flesh see corruption. This Jesus*

God raised up, and of that we all are witnesses. Being therefore exalted at the right hand of God, and having received from the Father the promise of the Holy Spirit, he has poured out this which you see and hear. For David did not ascend into the heavens; but he himself says, 'The Lord said to my Lord, Sit at my right hand, till I make thy enemies a stool for thy feet.' Let all the house of Israel therefore know assuredly that God has made him both Lord and Christ, this Jesus whom you crucified."» (Act 2,14. 29-36).

Thus there can be no doubt that Jesus really did ascend into Heaven. Therefore, we believe it and, with the Church, we confess our faith, saying: *"On the third day He rose again from the dead; He ascended into Heaven; is seated at the right hand of God, the Father almighty; from thence He shall come to judge the living and the dead".* (The Apostles' Creed).

Ave Maria!

Third Glorious Mystery: The Descent of the Holy Spirit.

In the this decade of the Rosary, we recall the descent of the Holy Spirit on the Apostles.

The Acts of the Apostles tell us what happened. After the Lord's Ascension into Heaven, the Apostles and disciples left the Mount of Olives and returned to Jerusalem:*« When they had entered, they went up to the upper room, where they were staying, Peter and John and James and Andrew, Philip and Thomas, Bartholomew and Matthew, James the son of Alphaeus and Simon the Zealot and Judas the son of James. All these with one accord devoted themselves to prayer, together with the women and Mary the mother of Jesus (...) When the day of Pentecost had come, they were all together in one place. And suddenly a sound came from heaven like the rush of a mighty wind, and it filled all the house where they were sitting. And there appeared to them tongues as of fire, distributed and resting on each one of them. And they were filled with the Holy Spirit and began to speak in other tongues, as the Spirit gave them utterance.»* (Ac 1,13-14. 2,1-4).

In the discourse at the Last Supper, Jesus Christ spoke several times about the Holy Spirit, which He was to send from the Father when He had returned there, to teach them all truth, whose fullness they were not yet sufficiently prepared to understand. He said to them: *« "It is to your advantage that I go away, for if I do not go away, the Counsellor will not come*

to you; but if I go, I will send him to you."(...) "I have yet many things to say
to you, but you cannot bear them now. When the Spirit of truth comes, he will
guide you into all the truth; for he will not speak on his own authority, but
whatever he hears he will speak, and he will declare to you the things that are
to come. He will glorify me, for he will take what is mine and declare it to you.
All that the Father has is mine; therefore I said that he will take what is mine
and declare it to you.*» (Jn 16, 7-15).

As we see by the use of the word "My", there is full communion and
reciprocity between the Father, Jesus Christ and the Paraclete.

Jesus said also: «*I came from the Father and have come into the world;
again I am leaving the world and going to the Father.*» (Jn 16, 28). On another occasion, He declared: «*I came not of my own accord, but he sent me*»
(Jn 8, 42), without, however, ever separating from each other, because, as
Jesus says: «*I and the Father are one*» (Jn 10,30).

He stripped Himself of the glory which He had with the Father as his
only-begotten Son and came into the world, becoming man through the
action of the Holy Spirit, as the Angel explained to the Virgin Mother:
«*The Holy Spirit will come upon you, and the power of the Most High will
overshadow you; therefore the child to be born will be called holy, Son of God.*»
(Lk 1, 35). In any action or initiative of one of the Persons of the Blessed
Trinity, the other two, also, are always involved.

And it was in their name that Jesus sent the Apostles: «*Go therefore and
make disciples of all nations, baptizing them in the name of the Father and of
the Son and of the Holy Spirit*» (Mt 28, 19).

In our faith we proclaim one God in three Persons: "*I believe in the
Holy Spirit, the Lord and Giver of life, who proceeds from the Father and the
Son; with the Father and the Son He is adored and glorified. He has spoken
through the Prophets*". (Nicene Creed).

Ave Maria!

Fourth Glorious Mystery: The Assumption of Our Lady into Heaven.

In the fourth glorious mystery of the Rosary, we recall the Assumption of Our Lady, Mother of God, into Heaven.

The Church, having studied this event for many years, and being enlightened by the Holy Spirit, declared as a dogma of faith the "*assumption
of Mary, Mother of God, body and soul, into Heaven*".

Preserved from original sin from the first moment of her conception by a singular privilege of God, Mary was exempt also, by His grace, from the punishment, which condemned the human race to the corruption of the grave. «*You are dust, and to dust you shall return*» (Gn 3,19). This was the sentence imposed by God in consequence of, and as a punishment for, the sin of Adam and Eve. Mary did not inherit this sin and so she did not incur its punishment.

Even before pronouncing this sentence, God declared that there was to be an exceptional Woman in whom and with whom He would realise the purpose He had in mind when He created man. God could not be thwarted in his plans for creation! Having created man and destined him for eternal life, He could not leave him forever in the death of sin and the dust of the earth. So He thought of Mary, a humble daughter of the human race but, by reason of the singular privileges with which He had endowed her, raised above every other creature and free from the stain of original sin. He thought of Mary, pure and immaculate, from whom He would assume his human nature, something which He needed to do in order to accomplish the work of our Redemption. God clearly could not take to Himself and unite to his divine nature a human nature stained by sin.

As soon as the first sin which brought condemnation on human beings had been committed, God, speaking to the Devil who had taken the form of a serpent and who had incited the first human beings to do evil, said to him: «*I will put enmity between you and the woman, and between your seed and her seed; he shall bruise your head, and you shall bruise his heel*» (Gn 3, 15).

This woman, predestined by God to give Christ a human nature and to be, with Him, co-Redemptrix of the human race – "*I shall put enmity between you and the woman, and between your offspring and hers*" – this woman, He said, could not remain in the shadow of death, because she did not incur the sentence of punishment. Hence Mary is the first fruit of the Redemption wrought by Christ; and, through his merits, she was carried up to Heaven in body and soul, where she lives and reigns, in God, with her Son and his.

In fact, her Son, Jesus, true God and true man, is the source of that life to which we shall all rise one day, because God created us for life, and cannot leave us in the shadow of death. This is what Jesus said of Himself to Martha in Bethany: «*I am the resurrection and the life; he who believes in me, though he die, yet shall he live, and whoever lives and believes in me shall never die.*» (Jn 11, 25-26). And He confirmed the truth of his words with the resurrection of Lazarus. Moreover, in the discourse on the Bread of Life, in Ca-pharnaum, He said: «*For this is the will of my Father, that every one who sees the Son and believes in him should have eternal life; and I will raise him up at the last day.*» (Jn 6,40). But the final result depends on our faith and our attachment to Christ: «*Truly, truly, I say to you, he who hears my word and believes him who sent me, has eternal life; he does not come into judgment, but has passed from death to life.(...) For as the Father has life in himself, so he has granted the Son also to have life in himself, and has given him authority to execute judgment, because he is the Son of man. Do not marvel at this; for the hour is coming when all who are in the tombs will hear his voice and come forth, those who have done good, to the resurrection of life, and those who have done evil, to the resurrection of judgment.*» (Jn 5,24-29).

Thus we believe and thus we hope while with the Church we sing: "*Assumpta est Maria in Caelum!*", Mary has been assumed into Heaven.

Ave Maria!

Fifth Glorious Mystery: The Coronation of Our Lady in Heaven.

In the very last mystery of the Rosary, we recall the Coronation of Our Lady in Heaven as Queen of the Angels and Saints.

God alone is King, and his kingdom has no end.

When Pilate asked Jesus if He was a king, the Lord answered" «*My kingship is not of this world; if my kingship were of this world, my servants would fight, that I might not be handed over to the Jews; but my kingship is not from the world (...) I am a king. For this I was born, and for this I have come into the world, to bear witness to the truth. Every one who is of the truth hears my voice*» (Jn 18,36-37).

The kingdom of Jesus is a kingdom of truth. And even if Pilate did not bother to wait for the answer to the question, which he himself had asked, about the nature of truth, at least he acknowledged the accusation which the Jews had made about Jesus, that He had claimed to be king. Accordingly, Pilate ordered an inscription to be affixed to the cross with these words: «*Jesus of Nazareth, the King of the Jews*» (Jn19, 19).

Jesus often spoke of the kingdom of God. About its irruption into time, He said: «*The law and the prophets were until John; since then the good news of the kingdom of God is preached, and every one enters it violently.*» (Lk16, 16). But not everyone will inherit it: «*The Son of man will send his angels, and they will gather out of his kingdom all causes of sin and all evildoers, and throw them into the furnace of fire; there men will weep and gnash their teeth. Then the righteous will shine like the sun in the kingdom of their Father.*» (Mt 13, 41-43).

When the Angel announced to Mary the incarnation of the Word, he said to her: «*You will conceive in your womb and bear a son, and you shall call his name Jesus. He will be great, and will be called the Son of the Most High; and the Lord God will give to him the throne of his father David, and he will reign over the house of Jacob for ever; and of his kingdom there will be no end.*» (Lk 1, 31-33). God is the one and only eternal king; the Son is made man and is born in order to allow humanity to have access once more to the eternal kingdom of God: «*I am a king. For this I was born, and for this I have come into the world,*» (Jn18, 37), and his kingdom will have no end.

In giving birth to the Son of the Most High, everlasting king with the Father and the Holy Spirit, Mary is truly the Mother of God and Spouse of the Holy Spirit, having conceived by his intervention: «*The Holy Spirit will come upon you, and the power of the Most High will overshadow you; therefore the child to be born will be called holy*» (Lk 1, 35).

Thus Mary, in virtue of being Mother of God and Spouse of the Holy Spirit, is, we might almost say, by right, Queen. Hence, God could not fail to bring her to Heaven in body and soul, and crown her as Queen of the Angels and Saints.

In the Apocalypse, St. John tells us that He saw, in Heaven, «*a woman clothed with the sun, with the moon under her feet, and on her head a crown of twelve stars*» (Rev 12, 1). We believe that Mary is this woman, crowned by God.

And the Church celebrates the feast of Our Lady, Queen and Mother, on 22nd August. With the whole Church, we venerate her and proclaim her Queen of heaven and earth! Daily, we salute her and invoke her as we sing these words: "*Hail, holy Queen, Mother of mercy, hail our life, our sweetness and our hope!*".

Ave Maria!

25th March, 1997. With the help of God and in order to carry out his will, I have today finished this humble work of explaining and interpreting the appeals of the Message of Fatima. I place it in the pure hands of Mary, for Her to present to the Lord, begging Him to make use of it for his glory, and for the good of souls and of his Church

Ave Maria!

Sister Maria Lúcia of Jesus and of the Immaculate Heart (O.C.D.).

CONTENTS

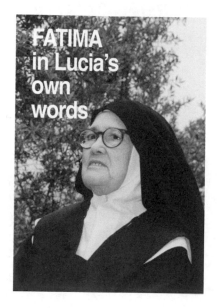
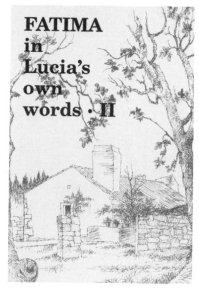

In 1964, the Vice-Postulator's Office (Secretariado dos Pastorinhos) was officially authorized to publish Sister Lucia's Memoirs and to arrange for them to be translated faithfully in other languages.

This important book is a help towards a deeper knowledge and love for Our Lady and her little collaborators, Blessed Francisco and Jacinta Marto.

The "Memoirs" («Fatima in Lucia's Own Words») are on sale at the Secretariado dos Pastorinhos in two volumes of which volume I contains the first four Memoirs and volume II contains the 5th and 6th Memoirs.

Execução Gráfica – Gráfica Almondina – Torres Novas